HMONG AMERICA

THE ASIAN AMERICAN EXPERIENCE

Series Editor
Roger Daniels

*A list of books in the series
appears at the end of this book.*

CHIA YOUYEE VANG

Hmong America

RECONSTRUCTING

COMMUNITY IN DIASPORA

UNIVERSITY OF ILLINOIS PRESS

URBANA, CHICAGO, AND SPRINGFIELD

∞ This book is printed on acid-free paper.

Library of Congress Cataloging-in-Publication Data
Vang, Chia Youyee, 1971–
Hmong America : reconstructing community in diaspora / Chia Youyee Vang.
p.   cm. — (The Asian American experience)
Includes bibliographical references and index.
ISBN 978-0-252-03568-5 (cloth : alk. paper)
ISBN 978-0-252-07759-3 (pbk. : alk. paper)
1. Hmong Americans—History. 2. Hmong Americans—Social conditions.
3. Hmong Americans—Social life and customs. 4. Immigrants—United States—
History. 5. Refugees—United States—History. I. Title.
E184.H55V35   2010
305.895'972073—dc22   2010024456

To my parents,
You Yee Vang and Pang Thao,
for their sacrifices.

Ncu txug kuv txiv hab nam,
Ntsum Yig Vaaj hab Paaj Thoj,
txujkev khwv.

Contents

Illustrations

Foreword

Unlike most books about the fate of Southeast Asian refugees groups in the United States, *Hmong America* is not primarily about victimization, demoralization, and loss of traditional culture, although those elements are an inevitable part of the story of any refugee group. Instead, its author describes and explains the special circumstances that have distinguished the Hmong experience from that of other Southeast Asian refugees. Chia Youvee Vang, now a professor at the University of Wisconsin–Milwaukee, was flown to the United States as a nine-year-old from a refugee camp in Thailand with her family after fleeing their native Laos. She is thus a member of the 1.5 generation, young enough to be able to adjust effectively to her new environment but old enough to have some memories of Southeast Asia, memories that are clearer about life in a refugee camp than in war-torn Laos. But this is not a memoir of personal experience, although she does provide small bits of autobiography as partial authentication. It is a mature work of scholarship involving a variety of archival and printed documentation, research on three continents, oral histories, and participant observations.

Vang briefly explains the still-dim origins of the Hmong in southwestern China, their migration to Laos, and their subsequent eighteenth-century encounter with French colonialism. She then details how, during the more than thirty years of fighting that engulfed much of Southeast Asia after World War II, the Hmong became the long-secret foot soldiers of the Central Intelligence Agency, surrogates for the force that no American president dared send, deserted when U.S. power in Southeast Asia collapsed. A substantial proportion of the Hmong people fled Laos, creating a diaspora, whose largest segment—130,000 persons—came to the United States in the late 1970s and early 1980s.

Vang concentrates on the largely successful struggle of Hmong Americans to adapt and acculturate themselves to a land vastly different from anything in their previous experience, but she understands that their experience is also another chapter in America's larger immigration story and the U.S. place in the global arena. She shows that, in common with other refugee groups, Hmong successfully resisted the efforts of both the government and nongovernmental agencies to disperse refugees widely so that they would be less visible. As immigrants have always tended to do, Hmong clustered in specific localities, chiefly Northern California and Minnesota's Twin Cities. While she treats many areas of Hmong resettlement, including France and parts of South America, her major focus is on St. Paul–Minneapolis. Her thick description of annual Hmong cultural events in those cities over time enables her to depict the acculturation process in a specific and understandable manner. Another unique aspect of Hmong acculturation was the community leaders' ability to tell and retell the story of Hmong participation in the struggle against communist forces to gain special government support and win allies from forces in American society rarely favorable to immigration, such as the American Legion.

Her account is strengthened and made more vivid by her nuanced use of her interviews of older Hmong with little effective use of English. Her analysis is informed both by her own experience and by her use of the traditional methodologies of ethnic scholarship.

While it is not appropriate at this time, with the first generation of Hmong still very much on the scene, to talk about a definitive study of that generation, *Hmong America* is surely the most valuable single volume that we now have.

Roger Daniels

Preface

I am a member of the one-and-a-half generation of Hmong who came to the United States as a nine-year-old child in 1980.[1] I grew up in the Twin Cities, and my personal experiences, whether as witness to the transformations in this community or as participant in the many events here, greatly influenced my research and writing. My parents had tried to escape from Laos in 1975 when the military leaders fled, but the shooting of some escapees ahead of our group convinced my parents that the risks outweighed the unknown future benefits. They returned to our village, Tashelaan (*Taj Siv Laav*), and from 1975 to 1979, tried to bring some normalcy to an unstable situation by working hard to rebuild their lives, their agrarian lifestyle. Like thousands of other villagers, however, their efforts were interrupted by sporadic bombs dropped on villages that were thought to harbor resistance fighters. The fear intensified. Each time the noise of an airplane was heard approaching, villagers would disperse like ants to the surrounding thick jungle. In 1978, my father's youngest brother, Tong, who had escaped in 1975, sent a message through Hmong men who had returned from the refugee camp in Thailand to let my father and his other brother know that he was safe in America. He encouraged all of the villagers to find a way out of the country. However, my father and the elders hesitated. Following the bombing of our village in the summer of 1979, the elders convened a meeting and decided to make another escape attempt.

We made the journey from northern Laos to Ban Vinai refugee camp in Thailand in September 1979 along with our extended family members and relatives. Upon arrival on the Thai side of the Mekong River in October, our group was held by Thai officials for several days until international relief workers were allowed to examine us.[2] After being registered by refugee-camp workers, Uncle Tong urged my parents to apply for resettlement in the United States as soon as possible. We were fortunate in that we spent only six months in the refugee camp before being resettled in Minnesota in April 1980.

I remember only bits and pieces of being tired and hungry traveling through the jungles and crossing the Mekong River in the darkest of the night hours. I also remember being consumed by new experiences such as drinking soda and holding a pencil for the first time in Ban Vinai. The truth of the matter is that I have limited personal recollections of the actual journey. When I am asked to describe the journey from Laos to Thailand, I often describe it as a film one had seen a very long time ago. One may be able to recall the themes and a few scenes here and there; however, one cannot accurately recount the entire story. As my mother frequently reminds me, perhaps I could not remember much because the smell of diesel fuel made me sick. Vomiting and being "near death" were my state of being from the bus ride from Ban Vinai to Bangkok International Airport. On the plane ride from Bangkok to San Francisco, California, where we stopped to go through U.S. customs, my health condition troubled my parents greatly. Unlike my siblings, motion sickness overwhelmed me, and I could not eat anything. While we waited in San Francisco, my mother literally begged the Hmong interpreter helping with customs check to find me some rice. When he came back with a small bowl of steamed rice, she mixed it with water and fed it to me. My mother tells me that this bowl of rice saved my life. We arrived at the Minneapolis–St. Paul International Airport on April 13, 1980, and were welcomed by my Uncle Tong and his family, who had been in Minnesota since 1976. So, our life in America began.

It is common for scholars of non-Hmong ethnicity to describe their sometimes intentional and other times surprising encounters with Hmong subjects. In studies about Hmong in the United States, in other Western nations, in Thai villages, and in Laos before the Vietnam War era, researchers describe their increasing knowledge and understanding of various aspects of the Other's culture and traditions. Frequently, it is through observations and both structured and nonstructured interviews with their subjects that outside researchers discover cultures and traditions that contradict or complicate their own worldviews while providing them with a better understanding of Hmong worldviews. By immersing themselves in the lives of their subjects, these researchers position themselves as cultural bridges where they assume responsibility and expertise in explaining to Western audiences exotic Hmong cultural practices.

If these are common processes by which researchers of non-Hmong ethnicity take, what path do those who are of Hmong ethnicity follow? What difference does it make when one has lived and/or experienced the topics of interest? How does one's status as an insider influence the process and outcome of research studies? In one community study after another, it is also a widespread strategy for researchers to engage key informants or cultural brokers who serve as interpreters. When language is not a barrier between researcher and interviewee, I believe that stories are told or experiences are explained differently due to the existence of common cultural knowledge. Furthermore, insider status increases the researcher's access to information that marginalized groups such as the Hmong may not feel comfortable sharing with an outsider. This stems from their attempt to portray a positive image of the ethnic group to outsiders. As a historian, I want to increase the possibility of understanding the forces, choices, and circumstances that brought the Hmong people to our current situation. It is important to recognize that what one knows of the past is not static but constantly evolving as new information become available. Additionally, historical understanding requires studies that encompass all aspects of human experiences and recognize that the lives of ordinary people are as full of interest and significant as those of famous leaders.

My interest in Hmong diasporic experiences has evolved over the years with travels to many enclaves throughout the United States. My research is also informed by numerous trips abroad since the early 1990s. As an undergraduate student, I spent my junior year (1992–93) studying in France where I had the opportunity to visit and interact with different Hmong populations throughout the country. In 1999, I visited Argentina and was able to interact with Lao refugees who had resettled there. I spent two weeks in Thailand in March 2006 where I was able to visit with the several hundred refugees who remained at Wat Tham Krabok, a Buddhist monastery northeast of Bangkok where many Hmong refugees fled following closure of United Nations–sponsored camps in the mid-1990s. In January 2009, I had the opportunity to lead a short-term study-abroad program to Laos where I reunited with my aunts and uncles from my mother's side for the first time since 1979. Although it felt as though I was returning "home," I came away realizing how different our lives were and how out of place I was in the village. The life I was born to lead and the life I am currently living are clearly worlds apart.

Overall, I have tried to present perspectives from a variety of people. Despite my status as an insider, I am sure that not all people of Hmong ethnicity will agree with my portrayal of the Hmong American community and my conclusions. What I do hope is that this project will encourage other researchers to engage in the production of more-critical work on Hmong in the diaspora.

Acknowledgments

Many authors have shared the wisdom that a book is rarely ever written alone. Although this project did require endless hours in archives and months writing in isolation, the end product came about because of support from mentors and colleagues. Jennifer L. Pierce, Roderick Ferguson, Erika Lee, and Helga Leitner gave me critical feedback in the early stage. Comments and questions from Rachel Ida Buff on earlier drafts were instrumental in shaping the manuscript.

I now believe more than ever that our accomplishments in life are influenced by the people we encounter. I met Roger Daniels when he came to speak during Constitution Day at the University of Wisconsin–Milwaukee in October 2007. My colleague Margo Anderson introduced me to him. When she mentioned my research on Hmong, he encouraged me to send him my book. His thoughtful comments and suggestions greatly enhanced it. I cannot imagine this book at its current stage without his continued support. I am deeply honored to have received his guidance.

Although he did not know me, Jeremy Hein, who has conducted extensive research about Southeast Asian refugees offered helpful suggestions. UW-Milwaukee graduate student Karen W. Moore took time out of her own busy graduate studies to provide feedback. The anonymous reviewer's suggestions helped me greatly in placing the book in the larger Asian American and United States immigration historiography.

A Faculty Diversity Research Award from the University of Wisconsin's Institute on Race and Ethnicity released me from all teaching responsibilities during spring 2008 in addition to providing financial support for additional research.

Finally, thank you to senior acquisitions editor Kendra Boileau and the staff at the University of Illinois Press for guiding this project through the editorial process.

Because history is a matter of perspectives and what is included or excluded depends on the storytellers' interests, I had an obligation to make sure that I tell this story of the Hmong in America as best as I could. Although all interpretations and any errors are mine alone, I am indebted to the men and women who shared their personal life experiences with me. My questions did not only involve recounting events that happened to them but also their interpretations of what happened before and after their flight to refugee camps and then to third countries. Sometimes through tears and other times through laughter, their memories make visible how their lives were affected by a war that was decided by politicians on the other side of the globe. Through the powerlessness in which political refugees initially find themselves immersed, these men and women made strategic decisions that would change the course of history not only for themselves but also for all Hmong people in diasporic locations. Being able to learn directly from those who migrated was an invaluable experience. The oral histories they shared help me to include the lived experiences of ordinary people that often are not counted as official history. I am grateful for this opportunity to study and write about Hmong migration to the United States from an "insider" perspective. As I interpret their stories of uncertainties and strengths amidst much adversity, I begin to better understand my own journey as a refugee child.

Many people say that a Hmong family is the core of its members' existence. I thank my husband, Tong, and children, Simone, Tujntsuj (Junie), and Flasche, for their understanding when I had to disappear for days into the basement. I appreciate their excitement about the things I was learning and the many hours Tong spent helping transcribe interviews and read drafts. My brothers and sisters, Khou, Teng, Chance, Mao, Yang, and Cher, stood on the sidelines cheering as I moved through the various educational stages. Their belief that my success was also theirs helped me to see a greater purpose beyond my own interests. As the oldest child who was married at a very young age in Laos, my sister Khou did not have the opportunity to obtain formal education. My younger sister Mao earned her doctoral degree in 2009, and this has brought great joy to our immediate and extended family.

My in-laws, Xao and Yia Yang, gave me unending support. I am indebted to my husband's grandmother Shoua Vue for all the times that she took care of my children and cooked my favorite Hmong food when she knew I was on my way to pick up the children. My parents, Pang

Thao and You Yee Vang, deserve the highest praise. In 1979 they could not have imagined what our lives would be like in the United States. Seasonal farming and selling vegetables at farmer's markets in the Twin Cities have contributed to supporting six of us through college. Their love and sacrifice have allowed me to travel and discover the world. As I visit the various locations that Hmong people now call home, I feel blessed that they made the decision to come to the United States because only here in America would someone like me have the privilege of obtaining a higher education. My greatest regret is that my father passed away in March 2005 and did not live to see the completion of this book.

Chronology of Relevant Events

Date	Key Event
Early 1800s	Hmong begin migrating to the Indochinese peninsula from southern China.
1850s	Migration increases southward, to Vietnam, then Laos, and eventually to Thailand.
1893	French empire establishes protectorate over the Kingdom of Laos.
1896	Hmong revolt against French taxation.
1918–21	Mad Men's War fights against colonial regime.
1945–54	Some Hmong support French attempt to reinstate its colonial rule while others align with revolutionaries seeking end to colonialism.
1961–73	Many Hmong in Laos fight on both sides supported by the East and the West. Some participate in U.S. covert operations in Laos in support of larger war in Vietnam; January 27, 1973 "Agreement on Ending the War and Restoring Peace in Vietnam" allows the United States to disengage from the Vietnam; the February 21, 1973, "Vientiane Agreement" results in cease-fire in Laos.
1975	Saigon falls April 30; U.S. Congress enacts the Indochina Migration and Refugee Assistance Act to support refugees fleeing Vietnam and Cambodia; Hmong military personnel and families airlifted out of Long Cheng to Namphong, Thailand, on May 14; Communists take over Laos.

1976   The Indochina Migration and Refugee Assistance Act is extended to Laotians in June 1976, which includes ethnic Lao, Hmong, and other minority groups involved with Americans during the Vietnam War.

1977   Exiled leaders establish a mutual assistance association (MAA) in Santa Ana, California. Similar self-help organizations founded in other U.S. locations with sizable Hmong populations.

1979   First International Conference on Indochinese Refugees held in July in Geneva, Switzerland, to plead for more permanent resettlement places.

1980   U.S. Congress passes the Refugee Act, which formalizes programs and procedures for resettling refugees. The Office of Refugee Resettlement is established under the auspices of the U.S. Department of Health and Human Services.

1980s   Secondary migration from initial settlement to other U.S. locations results in formation of new communities.

1987   American leadership role is reduced in dealing with the Indochinese refugee problem.

1988   Interstate meeting in Bangkok begins as an informal consultation to set out the groundwork for the Comprehensive Plan of Action (CPA) for Indochinese refugees.

1989   Second international conference on Indochinese looks at the flow of economic and nonpolitical refugees.

1991   CPA is affirmed, and voluntary return commences; Hmong American Choua Lee elected to serve on St. Paul Public School Board, making her the first person of Hmong ethnicity to be elected to a public office in the United States.

1992   Plans to close United Nations–sponsored refugee camps in Thailand are implemented; Hmong leader Mai Vue leads group of refugees in Thailand back to Laos.

1995   Ban Vinai refugee camp closes; refugees refusing to resettle in third countries or repatriate seek refuge near Wat Tham Krabok monastery.

1997   Washington Commencement is held in Washington, D.C., to formally recognize Hmong secret-war veterans.

2000   Hmong Veterans Naturalization Act becomes law providing exemption from English-language requirement and special consideration for civics testing for certain refugees from Laos applying for naturalization.

2002   Hmong American Mee Moua is elected to the Minnesota Senate.

2003   In the fall, the U.S. State Department announces that it would resettle up to fifteen thousand Hmong refugees living in Wat Tham Krabok.

2004   The United States grants normal trade relations (NTR) to Lao People's Democratic Republic.

2005   Chai Soua Vang shoots six white hunters in northern Wisconsin.

2006   Wat Tham Krabok closes; memorial is dedicated in Sheboygan, Wisconsin, for Lao Hmong and Americans who served in Laos during the secret war.

2007   James Nichols's murder of Cha Vang in the Wisconsin woods intensifies race relations; former General Vang Pao and coconspirators are arrested for allegedly planning to overthrow the Lao government.

2008   Hollywood legend Clint Eastwood releases film *Gran Torino* with all Hmong American actors playing Hmong roles.

2009   Charges against former General Vang Pao are dropped in September by U.S. government for insufficient evidence.

Map 1. Indochina. In the pre–Vietnam War era, the majority of Hmong lived in Xieng Khouang province, Laos.

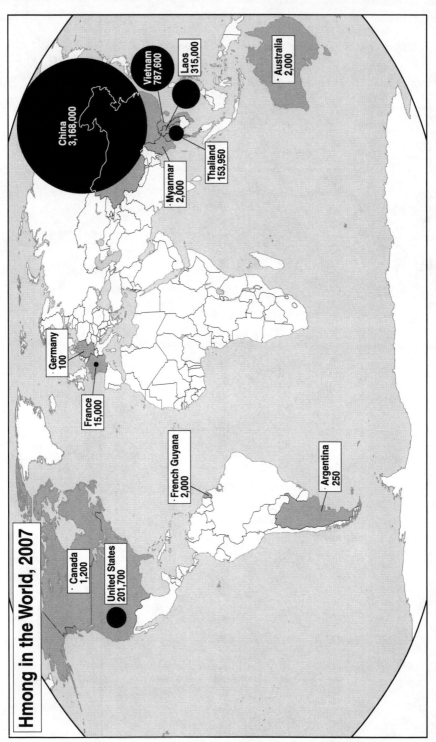

Map 2. Hmong in the world. The Hmong global diaspora is found in Asia, Australia, Europe, North America, and South America.

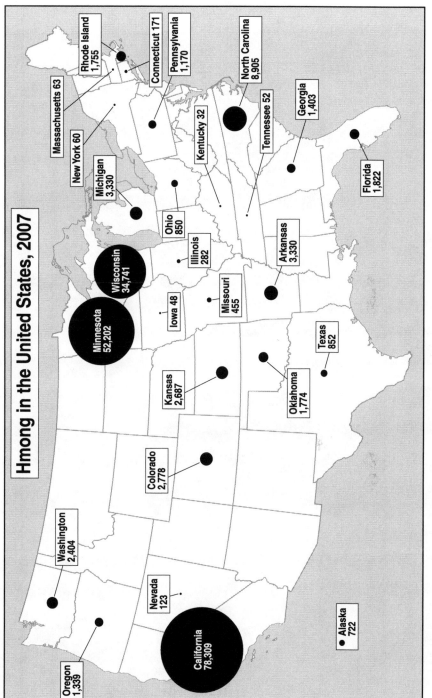

Hmong in the United States, 2007

Washington 2,404

Oregon 1,339

Nevada 123

California 78,309

Colorado 2,778

Kansas 2,687

Oklahoma 1,774

Texas 852

Alaska 722

Minnesota 52,202

Wisconsin 34,741

Iowa 48

Missouri 455

Arkansas 3,330

Illinois 282

Ohio 850

Michigan 3,330

Massachusetts 63

New York 60

Rhode Island 1,755

Connecticut 171

Pennsylvania 1,170

Kentucky 32

Tennessee 52

North Carolina 8,905

Georgia 1,403

Florida 1,822

Map 3. Hmong in the United States. Hmong presence is felt in large cities and small towns across America.

HMONG AMERICA

Introduction

> Transnational migrants today move about in a very
> different world than that of the mid-twentieth century,
> navigating faster and more dangerous circuits in
> pursuit of work and safety, but their journeys reprise
> past crossings in important ways. They travel with the
> ghosts of migrants past as they, too, traverse boundaries,
> negotiate with states over the terms of their inclusion,
> and alter the future histories of nations and the history of
> our world.
>
> —Mae Ngai, *Impossible Subjects*

More than 130,000 Hmong people came to the United States
as political refugees beginning in the mid-1970s. This book is a story of
why they left their country of birth and how they have rebuilt their lives
in the diverse places they now call home. Although they are one of the
ethnic minorities in America that frequently make it into the public consciousness, most Americans have little or no knowledge of who they are
and why they have been immigrating to the United States for more than
three decades. To better understand this, it is necessary to explore Hmong
social, cultural, economic, and political experiences during the twentieth century in Asia and their subsequent community-building efforts in
the United States in relation to dominant institutions, ideologies, and
aesthetics. What has occurred in the Twin Cities—St. Paul–Minneapolis,
Minnesota—Hmong American community is a microcosm of the larger
transformations taking place in different Western nations since the end
of the American war in Vietnam.

The central question this book seeks to answer is, How do refugees
build an ethnic community from scratch in the United States when they

arrive with almost no material resources but a long history of nation-building aspirations in their homeland? Several additional key questions are addressed: How is the Hmong sense of community in the United States different from what it was in Laos? What aspects of Hmong culture have changed the most, and what have changed the least? What were the central challenges to building a community, and how were they overcome? What were the main points of conflict between the Hmong and American society as they formed their communities? What were the main points of conflict among the Hmong? How are Hmong American communities at the beginning of the twenty-first century different from the initial communities established by the refugees circa 1975–85?

This book argues that Hmong community formation in the United States has been a multifaceted process utilizing both existing Hmong social-organization strategies and new resources available to them in the host country. Consequently, multiple layers of community building exist. These layers range from familial to extended kinship groups to formal institutions such as nonprofits and churches. The layers are complex because newly formed communities facilitate the invention of new identities while simultaneously generating intra-ethnic group tensions on multiple scales. Indeed, the early refugees exemplified unity and solidarity as they struggled to survive in the host society. It is not only a romanticized notion of refugee unity and solidarity. The early refugees tried to build alliances across clan lines, religious preferences, and ethnic groups. However, as the population increased and individuals and families had to negotiate their identities and traditions, new communities were then formed to represent the increasingly varied interests.

This book examines aspects of community building as they pervaded everyday life through the migration and settlement processes. In addition to recounting historical events, the voices of those who personally experienced the events and how they understood the specific situations are explored. The topics included were intentionally chosen to both illustrate Hmong solidarity and illuminate division within the ethnic group. Although refugees entering the United States are initially resettled in certain cities and towns due to the availability of American sponsors, most do not remain in these initial settlements. Consequently, these subsequent migrations have contributed greatly to community formation in disparate locations. The experience of multiple migrations within the United States suggests that Hmong American lives were, for the most part, in semipermanent mode; many Hmong expressed a desire to move to another location if and when conditions allow them to do so. By the new millennium, it appears that permanent roots are set in specific locations enabling the emergence of collective actions around many different issues.

Within the context of their diasporic conditions, this study further argues that Hmong Americans/refugees forge a collective identity based on memories of a shared past as they negotiate with racial and ethnic tensions in their new home. While many have fully invested in their lives in America and focused their energies on domestic issues, others continue to mobilize around the perceived declining quality of life of their coethnics (other members of the Hmong ethnic group) who remain behind in Laos. In doing so, they hope to change adverse conditions in the homeland. Clearly, different immigrant groups throughout American history have had contentious relationships between the homeland and the U.S. nation depending both on domestic challenges and foreign policy interests. The Hmong are no exception.

From the 1980s through the 1990s, many Americans working or interacting directly with Hmong refugees eventually went on to write about their experiences. Such books illustrate how Americans continue to be fascinated with Hmong refugees, in particular how Americans can learn about themselves by learning about the Hmong, a people consistently described as culturally very different.[1] Unlike these other studies, this book is written from the "inside" of the Hmong community and makes contributions to previous analyses of reasons for refugee flight and the multiplicity of migration experiences. It critiques representations of Hmong and reassesses Hmong history in relation to larger globalization processes. In contrast to some other studies from the "outside" and discourses on people of Hmong ethnicity that portray them as "primitive" and their culture as static, the diverse Hmong American voices heard throughout this book reveal significant heterogeneity regarding Hmong pre- and postmigration experiences. In addition to perspectives gleaned from political and military leaders, the book includes lived experiences of ordinary people, which are as important in helping us to understand key historical events as the experiences of the main actors. Another contribution this book makes to the existing literature is the rearticulation of how Hmong have not merely been victims of larger social and political transformations but have exercised much agency throughout their recent history.

It is not my intention to write a revisionist, celebratory history of Hmong migration to the United States. On the contrary, my goal is to illustrate that Hmong who live in the American context have been shaped by larger social, cultural, economic, and political transformations before, during, and after migrating to the United States and that diverse experiences have accompanied the migration and settlement processes. The agency the Hmong employed may not be apparent to those outside of their ethnic group. Due to the continued portrayal of this ethnic group as powerless victims, even those who may have worked directly with them cannot understand the depth of strategic actions taken by Hmong leaders of various levels to obtain resources for members of their ethnic group. Through the lens of events and activities that constitute the Hmong American experience, one is able to evaluate larger societal issues with respect to the notion that the United States continues to be a nation of immigrants who are not only changed by the new society but also contribute to the dynamic communities in which they settle.

Using a multidisciplinary approach, this book illustrates how Hmong American identities are socially constructed and constituted and how, with these identities, they are challenging popular assumptions about race, ethnicity, and culture in multicultural America. Its interdisciplinary approach makes contributions to Asian American, American, ethnic, and immigration studies. Beyond these fields, it touches on diplomatic and military history, in particular the ways in which diplomatic and military affairs often trigger migration flows, both forced and economic. This study goes beyond what sociologist Jeremy Hein calls the "official accounts" that refugees develop for the benefit of numerous individuals who want to know about them. Moving beyond such pretense requires knowing refugees as people rather than subjects.[2] In doing so, the stories gathered are contradictory, and some may even seem distorted as time passes and memory is lost and/or it is diluted with rhetoric and tactics constructed by exiled leaders and their supporters.

Theoretical Frameworks

Is *e pluribus unum* still a valid motto for the United States, or have contemporary immigration and diversity fractured society into separate communities? In what ways is the Asian American experience similar and different from that of minorities such as African Americans and Hispanic Americans in contrast to European Americans? How do Hmong American experiences fit into these larger frameworks? This book uses diaspora as the primary theoretical framework and engages in the debates around diasporic identities as empowerment against essentializing categories. *Diaspora* means a human scattering of peoples from their original site and location. The term has long been used to describe the forced dispersal and displacement of the Jewish, Armenian, and Greek peoples.³ Scholarship produced during the last quarter of the twentieth century has, however, expanded the term to describe the experiences of other dispersed groups.

Historian James Clifford defines the main characteristics of a diaspora as incorporating a "history of dispersal, myths/memories of the homeland, and alienation in the host country, desire for eventual return, ongoing support of the homeland, and a collective identity importantly defined by this relationship."⁴ Political scientist William Safran further describes diasporas as having the following characteristics: (1) dispersal of a "people" from an original "center" to two or more peripheral or foreign regions, (2) the presence of a collective memory or myth about the homeland, (3) a belief that the diasporic people cannot be fully accepted into the hostile host society, (4) the homeland as the true, ideal home to which the diaspora should eventually return when conditions are acceptable, (5) a commitment to the maintenance and restoration of the homeland, and (6) a continuing relationship with the homeland and a sense of ethnonational consciousness.⁵

Building on Safran's characteristics of diasporas, Robin Cohen in *Global Diasporas: An Introduction,* outlines the common features of a diaspora to include: (1) displacement from an original homeland, often traumatically, to two or more foreign regions; (2) alternatively, the expansion from a homeland in search of work, in pursuit of trade, or to further colonial ambitions; (3) a collective memory and myth about the homeland, including its location, history, and achievements; (4) an idealization of the putative ancestral home and a collective commitment to its maintenance, restoration, safety, and prosperity, even to its creation; (5) the development of a return movement that gains collective approbation; (6) a strong ethnic group consciousness sustained over a long time and based on a sense of distinctiveness, a common history, and the belief in a common fate; (7) a troubled relationship with host societies, suggesting a lack of acceptance at the least or the possibility that another calamity might befall the group; (8) a sense of empathy and solidarity with coethnic members in other countries of settlement; and (9) the possibility of a distinctive creative, enriching life in host countries with a tolerance for pluralism.⁶

Cultural theorist Stuart Hall's "anti-essentialist valorization of multiple identities" and sociologist Paul Gilroy's "Black Atlantic" have made the term *diaspora* relevant to current research on dispersed communities. Hall's discussion of identity, cultural practices, and cultural production, whereby cultural identity is understood as unstable, metamorphic, and even contradictory, argues that identity is marked at the same time by multiple points of similarities and differences. Hall promotes diaspora as a cultural identity that is enacted through difference, rather than through an emphasis on return to origins.[7] Gilroy argues against nationalist and essentialist models of cultural production by discussing the ways in which well-known black individuals have engaged in cultural exchange, production, and belonging that spans Africa, Britain, the Caribbean, and the United States.[8]

Building on these processes, Khachig Tölölyan suggests that diasporic existence does not necessarily require a return to the homeland; instead, he claims, it involves heterogeneous connections to both the homeland and other diasporic locations, through such practices as memory, travel, political commitment, and cultural production.[9] The idea that a diaspora may exist without this yearning to return to a homeland is particularly relevant to the study of Hmong in the United States as they interact with their counterparts in Europe, South America, and Oceania. These groups tend to negotiate their identities by situating themselves within the host society and their diasporic ethnic communities, rather than solely in relation to a shared physical homeland. Furthermore, people of Hmong ethnicity today define their homeland differently. Certainly, nostalgia and memory of a life very different from that of the host country are embedded in Hmong refugee/immigrant narratives, but the homeland means different geographic locations for different individuals and groups. For some of the elders, the true homeland is the People's Republic of China, the country from where their ancestors originally migrated. For the adult emigrants, that place is Laos. But for immigrant children, home may simply be Detroit, Minneapolis, Milwaukee, or Providence. To still others who were born and spent their childhood in refugee camps, home may mean Thailand.[10]

Anthropologist Steven Vertovec argues that discourses on diaspora have used the term in three distinct but related ways: as a social form, a type of social consciousness, and a mode of cultural production. Social form refers to individuals who live in different parts of the world but identify collectively with one another, with the countries or region from which they or their ancestors originated, and with the society in which they currently reside. Social consciousness makes reference to individuals who live in a variety of societies and cultures and who emphasize their sense of belonging or exclusion, their states of mind, and their sense of identity. Finally, cultural production shows how traumatic and wounding experiences construct identity and shape feelings of community in various social and political contexts and, thus, refers to the reproduction of cultural phenomena through creolization and hybridization.[11] Drawing on these diverse meanings of diaspora, this book highlights not only the ways in which Hmong Americans position themselves in relation to their homeland and their current country of residence but also the means by which they formulate an independent consciousness, transcending relationship to any particular nation-state for fulfillment.

Applying the various features described earlier, the Hmong diaspora is defined as the initial process by which members of this ethnic group went into exile and were then dispersed throughout the Americas, Europe, and Oceania. The dispersal from Laos is accompanied by the shared recollection of the traumatic so-called secret war (the U.S. covert operations in Laos during the Vietnam War era in which Hmong became entangled), which provides the memory of the great historic injustice binding the group together.[12] Furthermore, many migrants today rigorously conduct activities and maintain substantial commitments that link them with people (such as kin, covillagers, political comrades, fellow members of religious groups, and the like) who dwell in nation-states other than those in which the migrants themselves reside. Such connections are effectively maintained through the use of technology, travel, and financial mechanisms more intensely than ever before.[13] Migration within and across national boundaries has produced new transnational ties where Hmong Americans today interact with people of Hmong ethnicity not only in Laos but also in places such as Australia, Canada, France and French Guyana, and Germany. In the search for the true homeland, Hmong Americans have also made new transnational ties with their coethnics in China.[14]

In this sense, Stéphane Dufoix's concept of *referent-origin*, which could be a nation, people, land, or nonterritorial identity, is helpful in understanding Hmong experiences in the United States. As a stateless ethnic minority, their point of reference is not always tied to a physical homeland but rather is one of a people with common ancestry. Dufoix's framework for comparing the relationships between homelands and their dispersed populations consists of four ideal types that involve the structuring of the collective experience abroad. In the *centro-peripheral mode*, the home state is the controlling force with links extending between the country of origin and the community in the host country. The *enclaved mode* describes a locally organized diasporic community organized around individuals' shared identity within the host society. The enclave assists its participants in getting to know and stay in touch with each other. The *atopic mode* refers to a way of being in the world between states that is built around a common origin, ethnicity, or religion that does not reduce individuals to being subjects of a host country, nor, in this mode, does the diasporic community seek to acquire physical territory. The *antagonistic mode* essentially depicts exiled politics. In the host country, emigrants who do not recognize the legitimacy of the regime in power in their country of origin form rival groups, endeavoring to liberate their country, nation, people, or land.[15] Three of Dufoix's modes—the enclaved, atopic, and antagonistic modes—are particularly relevant to any study of the Hmong American diaspora since some Hmong have mainly focused on living at the local level, while others continue to engage in transnational activities in the hope of improving conditions for their coethnics left behind as well as building alliances among Hmong communities across the globe.

What does the term *community* mean in the context of Hmong migration? *Community* as a term is open to multiple interpretations and meanings among both scholars and the people who are in communities. It often does not mean geographical place or physical contact. In the case of stateless groups such as the Hmong, it may be best described as "imagined communities," as articulated by historian Benedict Anderson. This is not to say that the Hmong community is not real, but that the lack of a nation-state places them in a position where community transcends national borders. Anderson explains, "It is imagined because the members of even the smallest nation will never know most of their fellow-members, meet them, or even hear of them, yet in the minds of each lives the image of their communion."[16] As long as people are able to imagine this collective identity, the community will exist.

Be they economic or forced, diasporic communities form as a result of transnational migration. Linda G. Basch, Nina Glick Schiller, and Cristina Blanc define transnationalism "as the processes by which immigrants forge and sustain multi-stranded social relations that link together their societies of origin and settlement. . . . [M]any immigrants today build social fields that cross geographic, cultural, and political borders."[17] Whereas blacks have traversed diasporic paths throughout the Atlantic Ocean, Chinese investor-immigrants and professionals shuttle back and forth across the Pacific Ocean.[18] Because transmigrants are immigrants who develop and maintain multiple relationships—familial, economic, social, organizational, religious, and political—that span borders, Hmong American/refugee experiences can also be examined using this framework. If transnationalism is, however, understood using anthropologist Aihwa Ong's transnational cosmopolitans, where transnational shuttling is afforded by high levels of capital, then this framework becomes muddled when thinking about Hmong refugee experiences. In describing the strategies through which refugees are crafting Hmong/Miao[19] transnationality between the United States and China, anthropologist Louisa Schein clearly articulates that the players are neither "transmigrants" nor exemplars of migrants with "flexible citizenship" as Ong outlines.[20] However, Hmong refugees have moved along the continuum from "forced migrant" status to "transnational agents" over the course of the last few decades. Although transnational practices involving the flow of capital are in no way measurable to that of the Chinese transnational cosmopolitans, such flow has increasingly emerged since the 1990s. Business enterprises, remittances, and the popular practice of traveling to Asia to participate in New Year celebrations and/or to seek a spouse are now common Hmong American transnational activities. The difference is, the transnational ties and flow of capital are primarily between Laos and the United States and not China, where family and kinship networks have been cut off.[21]

The idea of a *perpetual refugee* is incompatible with notions of national identity where citizenship is required. Regardless of their immigration status and how long they have lived in the United States, images of Hmong continue to portray them as struggling refugees. In contrast to the American "melting pot" myth of national absorption, Hmong refugees have had to continuously define the meaning of their presence in the United States—they live in America, but what it means to be American is perplexing. The process of *becoming a refugee* has evolved into a problematic phenomenon for people of Hmong ethnicity and the nations and institutions involved. The dispersal set in motion in May 1975 was abrupt and caught many off guard as they tried to find ways to respond to the situation following American disengagement from the Vietnam conflict. Successful flight across the Lao-Thai border following the American air evacuation resulted in escapees being categorized as political refugees who were treated primarily as victims of communist oppression. As stateless people, refugees often become objects to be observed and scrutinized by outsiders, in particular the international relief apparatus. Their state of powerlessness was, however, also enabling. Despite their status as displaced persons, they are not simply objects but, often, conscious subjects who "take on an active role in carving out their new lives, making their own decisions along the way as they face new situations and cope with new contingencies."[22] Initially, people fled as a result of fear, and few, if any, could be certain about the future. As the escapees interacted with the international humanitarian regime, news spread across refugee camps and national borders about the resources inside certain camps, thus influencing some prospective migrants' decision to flee.

Refugee populations in poorer countries often struggled to survive and were a tremendous burden on local populations in first asylum countries. International relief organizations certainly lessened that burden. Yet, international involvement and attention also heightened or prolonged an internal conflict.[23] Encoded in the definition of refugee are "images of dependency, helplessness and misery."[24] In the international humanitarian regime, the refugee is both the means and the end—because it is the image of refugees that will encourage people to donate money for the relief programs that will then assist and protect them.[25] In the Hmong refugee case, when those left behind heard about the support system in place within refugee camps, some left to escape not only political persecution but also a declining economic situation with little prospect for improvement. When news from their relatives and friends who had resettled in Western countries traveled to the refugee camps and eventually to villages and towns in Laos, it had two primary effects. On one hand, the integration problems encountered by refugees in the West scared many and discouraged them from following their friends and relatives. On the other hand, the stories of economic success and educational opportunities inspired some who had not previously desired to leave the country to do so. While in the mid- to late 1970s most escapees were indeed those who had actively assisted former General Vang Pao, an officer of Hmong origin in the Royal Lao Army supported by American military personnel in Laos, others who fled later did so because they learned of the process of *becoming a refugee* connecting them with the refugee-camp bureaucracy and its benefits. As noted by political scientist Peter Nyers, "This process is not a seamless, sudden, or otherwise dramatic shift from one static state to another. . . . Rather, it is a site of struggle, a continual process of identity construction, and one that highlights how the activity and practices of refugees are recasting the terms of ethical and political discourse."[26] Learning how to become refugees enabled Hmong to enter the international humanitarian system and, for many, the opportunity to permanently settle in Western nations.

How did Hmong in Laos learn of this process? Often, men who had escaped to Thailand returned to Laos to lead other groups for a fee, sometimes paid by the escapees themselves and other times by relatives who had resettled in third countries, upon arrival of their family members in refugee camps. Although this process was dangerous, and many guides lost their lives, it became a lucrative business for some. In addition to guides, as early as 1977 there were those who had reached safety in Thailand but voluntarily returned to Laos to serve as informants for those who were interested in finding a way out of the country.[27] Additionally, Lao and Thai individuals with access to small boats made a living by working with Hmong guides to transport many escapees across the Mekong River dividing Laos and Thailand.

The forces behind Hmong refugee migration were undeniably complex. Once they began, the migratory processes became self-sustaining. With support from the United Nations High Commissioner for Refugees (UNHCR), Thailand served as the first asylum nation for Hmong refugees. Although Thailand, the United States, and Laos have all repeatedly attempted over the course of the last few decades to end the Hmong refugee situation, each time an end seemed near, a new crisis emerged. The resettlement process temporarily ceased with the closure of refugee camps in Thailand during the mid-1990s. Some chose repatriation to Laos, while others found unofficial refuge in Thailand. Before long, their semipermanent life would be repeated, and all had to decide which path to take. After years of living without the protection and supervision of UNHCR and international relief organizations, the Hmong residing in a village they themselves constructed next to Wat Tham Krabok monastery in northern Thailand were offered resettlement opportunities to the United States by the U.S. State Department in December 2003. This endeavor was characterized by U.S. policymakers as America's last payment to the Hmong for their role as U.S. allies during the American war in Vietnam. As soon as Hmong in Laos heard about the reopening of doors to America, many made their way to Thailand to find themselves labeled illegal immigrants. Although these new border crossers echoed previous arguments of either being former American allies and/or their descendants, they were not given the refugee status that their predecessors had been designated. They discovered that only those who had previously registered with Thai authorities at Wat Tham Krabok were qualified for resettlement.

This never-ending refugee crisis has partially contributed to the view that people of Hmong ethnicity in America, regardless of birthplace or immigration status, are perpetual refugees. This perpetual-refugee condition is not only imposed by individuals and institutions outside of the Hmong ethnic group. Many Hmong American community leaders continue to utilize Hmong's refugee status as justification for the allocation of various resources in the American context. They view themselves as *special* because of their involvement with American military advisers in Laos. This special status is often incorporated into discourses about their military sacrifices on behalf of American interests. Cold War anticommunist rhetoric is embedded in this discourse, which many secret-war veterans and their supporters learned to narrate in detail after being in the United States for some time.[28] Interestingly, however, this perpetual-refugee condition has placed some Hmong in America in a contentious position—in that they can make neither legitimate claims of belonging to the United States nor to Laos because a *refugee's* status is one of statelessness. Such a situation perpetuates the notion that Hmong are not integrating into American society and, like earlier views about other people of Asian descent, not assimilable into the U.S. nation.

In what ways are contemporary immigrants confirming that the United States is still a melting pot like it was for European immigrants, and in what ways are the new immigrants changing or refuting the idea of the melting pot? In fact, the varied Hmong experience in the United States is not unlike that of other refugee groups. Hmong adaptation to American society was initially heavily concentrated in the lower socio-economic strata within urban environments, but over a brief period of time, Hmong refugees developed survival mechanisms to change their socioeconomic status, in particular through forming ethnic communities to access economic opportunities and establish social support systems. Their adaptation in the United States has unquestionably hinged on a complex set of factors: some relating to the specific experiences that refugees bring with them, others to the specific environments they find in the United States, and yet others to the effects of the programs designed to facilitate their transition into American society.[29] Successful immigrant or refugee adaptation involves the total life experience, meaning success in all three dimensions: a successfully adapted refugee has attained a healthy psychological orientation, an active social participation, and a satisfactory occupation and income.[30] Refugee status often does involve forced departure; thus, such state of being may result in some having physically but not psychologically and/or emotionally arrived in a host society. Furthermore, their life experiences and socio-economic background also influence the adaptation process. Where they enter America in the socioeconomic continuum may determine their adaptation rate.

Sociologists Alejandro Portes and Min Zhou argue that immigrants today enter different segments of American life—for those who are non-white, downward assimilation into the ranks of low-income native minorities in poor urban neighborhoods is a distinct possibility, while others enter the middle-class mainstream and lose their ethnic distinctiveness.[31] Still others experience social mobility while maintaining strong ethnicities, competence in the immigrant language, and other kinds of bicultural skills.[32] Most Hmong refugees experienced "downward assimilation," in particular if they were resettled in urban, low-income neighborhoods.

They often competed for the scarce resources designed for disenfranchised populations. Those placed in suburban and/or small towns frequently became the few racial minorities in such locations. Some were welcomed by the local populations and received tremendous emotional and material support, while others encountered isolation and were targets of racially motivated violent acts. Regardless of local community reception, most longed to interact with people from their ethnic group and desired mutual support. The networks they eventually established assisted some in improving their personal and community conditions.

Immigrant networks were historically created to facilitate immigrant incorporation into host societies and to provide the basis for processes of adaptation and community formation.[33] Parallel to these processes, networks also enabled the development of transnational ties to the homeland. However, this also created possibilities for conflict within the population. This is due to the fact that although they may share a common background, have constant contact, and share similar migration experiences, these commonalities may not automatically breed cohesive and supportive networks due to politicoeconomic forces over which they have little or no control.[34] In addition, tension may arise as a result of former intra-ethnic conflicts in the homeland that are sustained in the disapora. In the Hmong refugee community context, clan rivalry, both implicitly and explicitly, affected the construction of social networks. For example, in the early 1980s community-based social-service organizations were viewed in high regard because refugees required assistance with basic needs. Board and staff members of these organizations were perceived as leaders with much power, both real and imagined. Consequently, members of various clans would promote individuals from their particular group to serve in these leadership positions, with the assumption that the members would then receive preferential treatment. One of the most visible examples is the establishment of Lao Family Community Inc. in early 1977 in California. Despite its advertised goals of serving all refugees from Laos, one of the ongoing criticisms of this agency was that its affiliation with former General Vang Pao assumed that members of the Vang clan would have an advantage over others. Additionally, his ties to Lao Family Community resulted in the organization being viewed as a front for homeland politics. Many Hmong Americans who disagreed with the politics of Vang Pao and his supporters either became uninvolved or formed their own organizations.

Although refugees arrive in the United States under different conditions, studies about them have focused on the extent to which they are incorporated into the new society. Their assimilation is measured by the extent to which the characteristics of members of the immigrant group and host societies come to resemble one another. Critiques of the immigrant incorporation model have been vast; thus, this study does not attempt to cite all relevant sources. It does, however, argue that the Hmongs' practice of *becoming a refugee* and their *perpetual-refugee status* complicates the incorporation model and makes a unique contribution to this ongoing debate. For example, do immigrants attain the "American dream" in the first, second, or third generation, or is that just an ideology to hide white privilege and racism? Clearly, the social integration and social solidarity of any migratory or refugee group are crucially affected by the existence or degree of their assimilation into the dominant culture. Refugees who arrive with little education, minimal occupational skills, and poor English are more likely to live on the fringes of American society.

The assimilation model of eventually merging new arrivals with the native population has historically not been successful, due to factors such as economic and labor processes, residential segregation, and ethnic-community formation. Most migrants were treated as either permanent settlers who would assimilate or temporary sojourners who would remain on the periphery. The general theory of immigrant incorporation in liberal democracies implies that incorporation is a one-way process and that the host society remains relatively unchanged if incorporation is successful.[35] Over time, negative stereotypes may evolve into more-positive ones, a transformation that is the principal outcome of immigrants' ascension into the mainstream.[36] This ascension, as Hein articulates, is complicated with refugees because their experiences are intimately tied to their homeland: "All forms of immigrant adaptation involve an interaction between immigrants' conditioning in their homeland and conditions in the host society. In the case of racial and ethnic adaptation, the relevant features of the host society are identities and inequalities based on perceived physical appearance and culture. Until immigrants are fully assimilated (if that ever happens), they rely heavily on their homeland histories, politics, and cultures to interpret and respond to American diversity."[37] Connection to the homeland is an integral part of how immigrants make sense of their lives and reconstruct community in diasporic locations. As further illustrated by Matthew Frye Jacobson in *Special Sorrows: The Diasporic Imagination of Irish, Polish, and Jewish Immigrants in the United States,* such interactions with those in the homeland are prominent phenomena among immigrants to the United States.[38] Enduring transnational linkages between the politics of the homeland and the culture of the diaspora are evident among Hmong in America.

Note on Methodology

This book is based on archival research, oral-history interviews, and community-event observations in St. Paul–Minneapolis, Minnesota, from 2003 through 2006. Archival research was conducted at the Immigration History Research Center (IHRC), along with examination of personal collections of Hmong American community members interviewed. The Minnesota History Center holds the State of Minnesota's refugee-program records from its inception in the late 1970s to the present. Data regarding the establishment of the first couple of Hmong community-based organizations, correspondences, policy briefs, newsletters, and reports were examined. These documents were instrumental in understanding the State of Minnesota's evolving responses to Hmong and other refugees. At the IHRC, the Refugee Studies Collection (RSC) and the International Institute of Minnesota's (IIM) refugee-resettlement case records were examined. Sources reviewed included newsletters, community-newspaper articles, policy and organization reports, pamphlets, and New Year celebration videos during the early 1980s. Additional celebration videos were provided by interviewees who were active in organizing the cultural events. Observations of New Year celebrations from 2005 to 2007[39] and many church services in the Twin Cities, as well as in other locations discussed in this book, further enhanced the archival data. Three trips were made to Arkansas, Missouri, and Oklahoma to collect additional information on Hmong poultry farmers. The phenomenon of liquidating all assets accumulated in order to purchase farms in southern states beginning in the late 1990s reveals tremendous agency among migrants. To highlight additional settlements across the United States, data was gathered in Wausau and Milwaukee, Wisconsin, and Philadelphia, Pennsylvania, during winter/spring 2008. In addition, archival research regarding the secret-war years was conducted in May 2008 at the University of Texas–Dallas, which holds the History of Aviation collection, including the Civil Air Transport–Air America special collection.

Individual interviews were conducted with thirty-six Hmong Americans, one former International Volunteer Service / U.S. Agency for International Development (USAID) employee who trained Hmong nurses in Laos during the war years, a former state refugee coordinator to help clarify programmatic issues, and one real estate agent in Arkansas who provided service to many Hmong Americans interested in purchasing poultry farms. Hmong American interviewees were asked to share their migration stories, reactions to challenges they faced, and reflections of how they have accommodated and challenged the forces of state regulations, racialization processes, identity formation, and changes in gender roles and cultural expectations. Access to interviewees was enabled by community-organization records at archives and by my insider status. I broke several canons of traditional research by asking interviewees to identify other prospective participants. This was done to ensure that those recruited included people whom I did not previously know. Careful considerations were made during the recruitment process to ensure a balance based on sex, age, immigration experience, and types of work and/or community involvement. Hmong interviewees were informed that unless they preferred a different documentation tool, interviews would be videotaped. Five interviews took place in formal office settings; the rest occurred in interviewees' homes. Because I am a trilingual researcher (Hmong, English, and French), interviewees were asked to choose the language they were most comfortable in using during the interview. Although the Hmong individuals spoke some English, almost all chose to speak Hmong. For the Hmong interviewees, communicating in their first language seemed to allow them to have natural conversations. The prepared questions guided the interviews; however, interviewees often told their stories according to what they felt was most important.

Culturally, it is difficult to enter the home of a Hmong family and directly begin the interview. It is common to take time to establish trust and mutual understanding before the formal interview. In several cases, the interviewees prepared a meal for me, which is common practice for Hmong families when receiving visitors. Thus, rather than the two-hour time requested for the interview, I have spent three to four hours talking to and learning from interviewees. Many went through boxes in their basements, attics, and photo albums to show me various items that were important to them, some of which they had not looked at since their arrival in the United States until I brought up the topic.

Because interviewees' "lives are now inextricably linked with representations," as described by Arjun Appadurai, I "incorporate the complexities of expressive representation into my ethnography not only as technical adjuncts but as primary material with which to construct and interrogate the representations."[40] I treat ethnic newspapers, newsletters of community-based organizations and articles in both English and Hmong languages, semiprofessional videos or documentaries of events, and music production as important primary data. In addition to my own interviews, I include a few relevant interviews from Concordia University's Hmong Oral History Project to enhance my own data.

1 Hmong History and Migration Prior to America

> History sets off its own chain reactions; one great event touches off another.
>
> —David Halberstam, *Ho*

Debates about Hmong origin have evolved since the first Western text, *Histoire des Miao,* was written by French missionary François Marie Savina in 1924. Savina's speculations, with biblical references, about Hmong having lived in a place of ice and snow before settling in China have been perpetuated in many writings since. Due to Hmong cultural and religious rituals and the lack of historical evidence to support such speculations, most scholars today believe that the Hmong residing in the United States today originated from southern China.[1]

It is generally agreed upon by scholars that the Hmong were pushed southward sometime after the beginning of the nineteenth century from the southwest area known today as Kweichow (the old spelling of this province) or as Guizhou Province in China, to the southern frontier along the border with Vietnam by the expanding Chinese empire. Exactly how many people migrated is not possible to estimate due to this movement occurring in a sporadic fashion over a hundred years and the lack of written documentation of the migration.[2] Most scholars also agree that significant migration has occurred only since the mid-nineteenth century. By this time, French and British colonial powers were fighting for access into southern China for its lucrative resources and markets. They often brought along Christian missionaries who would target Miao ethnic minorities for conversion, thereby seriously annoying the Manchu dynasty.[3] Miao relations with Chinese authorities had deteriorated, generating bloody wars. In the shadow of larger insurrections, such as the Taiping Rebellion from 1851 to 1864 in which an estimated 25,000,000 deaths occurred, the Miao rebellion in Guizhou from 1854 to 1873 "resulted in widespread destruction, including, by one estimate, the deaths of as many as 4,900,000 people out of a population of 7,000,000."[4] No single group dominated the rebellion during its course, and it involved more than a score of important rebel groups. Ironically, however, the rebellion came to be labeled "Miao," suggesting the historical antagonism toward the Chinese people who were not Han, the largest, dominant ethnic group in China.

The Miao category today comprises at least four linguistically and culturally related subgroups: Hmong, Hmu, Qoxiong, and the Hmau.[5] Among these ethnic minority groups referred to as Miao in China, only the Hmong were found in the Indochina peninsula where they were referred to as Méo.[6] Resistance to assimilation pressures, war, and taxation were push factors for Hmong migration southward.[7] The need for land to cultivate opium has also been suggested as a pull factor to settle in less-densely inhabited areas.[8] Because opium enabled Hmong to participate in trade with others and to make a living, its cultivation served as a key factor in determining migration and settlement in Southeast Asia. Those who moved first settled in the northern regions of Vietnam and Laos and then eventually in Thailand. Some made the journey to Burma (Myanmar), where today a couple thousand live.

Social Structure

Before examining their migration and settlement experiences in Southeast Asian locations, a brief overview of Hmong social structure may be helpful because this structure shaped Hmong worldviews and the relationships they developed within their ethnic group and with outsiders—a social structure that persists to this day. Hmong society was and still is based on a kinship system that is divided into patrilineal clans and further separated by subclans based on lineages. The clan (*xeem*) system serves as both a unifying and a dividing force. It determines how people relate to one another. Clan membership is a birthright and could be obtained through adoption. As a religious practice, ancestral worship historically served as a constant across clans. However, religious rituals and other traditions varied from one clan to another and may exclude nonclan members.[9] Across the approximately eighteen Hmong clans, elders served as leaders to oversee the health and well-being of the immediate and extended family. Elder males primarily supervised and directed a system of conflict resolution, addressing disputes of every nature, and supervised the performance of religious rituals. As a precursor to knowledge and wisdom, age influenced who could become clan leaders.[10]

Members of the same clan—whose clan name was their last name—considered one another to be part of a larger family; however, not all Hmong with the same surname were related. Marriage among clan members was not allowed, as men and women from the same clan were broadly considered brothers and sisters.[11] In order to be considered close relatives, clan members had to be able to trace their lineage to a common male ancestor. As explained by anthropologist Gary Yia Lee, "Clan identification is made on the basis of a common surname. When two persons have a similar surname, they are said to belong to the same clan. If they further share similar rituals but without any genealogical connection, then they are of the same subclan, a grouping intermediate between the clan and lineage. A lineage is known in Hmong as a 'cluster of brothers' (*ib cuab kwv tij*), and a subclan as 'one ceremonial household' (*ib tus dab qhuas*). One of the distinguishing features between kinship categories is that members of a lineage can die in one another's house and will be given a funeral but not people related only by clan or subclan membership."[12] White Hmong (*Moob dlawb* / *Hmoob dawb*)[13] and Green Hmong (*Moob Ntsuab* or *Moob Leeg* / *Hmoob Ntsuab* or *Hmoob Lees*) shared one language with two dialects that are mutually intelligible. In the pre–Vietnam War era when they lived in isolated villages, it was possible to distinguish between the two groups by physical markers such as clothing; however, in the diaspora, Hmong have access to a variety of costumes and dress according to their taste rather than dialect. Clothing is no longer a useful distinction. Furthermore, white Hmong and green Hmong shared many of the same eighteen clan names. Today, the two most common Hmong surnames in the United States are Vang and Yang. The others include: Cha (Chang), Cheng, Chu, Fang, Hang, Her (Heu), Khang, Kong, Kue, Lo (Lor), Lee (Ly), Moua, Pha (Phang),Thao (Thor), Vue, and Xiong.[14]

The Indochinese Peninsula

The Hmong migration from China to the Indochinese peninsula has been described both as "fleeing en masse from specific dangers in China" and as "pioneering households" simply trying their luck.[15] Hmong, sometimes consisting of mostly members of the same clan, settled in small villages in the mountainous regions. When allowed to coexist with other groups, they lived in relative peace. However, when their way of life was threatened, they often rebelled. Their practice of slash-and-burn agricultural methods, requiring frequent searches for fresh, fertile land, resulted in the consistent description of this ethnic group as nomads, "mountain dwellers," and "isolationists" who did not mix with other peoples. The primary method for incorporating Hmong into Lao, Vietnamese, and Thai societies was taxation. Other than that, they existed primarily on the margins of these societies. Most survived by subsistence farming, hunting, and gathering. Although some interacted with other indigenous peoples of the northern regions, few ventured into larger towns and cities in the lowland.

Hmong lives would change dramatically with the arrival of French colonists in the late 1800s. Although rebellions had occurred in southern China prior to their migration southward, Hmong did not have the kinds of political opportunities that came with French colonialism. French conquest of the region began with the southernmost part of modern-day Vietnam and continued into southern Vietnam in 1862, Cambodia in 1863, Annam (central Vietnam) and Tonkin (northern Vietnam) in 1883, and ended with establishing Laos as a protectorate in 1893.

To consolidate its power, France created the Indochinese Union (l'Union Indochinoise) as a federal administrative structure to rule the region's culturally diverse peoples. Of the colonies, Laos was considered to be the least important.[16] As such, it remained a colonial backwater within the French empire, experiencing little economic, social, and political change.[17] With anticolonial sentiments among some segments of the population in Paris, the colonial administration not only had to demonstrate that colonialism contributed to France's grandeur but also that it was self-sustaining. Imposition of heavy taxes upon colonial subjects and a monopoly over opium production and sale became a major portion of the colonial administration's budget and reduced the burden on French citizens, thus pacifying anticolonialist voices.

In line with France's civilizing mission (la mission civilisatrice) to spread its republican ideals, racist colonial administrators often regarded the local population as primitive people who might eventually modernize. The extent to which colonial subjects gained approval depended largely on their acceptance of the colonizers' ways. France administered the colonies with a gouvernor général to oversee a lower bureaucracy staffed primarily by educated Vietnamese, who were viewed by the French as industrious and more intelligent than the other colonial subjects. The concept of the Indochinese Union encouraged ambitious Vietnamese to migrate to Laos and Cambodia where they dominated in government jobs and businesses. This domination would later contribute to anti-Vietnamese sentiments among some Laotian and Cambodian nationalists.

Colonists were welcomed by some from the local population who benefited from their presence. Corrupted native intermediaries often imposed additional taxes on ethnic minorities, which at times resulted in revolts against native intermediaries and colonists.[18] The first Hmong-led revolt in Laos against such practices occurred in 1896 and resulted in the appointment of a representative, *kiatong*, by the French from the Moua clan in one northern district (*tasseng*). Two decades later, Hmong within and beyond Laos revolted against corrupted native administrators and the colonizers, in what is referred to by the colonial regime as the "Guerre du fou" (Madman's War) from 1918 to 1921.[19] The colonizers' practice of divide and conquer put an end to this revolt. Those who collaborated with the French to defeat revolt participants were rewarded. Because of his role in the killing of revolt leader Pachay Vue (?–1921), Blia Yao Lor (?–1933)[20] was appointed *tasseng* of Nong Het district in Xieng Khouang province to represent Hmong interests to the colonial administration. Consequently, he became the wealthiest Hmong in Indochina during the early 1900s.

The relationship that people of Hmong ethnicity initially forged with French colonists would set the stage for future ethnic divisions throughout the twentieth century. The small gains made by the 1896 and 1918 revolts taught ambitious Hmong that alliance with the colonizers was beneficial and thus instigated Hmong clan rivalry for political and economic power. Other Hmong envied the wealth that Blia Yao Lor acquired from representing his ethnic group to the colonial administration. After witnessing the power that Blia Yao Lor possessed during the early 1920s, a member of the Ly clan, Xia Foung Ly, strategically established family ties by marrying one of Blia Yao Lor's daughters, May. It has been assumed that he formed this union to give him access to the leader's wealth. He became Blia Yao Lor's secretary.[21] As a determined man, Xia Foung Ly gained great wealth from opium sales and was able to hire a Laotian teacher to come to Nong Het and teach his three sons, who would later study in Xieng Khouang town and in the Lao capital, Vientiane.[22] It is believed that May's suicide in 1922 angered Blia Yao Lor greatly and resulted in severed ties between the Lor and Ly clans.

When Blia Yao Lor died in the early 1930s, his power was passed down to his oldest son, Chong Tou Lor, who eventually mismanaged his father's wealth. His inability to collect taxes for the colonial administration led to a transfer of the leadership position to Xia Foung Ly, who used his personal wealth to make up the due taxes. The rivalry escalated. The final blow to the Lor clan would come in 1939 when Xia Foung Ly died. Rather than transferring the position back to the Lor clan as promised to Blia Yao Lor's widow and Chong Tou's younger brother, Faydang, the French gave the position to Xia Foung Ly's youngest son, Touby (1917–79). With formal education of about the tenth grade behind him and a fascination with all things French, Touby was the preferred candidate for the Hmong leadership position. Touby Lyfoung's appointment offended the Lor clan greatly, in particular, Faydang Lor, and it produced a layer of ethnic conflict that persisted through the end of American involvement in Southeast Asia. In addition to serving as district chief, Touby Lyfoung was appointed to the Opium Purchasing Board by the colonial administration in 1940, which brought about great wealth not only to himself but also members of his extended family and clan. He was also revered by many Hmong due to his advocacy for a village school for Hmong children. He saw access to formal education as a means to improve his ethnic group's position in Lao social and political life.

Prior to the arrival of the French, a Lao national identity did not exist. What is now the Lao state was under the control of different royal families in three regions: Luang Prabang in the north, Vientiane in the center, and Champassak in the south. Unique opportunities emerged during World War II for those who desired freedom from colonial rule. World War Two facilitated anticolonial movements in much of the Third World and transformed the lives of disparate peoples like the Hmong. Lao nation-building efforts in the aftermath of the war provided Hmong with new opportunities to align with various factions. The alliances would determine their positions in the ensuing political struggles. Nationalist Prince Phetsarath Rattanavongsa established the *Lao Issara* (Free Lao) movement on October 12, 1945, to counter French occupation and uphold the Lao declaration of independence proclaimed by King Sisavangvong on April 8, 1945. Most members of *Lao Issara* were anti-Vietnamese, due to their fear of Vietnamese encroachment. This fear was based on the fact that, with the exception of Luang Prabang, all major towns in Laos were dominated by Vietnamese. Therefore, the Laos' struggle was not only to free themselves of French colonialism but also Vietnamese domination.

Like the *Viet Minh* nationalists in Vietnam, *Lao Issara* members had hoped that the United States would oppose the return of French colonial rule following World War II. However, U.S. interest in a strong France to resist communist expansion in Europe eliminated any hope of American support. Following the Japanese surrender to the Allies, British troops sent to disarm the Japanese south of the sixteenth parallel facilitated French return; consequently, on August 27, 1946, the Western powers signed a *modus vivendi* that endorsed the unity of Laos as a constitutional monarchy within the French Union. Internal political struggles became intense because some nationalists desired complete liberation from foreign powers. The political situation was filled with confusion, defying an accurate assessment of power relationships in the region, due to rivalries among numerous factions at all levels.[23]

Within the Hmong ethnic group, Touby Lyfoung aligned himself with those who were pro-French and, in fact, helped French parachutists in France's attempt to reinstate its colonial rule. Young Vang Pao, who would go on to play a major role in U.S. covert operations in Laos, worked within the Royal Lao Army and sided with Touby Lyfoung during the First Indochina War (1946–54). Both were interested in protecting the Hmong way of life, as well as increasing opportunities for Hmong in Lao political life. Reinstatement of French colonial rule after World War II resulted in Touby Lyfoung's appointment as district governor (*chao muong*) of the Hmong of Xieng Khouang province in 1946.[24] The following year, one of his older brothers, Toulia, became one of the province's representatives in the new Royal Lao Government (RLG) National Assembly, which was established by nationalists aligned with France in 1947. Because the French were plunged into the First Indochina War against the Vietminh, the Lao relationship with France would gradually change. In July 1949, France and the RLG signed a new general convention to grant Laos greater autonomy. By October 1953, the RLG attained full sovereignty, and the military defeat of the French at Dien Bien Phu in spring 1954 formally ended French colonialism in Indochina and resulted in a declaration of Lao neutrality.

Internal political strife between Lao elites of royal background resulted in factions aligning themselves with either the United States or the Vietnamese nationalists supported by China and the former Soviet Union. By the mid-1940s, Communist-led Vietnamese nationalists began recruiting Lao supporters. In 1949, Prince Souphanouvong (1909–95), who was the half-brother of royalist Prince Phetsarath and rightist Prince Souvanna Phouma (1901–84), resigned from *Lao Issara* and aligned himself with the Communists. The following year, he and other leftist nationalists formed a new organization, *Neo Lao Issara* (Lao Freedom Front), which would become the *Pathet Lao* (Lao Communist Party) in 1955.[25] Past political divisions meant that Faydang Lor chose to act in opposition to Touby Lyfoung, therefore throwing his support to the *Pathet Lao.*

Today it is known that U.S. covert activities on Lao territory were carried out in support of the larger war theater in Vietnam, but at the time, they were hidden from the American public. As in other parts of the world, the principal Eisenhower administration cold-war strategy of appealing to the rights of ethnic minorities against communist domination reached Laos. In the 1950s, some Lao politicians began to reproduce American-inspired anticommunist rhetoric. Lao leaders became masters at channeling and twisting the U.S. rhetorical and policy imperatives to their own aims, which kept American aid flowing in by the millions. The 1954 Geneva Peace Accords declared Lao neutrality, but, before the ink dried, cold-war political struggles resulted in both the East and the West interfering in Lao politics. As a result of the Truman Doctrine committing American support in the fight against communism anywhere in the world, U.S. policy makers pushed for not only a neutral Laos but also one that was pro-American. In its attempts to win over the Lao people, U.S. officials established a military-aid program in 1955 to train the Lao army.

United States' proselytizing efforts in Laos had achieved minimal success by the late 1950s. Interfering in the 1958 Lao national election still did not produce a pro-American National Assembly. American military personnel had been training the Royal Lao Army and upgrading the Royal Lao Air Force, but they became frustrated with Lao leaders as well as the performance of soldiers under their guidance. As a consequence of Vietnamese communist penetration of men and supplies through Lao territory, in what came to be known as the Ho Chi Minh Trail, the U.S. intelligence community changed its tactics in 1961 to ones that would involve counterinsurgency. An agent with the U.S. Central Intelligence Agency (CIA), James William (Bill) Lair proposed the recruitment, armament, and training of highland ethnic minorities through the creation of special guerrilla units (SGUs) to harass Vietnamese and Lao communists. He had been successful in training Thai paramilitary units (PARU) in northeastern Thailand.[26] His superiors embraced the proposal because it promised to be a good deal for the Americans since U.S. soldiers would not be required. In addition to putting pressure on the North Vietnamese and their *Pathet Lao* ally, it would be a low-cost, low-profile operation. Policymakers' embrace of this strategy set in motion what would come to be called America's clandestine war in Laos, where Hmong and other ethnic minorities became entangled in cold-war political struggles.[27]

By the time the only Hmong military officer met with Lair in 1961, Vang Pao had attained the rank of major within the Royal Lao Army.[28] He was born about 1930 in Xieng Khouang, Laos, where he and his family farmed like most other people of Hmong ethnicity in northern Laos.

Figure 1. Hmong soldiers practice using grenades. Pat Landry, Box 1, CAT/ Air America Archive, the History of Aviation Collection, Eugene McDermott Library, Special Collections at University of Texas–Dallas. Photo courtesy of Special Collections Department, McDermott Library.

They also had limited means and did not have the privilege to attend school. Similar to other Hmong leaders before him, Vang Pao's rise to power depended largely on collaborating with powerful foreigners. Having worked with Touby Lyfoung and the French, he understood the importance of such collaborations. Following the French defeat at Dien Bien Phu in May 1954, Hmong in Laos who had aligned with the colonizers no longer had the support they once received. Vang Pao and others participated with Royal Lao forces in engaging the *Pathet Lao* on a small scale throughout the late 1950s, but no significant changes took place.[29] A self-described devout anti-communist, Vang Pao was interested in protecting northeastern Laos, where most people of Hmong ethnicity lived, from Communist domination. Because he had limited capacity as an ethnic minority officer, he also became frustrated with the performance of soldiers under his command.

Due to experiences of benefits from alliance with the French, it is not a surprise that Vang Pao welcomed Lair's offer to arm Hmong and other ethnic minorities. In return for supporting American communist-

Figure 2. Thai paramilitary train Hmong to use machine guns. Pat Landry, Box 1, CAT/Air America Archive, the History of Aviation Collection, Eugene McDermott Library, Special Collections at University of Texas–Dallas. Photo courtesy of Special Collections Department, McDermott Library.

containment policies, Vang Pao and his people received military and humanitarian aid. However, what exactly took place between Vang Pao and Lair in 1961 has been contested. According to Lair, the only thing Vang Pao said during their meeting was, "We can't live with the communists. . . . If you give us the weapons, we will fight them."[30] What is certain is that the meeting did take place, and that, following this encounter, arms, financial support, and humanitarian aid materialized. The lack of written documents regarding the deal struck between the two men has led to a much-mythicized meeting where, in addition to the above, Hmong were promised a homeland if the United States was successful in its communist containment initiatives. Historians may never discover whether Vang Pao truly understood geopolitics on an international level at the time. While it was impossible for him to foresee the future of his people, it is clear he viewed Lair's offer as one he could not refuse. It came at a time when he had made no progress in his career as an officer in the Royal Lao Army. His lack of power and the discrimination from his superiors and subordinates due to his status as an ethnic minority officer created a difficult situation for him. Lair's ability to deliver on the material promises increased Vang Pao's status both in the

Hmong population and among the Lao elite. Clearly, the CIA was using him and his people, but he also used the CIA to meet his personal goals and, eventually, the needs of those from his ethnic group who sided with him.

Recruitment of prospective soldiers was intense because few people understood the underlying reasons why they were asked to take up arms. The first Hmong recruits received basic training in the early 1960s at Hua Hin, in northeastern Thailand. Thai paramilitary officers conducted the training under the direction of American advisers (see fig. 3).[31] The recruits would arrive and receive instruction in weaponry and counterinsurgency tactics while continuing to wear their native clothes. As American involvement increased and the clandestine army evolved into a near-conventional army, soldiers were provided with military uniforms. Vang Pao's army eventually grew from about nine thousand in 1961 to forty thousand men in 1969.[32] High casualties, in addition to the need for thousands to construct several airstrips on Laos's mountainous terrain,

Figure 3. American military advisers observe weapons training of Thai paramilitary with Hmong men and boys. Pat Landry, Box 1, CAT/Air America Archive, the History of Aviation Collection, Eugene McDermott Library, Special Collections at University of Texas–Dallas. Photo courtesy of Special Collections Department, McDermott Library.

meant that leaders had to continuously seek fresh recruits. The quality and length of training diminished as the war progressed. CIA case officers advised the clandestine army and helped decide targeting for air warfare. Over time, as CIA power grew, so did Vang Pao's military status—to the rank of major general. In addition, many others acquired military rank as never before in Hmong history.

This secret war of Laos was directed by the U.S. embassy in Laos in collaboration with the CIA. The CIA airline, Air America, was on contract to provide support, operating from Thailand (see fig. 4).[33] Bill Lair explained, "Fairly early in the game we wanted to keep everybody out of the Hmong headquarters operation area. We were trying to keep newspaper people out."[34] The military activities in northern Laos were considered top secret, especially the CIA-supported military base at Long Cheng. Long Cheng served as headquarter for Vang Pao's army, which ran espionage, sabotage, and propaganda missions between the base and

Figure 4. Udorn Air Base was constructed around 1964 in northeastern Thailand by the United States to provide air support to war efforts in Laos and Vietnam. Photo courtesy of Clarence J. Abadie Jr., Box 2, CAT/Air America Archive, History of Aviation Collection, Eugene McDermott Library, Special Collections at University of Texas–Dallas. Photo courtesy of Special Collections Department, McDermott Library.

across the frontier with the assistance of CIA operatives. Guerrilla fighters under Vang Pao's command conducted long-range reconnaissance patrols into Pathet Lao territory and North Vietnam and became America's foot soldiers in Laos. To cover up U.S. military activities, a humanitarian location at Sam Thong, roughly twelve miles from Long Cheng, was established from which U.S. Agency for International Development (USAID) staff operated. A hospital and schools for village children were constructed on this location, and it served as the showcase for visiting U.S. dignitaries. This diversion was carried out to show American policymakers only the humanitarian aspect of U.S. involvement in Laos.

To a large extent, the humanitarian work was intimately tied to the military operations. As the war continued and the United States' commitments in Vietnam increased, so did U.S. involvement on the Laos side. At the request of Lao Prime Minister Souvanna Phouma, U.S. secret missions began striking targets in Laos along the North Vietnamese infiltration routes into South Vietnam.[35] Escalation of the war resulted in

Figure 5. Thai paramilitary instructs Hmong men and boys on weapons. Pat Landry, Box 1, CAT/Air America Archive, the History of Aviation Collection, Eugene McDermott Library, Special Collections at University of Texas–Dallas. Photo courtesy of Special Collections Department, McDermott Library.

another request by Souvanna Phouma on December 1, 1964, for American aerial support of Vang Pao's forces through Operation Barrel Roll. In March 1965, Operation Steel Tiger continued this massive bombing campaign aimed at the Ho Chi Minh Trail.[36] Additionally, Royal Lao Air Force T-28s flew between two hundred and three hundred missions per day attacking enemy positions, which were often difficult to determine. Some of the pilots were Hmong. The most famous was a young man by the name of Lue Lee (1935–69), who flew over forty-two hundred combat sorties before losing his life on July 12, 1969. He was considered Vang Pao's right-hand man. Those who worked with him described Lue Lee as intelligent and daring because he possessed "unorthodox flying manners."[37] U.S. strike missions increased more significantly during the next few years. Ironically, the temporary bombing halt of North Vietnam that President Lyndon B. Johnson announced in 1968 freed additional planes for sorties over Laos, resulting in Laos being one of the most bombed locations in world history. In many locations along the Laos-Vietnamese border, unexploded ordinances have become a part of the landscape. Each year, hundreds of innocent people are killed and/or injured as a result of accidently coming into contact with them.

In 1969, U.S. military and civilian leaders still pretended that American presence in Laos was merely humanitarian and that the United States was not directly participating in the Laotian civil war. The portrayal of American military activities in Laos as a "secret" suggests that no one knew about the situation. In actuality, it was a secret only because open, public discussions were not taking place. Indeed, "[congressional] committees were well aware of what was happening. Appropriations subcommittees provided the funds and were briefed at regular intervals. [Senators] were 'very approving.' They believed 'it was a much cheaper and better way to fight a war in Southeast Asia than to commit American troops.'"[38] The war effort was cheap because the vast majority of lives lost in Laos were not American, thus preventing the kind of antiwar outrage that events in Vietnam generated among a segment of the U.S. population. The absence of U.S. combat troops facilitated perpetuation of this secret for eight years, until an unauthorized visit paid to Long Cheng (also known as Lima Site 20A) by *Time/Life* correspondent Timothy Allman and a French reporter exposed the operation in 1970.[39] This exposure set in motion outsiders' fascination with Long Cheng and the Hmong guerrilla fighters. Furthermore, refugee stories of heavy U.S. bombing made it difficult for American officials to continue denying U.S. military activities in Laos.[40] Although prevented before from entering the entire war zone surrounding Long Cheng, news reporters

Figure 6. Hmong soldiers train in parachuting. Pat Landry, Box 1, CAT/Air America Archive, the History of Aviation Collection, Eugene McDermott Library, Special Collections at University of Texas–Dallas. Photo courtesy of Special Collections Department, McDermott Library.

subsequently disregarded previously accepted denials. In 1971, the U.S. mission relaxed many of the secrecy restrictions, and for the first time, journalists were finally allowed on the premises. Long Cheng's legend continued to attract outsiders, as illustrated by journalist Don Ronk's description of the city: "The secret city itself. Buildings bristling with exotic antennas, filled with intricate electronic systems for airplane guidance and listening, computers, millions of dollars worth of gadgets. On the valley's runway airplanes, their chief asset being able to approach and depart ahead of their own sound, land and take off with virtually no runway. Helicopters and lumbering cargo planes—all of it hidden deep in a forbidden city."[41] High-technology gadgets, helicopters, and cargo planes seemed to contradict all other portrayals of Hmong life experiences in Laos as people surviving only from subsistence agriculture. The depiction of Long Cheng as a "forbidden city" suggests that it was an aberration. How could people who have been described by colonial administrators and missionaries as primitive be operating airplanes, trucks, and complex computer and radio systems?

What impact did the American military and humanitarian bureaucracies in Laos during the 1960s through the early 1970s have on Hmong society? What occurred because of the U.S. presence in Long Cheng was nearly a decade of social, cultural, and political transformations affecting the lives of thousands of Hmong and other ethnic minorities. No longer able to remain in their villages, the displaced people regrouped in and around Long Cheng. At the same time that war inflicted extreme pain and suffering, it also presented new opportunities. Although subsistence farming had clearly been the dominant daily activity in prewar Hmong society, war-generated disruptions beginning in the early 1960s changed this, heralding subsequent social and cultural changes in familial and community life.

The most dramatic change brought about by life in the resettlement centers in Laos was the loss of self-sufficiency. With neither enough land nor enough able-bodied men to grow their own food, the once self-sufficient Hmong became dependent on U.S. food airdrops, and a generation of Hmong children grew up without first-hand knowledge of farming practices.[42] While the war produced a dependent segment of the internal refugee population, it also brought about educational, employment, and business opportunities, all of which changed the ways in which Hmong people lived and imagined their lives. Most accounts of Hmong history and culture have largely overlooked such transformations.

Men's absence during war time in any society requires dramatic adjustments in women's roles. When their men went off to war, women took on all of their responsibilities. The conversion of Hmong fighters from a guerrilla force into a conventional army meant growth of an increasingly complex military bureaucracy that required military scribes whose job involved writing on behalf of the clandestine army.[43] While only members of a few families were appointed to chief provincial and village positions during French colonialism, Hmong association with American officials made possible a plethora of positions. Paid positions were available in quasi-military, economic aid, and rural development arenas, including the clandestine army, health care, education, refugee relief, and psychological warfare. This massive collection of people further changed Hmong lives immeasurably. The prestige that came with obtaining an education resulted in General Vang Pao's request for USAID to construct schools near the refugee-relocation centers. Efforts were made to recruit teachers to teach at these schools. The drive to increase education in the Hmong population meant that those who had some formal education became highly respected teachers. From the early 1960s through the early 1970s, numerous village schools were built around Long Cheng and Sam Thong. During this same period, it was estimated that nearly ten thousand Hmong children attended primary school. Some students were sent to the capital city to attend high school or receive other specialized training.

As refugees moved into crowded relocation centers, their lives then became plagued with other challenges, such as illnesses and continuous exposure to the death of soldiers at the frontline. Injuries at the front line as well as from bombs dropped by both sides of the war required additional medical support. Young women were recruited to support the war effort; this challenged Hmong cultural practices that unmarried women were not allowed to live away from their parents. Over one hundred ethnic minority women, mostly Hmong, were trained as "nurses" to assist the hospital staff at Sam Thong (also known as Lima Site 20).[44] A dormitory was built at Sam Thong for the women. The prestige that such positions promised attracted many to the program, but some could not handle the extreme conditions and left following the training. Those who stayed often worked day and night as the casualties of combatants and civilians increased.

The events unfolding in Vietnam had a direct impact on battlefronts in Laos. Following the Paris Agreement on Vietnam on January 27, 1973, representatives of the Royal Lao Government and the *Pathet Lao* agreed to a cease-fire to end the Laotian civil war on February 21, 1973. The agreement called for the formation of a Provisional Government of National Union, equal sharing of responsibilities, and integration of military forces between the two factions. But because the United States wanted to get out of the war in Vietnam, Laotian interests, like those of Vietnamese in the south that the United States supported, were compromised. For example, previous negotiations in the larger Vietnam conflict had demanded withdrawal of North Vietnamese Army (NVA) troops from the southern part. In the final Paris negotiations, U.S. National Security Advisor Henry Kissinger agreed to remove that requirement in order to reach an agreement with Hanoi delegates. Knowing that thousands of NVA troops were present on Lao territory did not concern Kissinger, who strongly urged the Royal Lao government to sign the peace agreement with the *Pathet Lao* leaders in order to secure his own country's departure from the region. Without prior levels of U.S. funding, the Royal Lao government and its army were no longer able to maintain their previous military capacity. General Vang Pao and his soldiers, who existed within the military infrastructure of the Royal Lao government, were then forced to wait for outsiders to determine their fate, resulting in their ultimate political and military decimation.

Factionalism, however, prevented a peaceful resolution, despite an official cease-fire. From February 1973 through May 1975, an array of provocations from both sides took place due to intense distrust and fear on all parts. In these deeply troubled months, a slim hope of peace did emerge. The new government announced that military officers would be allowed to keep their rank when joining the new army. While some in the military coexisted during this interim period, many Hmong soldiers chose to go back to their villages and were ready to return to civilian life. But as the communist regime gained ground, purges of former American collaborators began to reach Hmong villages. People did not feel safe traveling, and, with no more food supplies from American airdrops, a sense of insecurity gave rise to anxiety about the future. Those who lived in Laos during these critical months, regardless of political affiliation, experienced a harsh reality. Without the American funds that had fueled the Lao economy for so long, many had to scramble to survive. Those displaced from their villages during the war and no longer able to practice their self-sufficient, agrarian lifestyles became despondent. With chaos, a sense of hopelessness developed, and few were motivated to conduct daily routines.

How did Hmong people interpret their reality at the local level from the early 1960s through the early 1970s? Hmong during the 1960s did not completely understand America's broader priorities in Southeast Asia. Most Hmong Americans who lived through the war years mainly learned about U.S. interests in Laos when they arrived in America. Hmong entanglement in Lao political struggles beginning during World War II had cast them as both potential allies and enemies by the different factions. Over the course of the last three decades, two competing debates have continued regarding the role that Hmong in Laos played during the war. Some describe Hmong as heroic homeland protectors and America's allies, while others argue that they were merely mercenaries. Regardless of one's perspective, the reality is that they suffered a high proportion of casualties. In comparison to the United States losing more than 58,000 citizens during the Vietnam conflict out of nearly 3 million who served, the Hmong lost approximately 17,000 soldiers out of an estimated population of 350,000 before the war.[45] Because Vietnam was an unpopular war, many American soldiers returned only to become targets of animosity by their own people for having participated in a war that most of those soldiers had no control over. Like these soldiers, Lao, Hmong, and other ethnic minorities who collaborated with the United States were ostracized and had to seek refuge elsewhere after the communist regime came into power in 1975.

The Air Evacuation

The fate of many people in Laos was influenced by the fall of Saigon on April 30, 1975, to the communists. Viewed by communist forces as a historic liberation of the Vietnamese in the south from American imperialism, this day represented an end to American victory culture. Near Long Cheng, it was as though a dam had broken in mid-May 1975. When word spread that American officials planned to airlift military personnel and their family members out of Long Cheng, chaos ensued. Danger loomed in the area as many were angry at the thought of being abandoned by their military leaders to face an uncertain future. Throngs of people arrived with every type of imaginable belonging that they could carry to await the airplanes. As soon as the airplanes landed, people—military personnel as well as civilians—fought for a place on the aircrafts. Some children were thrown inside while their parents struggled to climb up the ladder. Some climbed over others in order to get inside. From May 11 to 14, thousands showed up every day to find a way out of Laos.

Former residents of Long Cheng who would eventually all rebuild their lives in the state of Minnesota share their memories and observations of those last few days. Mai Yer Her, a mother of an infant and wife of a young soldier, recalls the fierce competition:

> When we learned about the need to flee, we actually went on the first day to wait for the planes. There were hundreds of people. You heard walkie-talkies going on and off. Everyone was scared and wanted to save themselves. Everyone fought to get in line first. People weren't kind to each other. Before the planes even arrived, I looked at the situation, and it scared me. I worried at that time that there was no way I could fight the crowd to get on the planes. Something miraculous happened for us. My husband had gone back to his office, and another smaller plane was going to land on the north side of the landing strip. My husband had come back to pick me up in a car. I carried my child on my back and a basket in my hand. We got in the plane with Jerry [Daniels]. We were so blessed because we were alone and were able to get out of there safely. . . . If we had waited with the crowd that day, there would have been no way for us to get on those planes. We weren't high-ranking officers, and we had a baby.[46]

Xang Vang, one of the men who were literate who served as a military scribe in the army, remembers being encouraged to remain in position.

Although he was in a privileged position, he acknowledged not being in-formed of any evacuation plans: "That very afternoon, I said OK, I'll grab my wife and child and then go into the C-130 to Thailand. The military officers were not told that the country was collapsing. All we were told was to stay in position and make sure our jobs were running. We were supposed to keep everything in place until the last minute when they told us to run for our lives. So, I ran to get my wife and child."[47]

Husband and wife Yia Lee, who was active in supporting Ameri-can propaganda activities, and Mao Vang Lee, a young woman who had learned to read and write in Hmong and who worked at the CIA-sponsored radio station at Long Cheng, gave up after witnessing the mob of people fighting to enter the airplanes. Mao explained their decision, "My hus-band and I waited with the crowd for three days, but we just could not compete with the crowd. Our son was only five months old. As soon as the airplane lands, the crowd was already packed underneath it before it came to a halt. . . . People did not fear death. They would fight, step on each other to get into the plane. If the husband gets in, sometimes the wife would be left behind and vice versa. After observing this for three days, we just decided that we would never both make it together with a small baby. We decided to stay even though we feared for our lives as having been paid by the Americans."[48] Yia added, "There are no words to describe that moment of departure from Long Cheng. The landscape remains the same, but the people had all dispersed. If you weren't sad, then you didn't have a heart. Everyone cried. In those moments, there was sense of hopelessness. No dreams for the future. You become like thin air."[49]

May A Yang is one of the few Hmong women to receive an educa-tion and who had the opportunity to work as a teacher. She was married to T-28 pilot Sue Vang, who died during a combat mission. May recalled being told by a male relative to not flee. The male leaders encouraged her to stay because they did not believe women and children would be in danger under the new regime. May A refused to listen to them and prepared her four children for the departure. Many years have passed, but she remembers that challenging day with clarity:

> When General Vang Pao and his officers were being airlifted out of Long Cheng, I was there to try to get on the planes because my husband was a pilot. He died while on duty. I had four children. I carried my son Kong Pheng on my back and held on to the three older children. Fortu-nately, some of the soldiers who worked with my husband helped my children into the airplane. At that time, I was told by my brother-in-law that the leaders were only expected to stay in Thailand for about one

month, then they would go to the U.S. General Vang Pao had discouraged me from leaving the country. He told my brother-in-law to tell me to stay in Vientiane. He suggested sending my children away with my brother-in-law. Because my husband was no longer alive, General Vang Pao didn't seem to be concerned about me. He suggested that because I was a woman, the communists probably would not do anything to me. I wouldn't listen and got the last flight out of there.[50]

Although these were clearly difficult moments for everyone, it appears that women whose husbands were present were in a better position. Like Mai Yer Her, May Ia Lee was married to one of the literate soldiers at the time. Her husband also worked in the clandestine army, and he made decisions for her. She explained that she merely followed his directions to pack her belongings. It was not until she was amidst the crowd that she realized the tragedy surrounding her. She recalls with teary eyes, "Fighting to get out of there was like a bunch of ants fighting to get into the ground. Everyone was fighting for their lives. Families all got dispersed. If you got in, you just prayed that your family members did, too. . . . Some people threw their personal belongings into the plane but then were not able to get into the plane. When we landed, it was great joy, but, oh, you could see people crying everywhere. Some children made it without their parents. I don't know who helped who at the time. You couldn't be concerned about anyone else because your heart was broken too."[51]

These narratives portray a state of uncertainty. While thousands fought for several days to get on one of the flights out of Long Cheng, only about twenty-five hundred were fortunate enough to secure a spot. The vast majority stood stunned as they watched the last C-130 leave Long Cheng, with no assurance that the airplanes would return for them. When the dust settled, those left behind staggered under the weight of confusion. Some sought a way out immediately thereafter.

Why were many compelled to leave Laos? What occurred to suggest that their lives were in danger? Many initially intended to stay and rebuild their lives after years of displacement; however, as communist control permeated Laotian towns and cities, they became troubled by evidence of retribution for past collaboration with the U.S. military personnel. Hmong and Lao in the diaspora have adamantly argued that the new regime, supported by Hanoi, broadcasted its intent to eliminate all American collaborators, thus creating widespread fear. Consequently, thousands would make the treacherous journey to seek refuge in Thailand (see table 1).

Some people immediately left by a variety of escape routes, including the jungle, others fled to the jungle to hide; those who did not have

Table 1. Highland ethnic minority movement to
Thailand, 1975–80

Year	Number of persons migrated
1975	44,469
1976	7,266
1977	3,878
1978	8,013
1979	23,943
1980	14,901
Total	102,479

Source: Glen L. Hendricks, Bruce T. Downing, and
Amos S. Deinard, eds., The Hmong in Transition (Staten
Island, N.Y.: Center for Migration Studies, 1986), 26.

military rank continued with their lives. Many of those already in the
Vientiane area crossed the border as though they were going on short vis-
its to Thailand by carrying few belongings. Others paid exorbitant fees
to boat owners for transport across the Mekong River. The means varied
by which refugees made the journey across the Mekong River dividing
Laos from Thailand, depending on when they began their trek. Some
traveled alone, while others moved in groups ranging from a few families to hundreds of people. Those attempting to flee right after the airlift
planned their escape strategically so that it would not draw attention
to them. Because it would seem suspicious if all members left together,
many families decided to leave some elders and small children behind
while young adults escaped. Many were successful in finding refuge in
Thailand, but others died of illnesses, hunger, and drowning. Still others
were captured along the way and received severe punishment, sometimes
including unexplained disappearances.

Refugee Camps and the Hmong Diaspora

The Hmong who were airlifted were brought to Ban Namphong, a military
base in northeastern Thailand. In comparison to the helicopter evacuation of nearly 130,000 Vietnamese when Saigon fell, the air evacuation
of only 2,500 Hmong from Long Cheng was quite small. At Ban Namphong, people regrouped and searched for family members from whom
they had been separated during the airlift chaos. Some were able to reconnect with their loved ones; however, less-fortunate refugees searched
for their families in vain and wondered whether they had lived or died.
From the initial 2,500 refugees, the camp population increased to over

10,000 residents by December 1975 as more and more people found a way out on their own. Food was provided to the refugees, but several individuals who spent months at Namphong recall that life in the temporary camp was not only monotonous but uncertain. Mao Heu Thao, a young woman who married a U.S. AID field assistant not long before the flight, explained her limited worldview at the time: "All you knew was that each week, they assigned your family members to help out with various activities. For example, I remember being told that I had to go help cook. People all took turns. You cooked for all of the people. Then, they told us to go to Ban Vinai. Of course I didn't understand anything more than the tasks I was assigned."[52]

Sai Lee, a former military scribe and soldier married to Mai Yer Her, explained an awkward situation he and other leaders encountered at Namphong: "I remember one time there was a donation of about forty bags of clothes to the refugees. I looked through them. There were a variety of sizes. A few pieces were still good, but most were either ripped or were in really bad conditions. I asked Colonel Xay Dang what we should do because if we were to take the clothes out to distribute them, those who receive the ones in bad conditions would definitely be unhappy. Colonel Xay Dang said that he didn't know what to do. I came up with the idea that we would announce to the people the conditions of the clothes. We would not open the bags and asked people to stick their hands in the bags. Whatever they grabbed, they had to keep those items regardless of the conditions. That worked."[53] Although it is difficult to understand why clothes in such poor condition were given to the refugees, the refugees' response suggests that the competitiveness for survival during the airlift had changed to a situation of compassion for one another because all were in the same situation. The situation was very dire, and they understood that these were all the clothes to be had. Clothes in poor condition were better than nothing at all.

While concern for one another seemed to have occurred among the refugees, the scarce resources would soon challenge their abilities to retain it. For example, Mai Yer Her recollected not having enough food to eat due to her small family size in comparison to rations distributed to larger families: "They divided us into little sections. The leaders were the ones who had to go cook. Well, all the leaders were men. The food was terrible. After three months, we complained because most of the food went to waste. So, everyone agreed to distribute the food so individual families can prepare their own food. For larger families, it was OK, but for small families like ours, the portion was so small that sometimes you just didn't know what to do with it."[54] It appears that the hierarchy first established within the clandestine army was subsequently sustained in the refugee camp. Sai Lee recalled that those with at least colonel status were separated from the rest: "They were well fed. The other group included people like us. We ate food that [was] prepared as though one would be preparing it for pigs. Here, I learned how to eat dried fish (*pathu*) with greens."[55] As more and more people fled Laos, United Nations–sponsored refugee camps were then established to receive and process them. The Namphong residents would all be relocated to the UN-sponsored refugee camp Ban Vinai, which by the early 1990s held more than forty thousand refugees. At Ban Vinai, the refugees were provided with some materials, which enabled them to build their own shelter. As more people fled across the border at different locations along the Mekong River, additional camps of varying quality were established. Although representing a safe refuge, the confined camp life would eventually pose new challenges for residents. It was in this state of confinement that refugees had to decide what to do about their future.

Anthropologist Julie Peteet argues that refugee camps present a condition where refugee identity is embedded in and takes off from a multiplicity of places, experiences, and positions in life that are variously accommodated, celebrated, and resisted. They are places where inhabitants become objectified and thus learn how to negotiate multiple identities for survival. She explains, "If we zoom in on the refugee camp as a particular local manifestation of a larger process of global politics, our picture of diaspora politics is complicated in productive ways. . . . As living spaces that are the outcome of powerful displacing forces, they embody the capacity to affect identities in particular acute ways, ways that can at one historical and spatial moment be conducive to essentialized identities and at another spawn cosmopolitan. Periods of near incarceration contribute to a sense of self and community as bounded. . . . Essentialism then becomes a political and cultural necessity, a construct if you will, pointing to the notion of such essences themselves as contingent."[56] Camp residents initially feel displaced and may begin to see their lives as static. Being held in a place where armed guards surround the area may be interpreted as a form of protection. However, the lack of freedom to come and go can also be viewed as a way to strip refugees of any sense of safety. This jail-like situation motivated many to leave when they could.

To this day, it is difficult to attribute credit to any one individual or group for Hmong gaining political-refugee status pursuant to international law. The chaotic conditions suggest that both Hmong leaders and the Americans who worked with them in Laos contributed in one way or another to obtaining help for those who were waiting for their fate to be decided. Once American leaders in Thailand learned of the Hmong's flight, an attempt was made to identify the various roles that different Hmong individuals had played in assisting Americans during the war years. As Dang Her, a former USAID field assistant, revealed, "At Namphong, the American leaders surveyed the refugees to find out who did what during the war. So, they knew how many USAID employees were in the camp."[57] Under the U.S. Attorney General's parole authority, he and his wife, Shoua Moua, were part of the few refugees from Laos allowed to resettle in the United States in December 1975 because they had been U.S. allies.

The number of ethnic minorities who fled Laos from May to December 1975 reached 44,469 persons. These numbers decreased dramatically during the next two years but picked up again in 1978 to reach 23,943 during 1979. The fluctuation of the number of people fleeing reflects not only political but also economic conditions within the Lao PDR. Of the 102,479 who arrived in Thailand by 1980, an estimated 95 percent were Hmong ethnics who spent varied lengths of time in refugee camps.[58] As refugees, they received food rations and became eligible for an array of international humanitarian assistance.

Refugee reflections regarding their escapes often change over time. Lived experiences and interactions with others in similar situations and with outsiders result in an evolving sense of self and others. Although the initial flight may have been accompanied by anxiety, once refugees overcome that particular state of being, they begin to reflect about their experiences and contemplate their present conditions and blurred future. Often, the most overwhelming task refugees face is the lack of anything to do. Mai Lee, a former elderly camp resident, comments, "The men just sat around, the women just sat around. Just sitting around."[59] Mao Heu Thao's awareness of her surroundings evolved as she realized a sense of powerlessness: "It was only after we've lived there for a while that you begin to realize you're stuck and that it is very difficult to leave the camp. You have to have written permission. It was only then that you realize you are being controlled. At first, you didn't understand. No one tells you what it will be like. It was only through experience that you begin to understand the place in which you lived. You are being watched and controlled."[60]

Not surprisingly, many of those who left the country immediately were young people in their twenties who had been involved in the clandestine army. Yia Lee remembers young refugees' struggles to make sense of what has happened to them: "Being a refugee is one of the most awful states of being. People became crazy. One young man cried loudly. Took off his clothes and didn't care who saw him. He missed his parents so much. One of the hardest parts is that the vast majority in this first group of refugees were young people. They just couldn't deal with the situation. Some people were alone. The majority were like my group, young. The elders stayed because they faced less risk. For the young, we feared being forced to join the new regime."[61] May Ia Lee adds, "In the camp, you became someone with no responsibility. Nothing to keep you occupied. You knew nothing. When it was time to eat, you went to line up for your food. It was a situation in which you became indifferent. You don't know your future. Just waiting. Only when you were made aware that Americans were interviewing people to go to America that you realize you may never be able to return to your home. I felt this way because I didn't think I would leave forever."[62]

Many months of living in a monotonous condition for this initial group transformed into hope, as new possibilities of resettlement in third countries, primarily in the West, came to fruition. When fighting for a place inside the airplanes during the evacuation or escaping across the Mekong River, these refugees never imagined that they would be unable to return. During this period, most thought of their escape as temporary and believed they would eventually return to their way of life. Beginning in early 1976, refugee-resettlement programs dispersed Hmong throughout North America, South America, Europe, and Oceania, thus creating the Hmong diaspora in the West. Migration within and across nation-states would eventually shape the Hmong communities within these disparate places. Interestingly, some Hmong risked their lives to arrive in Thailand only to agree to go back to Laos shortly thereafter. Others took the opportunity to return the original homeland by applying to be resettled in China.[63]

The dispersal commenced in 1975 resulted in new concentrations of Hmong people in France's *banlieux*, large clusters in American, Canadian, and Australian cities and small towns, and new villages constructed in French Guyana. The vast majority of Hmong refugees chose to resettle in the United States. Colonial ties explain why France was the second most common destination.[64] A smaller group followed French missionaries who had converted Hmong in Laos to French Guyana in 1977. Due to American pressures, traditional immigrant-receiving nations such as Canada and Australia grudgingly accepted a few thousand Hmong refugees as part of international burden sharing. These nations were restrictive in their selection processes in that they required applicants to demonstrate education and work experience indicating they would not become burdens to society. Argentina was the only South American nation that accepted any refugees, and that was about a dozen families. Today, a small Hmong community also exists in Gammertingen in southern Germany. However, their presence in Germany was not the result of that country offering resettlement opportunities. Germany allowed five Hmong and five Lao families from the Nam Yao refugee camp to resettle there only because Argentina had decided it no longer wanted these refugees it had previously processed and accepted.[65]

2   A New Home in America

In the age of globalization, unexpected people turn up
in the most unexpected places. . . . Despite the virtually
free movement of capital, in the age of globalization no
countries welcome mass migration. Even where selective
migration is sanctioned, states have officially sought to
prevent the settlement of unskilled, elderly or dependent
migrants.

—Robin Cohen, *Global Diasporas*

Where the Hmong live in the world today reflects the complex
post–World War II international humanitarian apparatus distinguishing
people in danger and worthy of support from those deemed mere economic migrants seeking a better life. As previously discussed, several
Western countries accepted Hmong refugees; however, similar to Hungar-
ian refugees in 1956, most preferred a new life in the United States over
other options.[1] As an ethnic group with limited ties to others outside of
their villages in Southeast Asia, Hmong presence in the United States
can be regarded as unexpected. Their admission to the United States was
largely due to their status as political refugees "voting with their feet"
against communism. Had they not been political refugees during the
cold war, Hmong and many others from the former Indochinese colonies
would not have qualified for admission to the United States through its
regular immigration programs.[2] Unlike the Vietnamese who were accepted into numerous Western countries, few nations offered resettlement opportunities to the Hmong and other highland ethnic groups. Most
policymakers feared that they would not be able to survive in modern
societies due to their agrarian background.

The first refugees during the mid-1970s were initially isolated and powerless; however, the resettlement process eventually enabled them to become active social, cultural, economic, and political agents in reconstructing community in the United States. How they formed community in particular locations in the United States was intimately tied to federal refugee-resettlement policies requiring their dispersal throughout the country. In contrast, the concentration of Hmong populations at the beginning of the new millennium reveals a complex process of community formation determined by both internal and external factors.

Migration and Settlement

Migration on any scale can be accompanied by a sense of loss and uncertainty. Narratives from former Hmong refugees suggest that the process was filled with contradictory emotions. The unknown future brought about much anxiety, but it was also accompanied by tremendous excitement about new possibilities. For many, their stay in refugee camps was brief. The camps served only as a transition location for processing papers to permanently resettle elsewhere. For some, residence in refugee camps was prolonged as they waited for other family members. Once reunited, some pressed forward with the resettlement process and left as soon as they could. For others, the desire to move neither forward nor back to Laos resulted in the acceptance of refugee camp life as the norm. Such individuals remained for an extended length of time and resettled in the United States only when forced to do so with the closure of refugee camps.

The number of Hmong refugees resettled in the United States ebbed and flowed depending on arrival patterns in refugee camps and the availability of sponsoring families or institutions in the United States. From 1975 to 1980, more than 47,000 persons of ethnic minorities from Laos had resettled in the United States as political refugees (see table 2). Of this population, more than 90 percent were Hmong; the remainder included other ethnic groups such as Khammu and Mien. The year 1980 saw the highest number of arrivals in the United States at 27,242.

Of the Hmong population counted in the 2000 Census who were foreign-born (102,773), 14.8 percent arrived during the mid- to late 1970s, 46.1 percent during the 1980s, and 38.7 percent during the 1990s (see table 3). A Hmong community did not exist in the United States prior to the arrival of refugees. The small number before 1975 consisted of the few students studying at U.S. higher-education institutions as a result of their alliance with American military and humanitarian personnel during the war years. Like other leaders who came to see America's great

Table 2. Resettlement of Laos' highland ethnic
minority to the United States, 1975–80

Year	Number of persons resettled
1975	301
1976	3,058
1977	1,655
1978	3,873
1979	11,301
1980	27,242
Total	47,430

Source: Glen L. Hendricks, Bruce T. Downing, and
Amos S. Deinard, eds., *The Hmong in Transition* (Staten
Island, N.Y.: Center for Migration Studies, 1986), 180.

power status as the answer to their struggles, Vang Pao advocated for educational opportunities for Hmong children in Laos and study abroad in
the United States for a handful of students. The lower percentage during
the last part of the 1990s reflects the closure of official United Nations–
sponsored refugee camps in Thailand.

The first group of Hmong refugees during the mid-1970s was dispersed in both rural and urban areas. These dispersal policies were instrumental in shaping early Hmong migration and settlement patterns and
created some unintended consequences. Within a short period of time,
the refugees were exposed to many environments across the country and
thus were able to compare and contrast different geographic locations. By
connecting with one another and sharing information, the early refugees
were subsequently able to reach informed decisions about the advantages

Table 3. Arrival of foreign-born Hmong in the United States, 1965–2000

Year of entry to United States	Number of persons arriving	Percentage of foreign-born Hmong of total persons (%)
1965–69	89	0.1
1970s	14,404	15.2
1980s	43,598	46.0
1990s	36,581	38.6
Totals	94,672	100.0

Source: Jennifer Yau, "The Foreign-Born Hmong in the United States," *Migration
Policy Institute,* 2005, http://www.migrationinformation.org/USFocus/display
.cfm?ID=281fs; Bo Thao, Louisa Schein, and Max Niedzweicki, eds., *Hmong 2000
Census Publication: Data and Analysis* (Washington, D.C.: Hmong National Development and Hmong Cultural and Resource Center, 2004).

and disadvantages of settlement in different areas throughout the country, and either recruited others to join them or moved elsewhere. Many of these connections among distantly situated immigrants can be traced back to the Laos cities of Long Cheng and Sam Thong, where they had worked together in the American military and humanitarian bureaucracy. Though many may not have been knowledgeable about U.S. geography, relatives and friends often knew the locations to which their friends and family members were being relocated. Connections between those resettled and others remaining in refugee camps further contributed to future migration and settlement options.

Besides dispersal resettlement practices, the most important factor contributing to the development of population centers was the sponsorship of Hmong refugees by already settled Hmong. By 1985, seventy-two Hmong communities had been established in the United States, ranging in size from under one hundred to over ten thousand people: 28 of these communities had populations under 299 individuals, 28 consisting of 300 to 999, six with populations of 1,000 to 1,999, four with 2,000 to 2,999, two with populations between 3,000 and 3,999, two with 4,000 to 4,999 people, and two with populations larger than 8,000. The two largest populations were Fresno, California (10,000) and Minneapolis/St. Paul, Minnesota (8,500).[3]

The practice of secondary migration (moving from the initial location in which a refugee is resettled to another location) began almost immediately after the initial resettlement.[4] Explanations for secondary migration by refugees include: employment opportunities, the pull of an established ethnic community, more-generous welfare benefits, better training opportunities, reunification with relatives, and a more congenial climate.[5] Climate did not refer only to better weather. Although extreme winter conditions in some states influenced people to move to areas with warmer temperatures, climate here also meant greater tolerance and/or acceptance by the host society. While they had been allowed little voice in the decision making for the location of their initial resettlement, secondary migration reveals refugee agency. No longer living in contained camps with limited power, refugees were free to explore other locations that met their personal needs.

Secondary migration was further influenced by "the shortcomings of the sending communities rather than on knowledge of what might lie ahead."[6] For example, reasons Hmong gave for moving to California's Central Valley during the 1980s were multifaceted, involving such things as: (1) absence of jobs or a history of repeated lay-offs in the host community, (2) desire for English classes and vocational training, (3) dream of farming, (4) the snowball effect of family reunification (young find it difficult to resist the call of elders either to move with a group or join the group in a new setting), and (5) change in national policy for refugee cash assistance. In the spring of 1982, refugee cash assistance was reduced from thirty-six to eighteen months.[7] Those living in states without generous welfare programs for unemployed two-parent families had their benefits cut off. Thus some moved to states with a generous public-assistance program that accepted intact families. These factors would eventually result in an increase or decrease of Hmong populations in certain areas by the mid-1990s.

Movement from the initial-settlement location sometimes created difficulties for both refugees and sponsors. Furthermore, frequent relocations raised great concerns at the local and national level for policy makers. Consequently, the federal government took strategic actions to discourage Hmong from moving to areas with already higher Hmong populations. Conversely, in such areas, local initiatives were implemented to encourage relocation to areas with little or no Hmong population.[8] Although some sponsors did not understand why refugees wanted to move and expressed disappointment, others did their best to support families who desired to be closer to relatives or to be closer to a community with a larger Hmong population. In studies about refugees, the focus is often on the confusion and difficulties that they experience. It is, however, equally important to note that many sponsors often lacked knowledge about the culture and traditions of people they tried to help. As such, some sponsors were not able to fully support those who arrived in their homes and communities.

On the other hand, evidence exists to suggest that close relationships often developed between some sponsors and refugees, as illustrated by a sample letter from a sponsor to a refugee family. The author clearly understood the family's struggles: "Lloyd and I enjoyed working with you by helping you with the difficult task of learning ways of our culture." Elsewhere in the letter, it becomes apparent that both sponsor and refugee family did their best to make the resettlement work. There is also evidence of concern by the sponsor about the family's health and well-being. In addition, the author makes an effort to respect something that she may not have understood in full. It is revealed in the letter that she found an envelope with the refugee mother's hair. Rather than discarding it, she sent the hair to the family. Although the family did not know how to write, the author pleaded with them to keep in contact.[9] This situation is an example of a broader and more significant phenomenon of sponsors altruistically attempting to support refugees.

Why were families generally discouraged from secondary migration? Was the desire by many refugees to relocate simply an indication of their dissatisfaction with their new homes? Government attempts to prevent secondary migration were not new inventions after the refugees arrived. This component was embedded in refugee-resettlement policies and practices; all applicants were asked to sign a "Statement of Understanding" when completing their resettlement applications. The statement describes initial services and the goal of sponsorship. Applicants were asked to sign that they understood the terms of sponsorship and agreed with the following statements:

> I understand that if I have close relatives in the United States, my sponsoring agency will make every effort to resettle me with them. If that is not possible, I will accept resettlement anywhere in the United States. Once I am resettled in one city, after arrival I cannot expect to be transferred to and assisted in another city. I will accept the initial housing arrangements provided for me and my family. If I am of working age and able to work, I will accept whatever work may be offered, whether this work is my specialty or not. I understand that I may change jobs at a later date, but that the voluntary agency or sponsor is not expected to assist me with finding another job.[10]

The statement lays out what refugees could expect from sponsors and voluntary agencies. Key elements are job-search assistance and the provision of basic needs support such as housing, which refugees must accept regardless of its conditions. The underlying goal of the sponsorship is, however, to bring refugees "to economic self-sufficiency as quickly as possible." Although the refugee's signature indicates understanding of expectations, many refugees presented with this document could not sign their names, as indicated by the presence of hundreds of forms with either fingerprints or an *X* on the signature line. Despite these agreements prior to settling in the United States, Hmong refugees frequently explored other locations following their arrival in the United States.

The rationale for the government's insistence during the early resettlement process of distributing refugees to many places rather than allowing them to concentrate in particular locations was twofold. First, the early refugees required the availability of American sponsors prior to departure. Because sponsors were volunteers from all over the country, refugees were sent to areas where the greatest number of Americans volunteered to open their homes and communities to them. Second, embedded in refugee policies were policies that aimed to assimilate refugees into the societies in which they resettled. Immediate participation in the workforce was the first sign of assimilation. Some sponsors had secured jobs for refugees. Shortly following their arrival, they went to work. Immediate work is a key disciplinary aspect of the resettlement process where refugees do not get to choose the type of work they preferred. Thus, to become American also involved sacrificing individual agency. Practicing secondary migration is an important symbol of resistance to this construction. Furthermore, the funneling of many into the social welfare system undermined established refugee policies and programs. Acceptance of public assistance by those who were unemployable due to their lack of transferable skills contravened fundamental immigration policies that rejected prospective immigrants who may become a burden to American society.

Common questions have been why and how Hmong refugees selected particular locations, especially locations such as Midwestern cities, which are significantly different from their place of birth in Asia. What considerations did they make in settling in certain locations? The process by which chain migration took place among Hmong refugees is not significantly different from that experienced by other immigrants throughout American history. One of the most significant factors influencing Hmong decisions regarding settlement locations was explained by an early refugee, Chaw Kue, to journalist Spencer Sherman in 1986: "We first came to Philadelphia in 1976. We first saw snow. It was near the end of the season. We wondered, 'what is going on here?' We were surprised. We did not know how to handle the situation at the time. So I went to Ohio, Detroit, Minnesota and Los Angeles, San Francisco, Santa Ana, Memphis, West Virginia, Virginia, Washington, Richmond. I thought Georgia was the place I was planning to come. But I went down there, but it looked very crowded too. So I come up here [McDowell County, North Carolina,] and thought it would be the best place for me."[11] Chaw Kue indicated that the North Carolina landscape reminded him of Laos. Those who followed bought houses with gardens, and nearly everyone found jobs in the local textile mill, furniture factory, or at the Baxter-Travenol pharmaceutical plant. As long as the number of refugees was minimal, local communities could ignore them. As the population increased, the Hmong community could no longer keep a low profile. They became more visible and, consequently, generated opposition from local residents.

Other refugees made similar relocation considerations. Ly Vang was trained as a nurse during the war years in Laos. She arrived in the United States in 1976 with her husband. She explained their decision to move to Minnesota from South Dakota: "Madison [South Dakota] is a small town. Very few jobs [were] available. There was painting company so that was our job. We got connected with Vang Leng [in Minnesota]. In the beginning, I think the voluntary agency connected us. They worked closely with us, and they visited us. When we asked them, they told us where other Hmong are. So, they helped us get connected. We came to visit them, and we learned that there were more jobs here. So, our sponsor helped us to move here."[12] On their own, Ly Vang and her husband may not have been able to locate fellow Hmong refugees. With the assistance of their sponsors, they learned about the whereabouts of other refugees and visited them before making the move.

Similar to Ly Vang, Shong Yang, who is a prominent businessman in St. Paul, Minnesota, found it difficult to survive in other locations without his relatives. Arriving in the United States as a teenager with his older brother's family in 1980, he moved around a few times before settling in Minnesota. He recalled the journey: "I came to L.A. in April 1980. The organization, USCC [United States Catholic Conference], something like that, that sponsored us. . . . We only stayed in L.A. for three months. With no other relatives, we just couldn't stay there. I then moved to Chicago, Illinois, and stayed there for two and a half years. I attended adult school. After Chicago, I went to Columbus, Ohio, for a little more than one year. Then I moved to Michigan."[13] Having lived in different U.S. cities enabled Shong Yang to determine the best place to set permanent roots. Despite its cold winters, the Twin Cities became his preferred location due to the large population of Hmong and the support that the host society gave to refugees.

The Midwest winter climate differed significantly from Laos. While many refugees desired an environment similar in landscape and temperature to their homeland, this was not always possible. Some relocated to Minnesota from locations with significantly more-pleasant weather conditions. Like Ly Vang and Shong Yang, Mai Yer Her's desire to be near family took priority over the beautiful Hawaiian environment. As a young mother alone with her husband, she could not see a future in isolation from her relatives. She shared the chain migration practiced by her extended family: "My mother-in-law and a brother-in-law had moved to Minnesota. They moved here because my older sister and her husband moved to follow their relatives in Iowa. Then on to Minnesota. They sent us cassettes to tell us how nice things were here."[14] News traveling via audiocassettes occurred due largely to few people having literacy skills. Rather than spending hours dictating their thoughts to literate individuals, many took advantage of the technology available to convey their feelings to friends and family members. Hearing the voices of their relatives also provided reassurance and encouragement to the refugees that a letter could not. Often, families would gather to listen to audiotapes from their relatives. Through the recorded messages, the listeners could better understand the emotions of the speakers.

While some moved to the Twin Cities based on positive news they heard from relatives and friends, Xang Vang, who arrived in Loganville, Wisconsin, on March 16, 1976, decided to explore both St. Paul, Minnesota, and Missoula, Montana, before making a decision for his family. As one of the few people with a formal education in Laos, he had worked as a secretary in the clandestine army. After visiting the two northern U.S. locations, he decided to move his family to Missoula, where former General Vang Pao resided at the time. Not long thereafter, the lack of suitable jobs forced him to once again move his family to St. Paul by late 1977, where he has since remained.[15]

Although the first refugees were invited by people in local communities and were significantly isolated from those of similar heritage, it did not take many refugees long before they would extend invitations to their friends and relatives. After establishing themselves, they recruited others, as Roy Beck succinctly explains regarding the phenomenon in Wausau, Wisconsin, during the 1990s: "When they agreed to become local resettlement sponsors, in the late 1970s, Wausau congregations did not simply provide refuge for a few Hmong, Lao, and Vietnamese families; they also inadvertently created a channel through which the federal government could send a continuing stream of refugees. . . . Wausau residents discovered that the refugees invited to stay in their hometown soon began issuing their own invitations and serving as local sponsors for their relatives."[16]

This account is also supported by former Minnesota refugee coordinator Jane Kretzman. "It was the refugees themselves who got the word out that Minnesota was a good place," she comments. "Around 1979, 1980 was when the International Institute made major changes by partnering with the Hmong Community Association to sponsor other families."[17] In seeking resources for their ethnic community, Xang Vang further clarified that those residing in Minnesota strategically recruited others they knew who possessed certain skills to relocate there. After advocating for employment positions for refugee families, the emerging community leaders invited their friends and relatives to fill such positions: "The following school year in 1978, when the school year started, we needed to find a Hmong bilingual bicultural teacher. We dragged people from other states, Ly Tong Lytsontseng from Hawaii, Chia Vang from Indiana for police, Yang Blong from Wisconsin. And, we brought others from North Carolina."[18] Again, these first refugees either recruited others to join them or were recruited to other locations.

The temptation to reconnect with others from their ethnic group has been an integral part of life for many Hmong refugees. Some moved to established Hmong communities based on positive evaluations from their kin about certain locations, while others take time to reflect, sometimes choosing to remain. If they move, it may be to a different area in the vicinity rather than across the country. Since arriving in Philadelphia, Pennsylvania, on March 6, 1980, Chai Lue Kue has considered moving on numerous occasions. His experience is an example of those who become attached to a place and no longer believe it is necessary to live in areas with large Hmong populations: "We have visited relatives in other places. Although most of the people who came to Philadelphia had moved to Minnesota and Wisconsin, we just don't like the cold. It's too cold there. I suppose we just got used to this area and now are settled in our ways here. It's hard not having a lot of our people around, but when you have lived this way for the last three decades, you get used to it. Also, our uncle who we followed here has not moved, so we don't see any reason to move."[19]

Population Change and New Settlement Patterns

Despite the prevalence of secondary migration, many early Hmong refugee settlement patterns persist today. Although individual motivations to move or set permanent roots are influenced by a number of factors, broader social, cultural, economic, and political dynamics have also impacted these choices. The 1980 U.S. census counted 5,204 people of Hmong ethnicity in the country. Because Hmong represented an estimated 95 percent of the more than 47,000 highland ethnic minorities resettled in the United States by 1980 from Laos, the census number is a significant undercount. Barriers to being counted, such as language and literacy, partially help to explain the low number. Additionally, the frequent movement of refugees after their initial resettlement suggests that many institutions lost track of them once they moved unless they became dependent on public resources that required documentation. Furthermore, the racial and ethnic categories currently available on the census did not exist in 1980; therefore, some persons may have been counted under the Asian American category. Although Hmong American community leaders continue to suggest that their population is undercounted, exponential growth has occurred due to high birth rates and continued admission of refugees and sponsorship of family members from other countries of resettlement as well as from Laos. By 1990, the Hmong population had increased to 94,439, and a decade later, the population grew to 186,310, representing a 97 percent increase. According to the 2007 American Community Survey (ACS), the estimated population had exceeded 200,000.[20]

To some extent, federal, state, and local voluntary organizations lost "control" of the refugees once they resettled in the country. As refugees learned to maneuver through the various systems, they made strategic decisions that they perceived to be in their best interest, decisions not necessarily viewed by outsiders as beneficial to their well-being. For example, Mary Pipher writes, "One common, and generally not very adaptive, way refugees deal with their pain and difficulties in America is to move. Moves are common among refugees as they find one town difficult and hear rumors that the grass is greener in other places. Generally these moves don't make things better; they are expensive, disruptive of the family's relationships with schools and community resources, and they don't solve the original problems. Still, it is understandable that geographical moves would appeal to refugees. After all, they have moved before to solve problems."[21] Although Pipher's analysis captures the mobility frequently practiced by refugees, it suggests something more convoluted. An embedded assumption in her observation is that refugee agency is problematic. She underestimates the benefits such movements have in solving problems the refugees face. This paternalist viewpoint is not completely out of the ordinary. It reflects perceptions developed by many others who worked to help refugees adjust to their new life. This critique of escape as based on "rumors that the grass is greener in other places" suggests that refugees are irrational, and their decisions to move are merely to avoid facing reality.

In the mid-1970s, some Hmong refugees were initially placed in southern locations such as Fort Smith, Arkansas, because policymakers envisioned that these agrarian people would readily engage in farming activities. Despite the pleasant climate, refugees' lack of capital and knowledge of modern farming technologies, compounded with extreme isolation, resulted in most Hmong leaving the area for larger concentrations in other states. Coincidently, flight from the southern regions was reversed beginning during the late 1990s as Hmong Americans flocked to buy land and enter the poultry industry. According to the 2000 census, this resulted in a 714 percent increase of Hmong in the south (from 1,272 in 1990 to 10,350 in 2000). Although significantly lower, the Midwest Hmong population increased by 115 percent, followed by increases in the northeast (71 percent) and the west (38 percent) during that same time period.[22]

At the time of the 1990 census, Hmong Americans were found in thirty-two states, and none were counted in Washington, D.C. Yet, interestingly, people of Hmong ethnicity were present in the District of Columbia and all states except Wyoming by the year 2000.[23] Twelve states were home to more than a thousand Hmong Americans.[24] However, 76 percent of the entire U.S. Hmong population resided in only three states: California, Minnesota, and Wisconsin, a reduction from 89 percent of Hmong in the United States living in these same states in 1990. Ten American cities with the largest Hmong populations included six in Wisconsin, three in California, and one in the metropolitan area of St. Paul–Minneapolis, Minnesota.[25] By the year 2000, the largest concentration had shifted to the Twin Cities from Fresno, California. Milwaukee ranked sixth in 1990, but, in 2000, the Milwaukee area had the fourth-largest Hmong population in America. In 2000, Hickory, North Carolina, and the Detroit–Ann Arbor–Flint area in Michigan pushed La Crosse and Eau Claire in Wisconsin out of the ninth and tenth places with significant Hmong populations.

Seven states experienced more than a 100 percent change in their Hmong American populations between 1990 and 2000.[26] There was also a pronounced shift in the Hmong population away from the west, and the Hmong population in the eastern seaboard states remained relatively small. Altogether, Hmong population in the southern states represented only slightly over 6 percent (10,350 persons) of the national Hmong population, a notable increase from 1.3 percent in 1990. The most substantial gains were seen in the Carolinas, where the Hmong population increased from 544 to 7,093 and 40 to 519 from 1990 to 2000 in North Carolina and South Carolina, respectively. The percentage of the American Hmong living in the Midwest increased from 41 percent to 49 percent between 1990 and 2000. Minnesota and Wisconsin remained the two Midwestern states with the highest Hmong populations, followed by Michigan. Though significantly smaller, the populations in Kansas and Ohio nearly doubled. The populations in Illinois and Indiana experienced much lower rates of growth, and population decreases were seen in the states of Iowa and Nebraska.[27]

Hmong migrations both to and away from certain large concentrations can be attributed to the lure of employment and business opportunities and the desire to avoid large urban concentrations. The movement to southern areas discussed above is the most visible example. However, northern places such as Anchorage, Alaska, have also seen increasing Hmong American settlements. The 2000 census counted only 300 Hmong in Alaska, but by 2007, about 722 Hmong lived in the state.[28] Of the 6,000 students in the Anchorage School District, about 600 are Hmong. While many headed south, Breddy Yang decided to find a new land in Anchorage, Alaska, after spending seventeen years in Minnesota. In 2001, he was encouraged to go north by the state's mild summers, which are similar to those he remembered from Laos. In explaining the newest settlement of Hmong in Anchorage, Breddy Yang describes the "origin" of the new settlers: "Some are from North Carolina, mostly from California, and some are from Minnesota. Some are from Michigan, some are from Rhode Island and many different states."[29] These "third migrations" explain an increasingly diverse Hmong American population where some prefer to live in large Hmong concentrations while others flee from these locations.

Establishment of Ethnic Enclaves

In the mid-1970s, no one could predict how the future flow of refugees would change the demographic composition of the numerous cities in which Hmong settled. Hmong visibility was greater in less racially diverse communities than in urban areas that already had a higher population of minorities. As previously discussed, California has had the highest Hmong population, but its large Asian American population enabled the Hmong and other Southeast Asian refugees to somewhat disappear into the Asian American community. The descriptions that follow provide a snapshot of the diverse Hmong communities that have been established throughout the country during their first thirty years in the United States.

How does the size of a Hmong population impact a particular locality as well as the immediate Hmong community? The population changes had a profound impact on certain cities and towns around the country. Throughout American history, newcomers were not only changed by the culture and traditions of communities in which they entered; they also changed the communities through their presence and contribution to society. The experience of refugees both replicates and diverges from the experience of other immigrants, both in terms of their adjustment to the United States and in terms of host communities' response to them both before and after their arrival.[30] The construction of ethnic enclaves is clearly not a new phenomenon in American society. On the contrary, immigrants have always established ethnic enclaves, which have played instrumental roles in immigrant incorporation processes throughout U.S. history. As immigrants arrive, they often seek out others from their home country for mutual support. These ethnic communities serve multiple purposes regarding an immigrant's entrée into mainstream America. The formation of ethnic enclaves has been attributed to the need for social support, interest in strengthening and preserving culture and traditions, and the need for shelter against discrimination. Such communities can serve various functions for members, such as sharing information on how to cope in the new culture, providing a somewhat familiar social life, and protecting the refugee or immigrant from culture shock.

Sociologists Alden E. Roberts and Paul D. Starr argue that ethnic subculture can preserve tradition and cultural continuity. An ethnic enclave often goes through three stages in relation to the host society. First, the group slowly changes through the process of assimilation. New and old behaviors and norms become gradually interspersed. Second, the ethnic group minimizes contact with the host society and attempts to remain as traditional as possible. Finally, the ethnic group determines to be even more traditional than it was in the home country.[31] To some extent, all of these processes have occurred with Hmong ethnic enclaves throughout the United States.

The development of ethnic enclaves enables Hmong refugees to provide mutual support, but at the same time they are perceived as not being properly incorporated into the host society. In her study about Chinatown in New York, sociologist Min Zhou argues that Chinatown does not keep immigrant Chinese from assimilating into mainstream society but instead provides an alternative means of incorporation into society that does not conflict with cultural distinctiveness.[32] Zhou further argues that community networks and social capital are important resources for reaching socioeconomic goals and social positions in the United States. As Chinese in New York have done for many generations, Hmong business owners have used family ties and ethnic resources to advance socially. Within these new enclaves, support systems were developed to assist new arrivals. As Jan Lin highlights about Chinatowns, mainstream society tends to portray ethnic enclaves as monolithic entities whose members intrinsically agree with one another; however, groups inside the enclaves are not homogenous. Indeed, they are complex and have internal disagreements over the community's future direction.[33] In the various Hmong ethnic enclaves, divisiveness may be seen along the lines of clan, generation, and gender. As Hmong struggle to create meanings in their new homes, different stakeholders argue over who should represent their interests to the larger community, in particular when financial resources are involved. Various groups compete for funding from local foundations, corporations, and government entities to serve *the Hmong community.*

"HMONG CAPITAL OF THE WORLD"

As discussed earlier, the Twin Cities emerged as the largest concentration of people of Hmong ethnicity in the United States by the beginning of the twenty-first century.[34] When Dang Her and Shoua Moua arrived in Minnesota in December 1975 before the resettlement programs were formally established, they never imagined that such growth would occur. They had thought that they would exist among strangers. However, two months later, Leng Wong (formerly Vang), who was also a military scribe, and his wife, May Ia Lee, reached Minnesota as part of the first group of Hmong to be resettled through the refugee-resettlement program.[35] More people arrived from refugee camps throughout 1976 and beyond. The growing population also meant growing social-adjustment issues, resulting in refugees seeking ways to help themselves. Consequently, these early arrivals realized that they needed to organize themselves.

Due to limited capital, many early refugees resettled in some of the Twin Cities' poorest neighborhoods.[36] Sociologist Jeremy Hein reveals, "In small Midwestern cities Southeast Asian refugees brought a new kind of diversity, but in Chicago and Milwaukee they were just the latest installment in a century of ethnic succession."[37] Often, refugees enter areas that other Americans at the lower end of the socioeconomic strata occupied. Some may initially reside with their sponsors in more affluent neighborhoods if housing arrangements had not been made by the time they arrived. Shortly after arrival, they would search for housing options that they could afford. From 1976 to 1978, they resided primarily in the Central, Near North, Phillips, and Powderhorn neighborhoods in the city of Minneapolis. These areas consist of predominantly low-income communities, primarily residents of color. Examining refugee addresses reveals that they were concentrated in five zip codes within the above neighborhoods. Some landlords began to rent entire apartment buildings primarily to refugees because they tended to pay their rent on time. Beginning in 1979, a shift began to take place where some moved to St. Paul and other areas. However, it was not until 1984 that residence in St. Paul neighborhoods began to increase significantly.[38] From then on, the majority of Hmong families lived in St. Paul. Refugees in St. Paul were also concentrated in low-income neighborhoods, which included Frogtown, parts of Summit University, North End, and, toward the late 1980s, the East Side, which was largely a working-class area. Few Hmong families lived in the suburbs before the mid-1990s, when economic mobility led to an exponential growth in homeownership. Such changes in neighborhood patterns suggest that many Hmong, like other immigrants before them, choose to flee urban centers when they are economically capable.

As their socioeconomic status changed, many moved to the most affordable first-ring suburbs and then eventually to more affluent suburban communities. For example, the largest percentage of Hmong living in the Twin Cities suburbs during the 1990s were concentrated in Brooklyn Center/Brooklyn Park, northwest of Minneapolis, where homes were more reasonably priced. Despite this residential shift to suburban communities, few communities were formed in other Minnesota cities. From the late 1980s through the early 1990s, attempts were made to relocate some families to the southwestern part of the state such as Worthington, Marshall, and Tracy; however, the number of people moving to these areas had never been significant. Hmong families who move often find the isolation and lack of job opportunities unbearable. The city of Duluth, in northeastern Minnesota, initially sponsored some families, but similar to those in the southwest, almost all left to settle in the Twin Cities metropolitan area. Although students attend colleges and universities in the various cities and towns, no significant community of Hmong residents had been established in greater Minnesota.

The availability of jobs helped many to determine where they would live at the same time that some people's decisions were influenced by the generosity of public-assistance programs in certain states. Dependence of the Twin Cities' Hmong population on public assistance since they began arriving in the United States had remained relatively lower than in California. The Minnesota population had not only grown in size but also in terms of prosperity in various sectors. Education, job opportunities, and the entrepreneurial atmosphere have attracted young, educated Hmong Americans in other parts of the country who wish to establish businesses that cater to this population. Like several other cities, the significant number of Hmong Americans concentrated within a geographic area has enabled them to host large community sports festivals and New Year celebrations. Unlike in places with warm climates, however, New Year celebrations had been held inside large convention centers rather than outdoors due to the cold weather. The large population concentration, active civic participation of its members, high number of small businesses, growing number of professionals working in various sectors, and young people graduating at the top of their high school classes every year has resulted in the Twin Cities being referred to by some community members as the "Hmong capital of the world."

FRESNO, CALIFORNIA

The first visible concentration of Hmong refugees was in the Twin Cities, but the population in Fresno, California, surpassed the Twin Cities by the early 1980s and remained larger throughout the 1990s. The Hmong enclave formed in Fresno was not the result of initial refugee resettlement. Movement to the California Central Valley (Fresno, Merced, and Stockton especially) during the early 1980s had primarily been described as unplanned, spontaneous choices by dozens of clan and subclan groups. Reunification of families and friends reduced isolation, but the local labor conditions during this period could not provide employment for the ten thousand Hmong in the city. Consequently, the number of individuals receiving public assistance from 1980 to 1983 jumped from 168 to over 7,000 individuals.[39] This high percentage of social-welfare usage would plague the community for years to come. Despite this challenging economic environment, Hmong continued to flock to Fresno. Due both to secondary migration and high birth rates, the census in 1990 counted 18,321 people of Hmong ethnicity in this city alone. This critical mass meant that cultural events such as New Year celebrations could take place on a larger scale than in other cities. The Hmong International New Year organization is a separate nonprofit organization that works with other ethnic community-based organizations.[40] Pleasant weather conditions also allow celebrations to be held outside as they are in Asia, drawing thousands of vendors, performers, and spectators from around the country.

WAUSAU, WISCONSIN

While the populations of Hmong in most Midwestern locations are quite small, Wausau, Wisconsin, is an exception. By 2000, the Hmong population there reached 4,000, about ten percent of the city's population, and much attention focused on it.[41] Many—perhaps most—of Wausau's citizens initially experienced mixed feelings toward sponsored people who were different from them. The small percentage of people of color in Wisconsin by the time Hmong refugees began arriving suggests that some sponsors may have had limited previous encounters with racial diversity. Clearly, Native Americans and other people of color such as migrant workers had been present in the community for many years. However, both of these groups tended to be isolated on farms and reservations and thus had limited encounters with members of the larger community.

Inspired by moral duty to respond to those in need, some Wausau congregations and individuals marched forward in welcoming Hmong refugees, despite opposition from fellow church members and others in the community. In 1976, four Wausau families decided to sponsor two Hmong families although their church, Trinity Evangelical Lutheran, voted against congregational sponsorship.[42] The first Hmong family to come to Wausau arrived on April 9, 1976.[43] As other congregations and individuals extended their invitations to other Hmong refugees and the refugees recruited friends and kin from other parts of the country as well as from refugee camps, many middle-class white residents began to feel a sense of invasion by a growing, uncontrollable Asian population. In describing the impact of the Hmong population on Wausau, anthropologist Jo Ann Koltyk writes, "The effect of Hmong migration to Wausau has been felt in practically every aspect of the community, from law enforcement and legal issues, to housing, education and development, social and welfare programs, economic and political structures, and in the medical community. At every level, the community has been faced with an immigrant group whose belief systems, in many ways, differ radically from their own."[44]

The high unemployment rate among Southeast Asian families, who were mostly Hmong, was due both to their lack of transferable skills and the condition of the economy.[45] Nevertheless, many Hmong encountered controversial treatments when seeking employment. Some employers saw language as a key barrier and did not hire Hmong workers, whereas some preferred Hmong "industriousness" and welcomed them into their workforce. Still others, such as Paul Hsu, owner of Hsu's Ginseng Enterprises in the town of Texas, north of Wausau, preferred the "small-statured Hmong people [who] seem well-suited for the ginseng fields, where most work is done close to the ground."[46] In addition to preferring their physical characteristics, Hsu favored them because "the Hmong workers don't object to the relatively low pay of ginseng field work."

By the late 1980s to mid-1990s, Hmong in Wausau had established a number of businesses. In 1989, the innovative L. Jay Inc. (formerly known as United Hmong American Corp.) opened its three-thousand-square-foot shoemaking facility. Fifteen Wausau Hmong community investors pooled their resources together and won a contract from the Weinbrenner Shoe Company to sew and glue the upper portion of shoes for the company's Marshfield plant.[47] Additionally, the Wausau Area Hmong Mutual Association was established in 1983 to assist in Southeast Asian community integration as well as economic and social advancement in the Wausau area.[48] Services such as Hmong radio and television programs also go beyond the provision of basic-needs assistance; such stations communicate news and entertain the Wausau Hmong American community.

HICKORY, NORTH CAROLINA

The decision to remain in certain places clearly depended on careful considerations beyond warm climate. But, the weather cannot simply be overlooked either, as many Hmong Americans intentionally moved southward to states with milder winter temperatures. A 2005 community-needs assessment by the United Hmong Association of North Carolina (UHANC) estimated North Carolina's Hmong America population to be around 15,000, which is 5,000 more than the number counted by the 2000 Census. The authors described what they considered a fairly successful community: "Most of [the Hmong in North Carolina] are in Catawba, Burke, Alexander, Caldwell, McDowell, and Iredell [counties]. We also have Hmong families living in Iredell, Rowan, Mecklenburg, Union, Stanly, Montgomery, Cabarrus, Gaston, Lincoln and Surry County. The Hmong are drawn to North Carolina because of its economic opportunities and favorable climate. Over 60% of Hmong in North Carolina are U.S. citizens. About 95% of all Hmong adults are employed. About 70% own their own home and other real estate properties. Most of them work in factories while others engage in various types of business."[49] This description suggests that a successful ethnic enclave consists of people who are working, have become American citizens, are homeowners, and are engaged in business development. To some extent, this fulfills the goal of resettlement policies in helping refugees to become self-sufficient.

After the federal authorities instituted a change in settlement policy that refugees remaining in Wat Tham Krabok could apply to come to the United States, North Carolina officials responded. In a July 2, 2004, news release, Carmen Hooker Odom, North Carolina Department of Health and Human Services Secretary, encouraged North Carolinians to extend a helping hand to their newest group of Hmong refugees: "We welcome the Hmong to North Carolina. These are hardworking people who have demonstrated an ability to become contributing members of our communities, finding jobs and paying taxes. They do need some support, however, to help them get started in their new life."[50] This statement stems from the fact that by 2000, Hickory's Hmong American population had grown beyond 4,000. Contrary to dispersal refugee policies during the 1970s and 1980s, this last effort strategically sought to place refugees within existing ethnic enclaves rather than isolating them across the country. This change in refugee resettlement was critical, in that it took into account the negative consequences of earlier dispersal strategies. Unlike resettlement during the late 1970s, where sponsors in the larger community played a significant role, this last resettlement program relied almost exclusively on Hmong kinship networks for sponsorship. Anchor families, consisting of both immediate and extended family members, determined where the refugees would be resettled. Consequently, the vast majority of this refugee group was placed in California, Minnesota, and Wisconsin, all home to the majority of Hmong Americans.

The Hmong population in Hickory established formal organizations such as the UHANC to "improve the quality of life for the Hmong of North Carolina."[51] In addition to organizing festivals, UHANC assists with hosting New Year celebrations. Although the organization provides social services, less than 10 percent of the Hmong population in this area receives any public assistance. Across the states in which Hmong Americans reside, there exist differences in the percentage of community members utilizing public programs. In 2000, more than half of the California and Alaska Hmong populations used some public assistance, whereas in states like North Carolina, Oregon, Oklahoma, and Georgia less than 10 percent did.[52] This difference may be explained by the fact that those who moved to southern states often were individuals who had accumulated enough capital to purchase farms. Others moved only after having found employment. Their movement is not inspired by a more generous welfare program, as was partially the case during the mid-1980s. On an aggregate level, dependence on public assistance has decreased from 67 percent in 1990 to 30 percent.

MOHNTON, PENNSYLVANIA

An example of a very small population is the settlement in Mohnton, Pennsylvania, which in 2008 was six families primarily from the Kue clan. About thirty Hmong families arrived during the 1970s in the farmlands of Pennsylvania and were "rescued by the Mennonites of Pennsylvania Dutch country."[53] By 1981, about a thousand Hmong refugees had settled in the Philadelphia area.[54] Racial tensions as well as the desire to live with extended families and pursue better work opportunities resulted in most families moving to other parts of the country. Some moved to Detroit because younger individuals were able to obtain employment in the automotive and other manufacturing industries. Others like Kue Chaw moved to North Carolina. In 2000, 758 persons of Hmong ancestry were counted for the state of Pennsylvania.

According to Pastor Shong Chai Hang, only three Hmong families currently live in the city of Philadelphia. The majority had moved to such suburbs as Upper Darby.[55] Two Hmong churches are in the area: Hmong Alliance Church in Leola, established in 1987, and the Hmong Community Evangelical Lutheran Church, formed in 1996 in Philadelphia but currently located in the small town of Pottstown, Pennsylvania. The latter's members are primarily the six families residing in Mohnton and a few extended family members from the Philadelphia area. The Hmong Community ELC worships in the St. John's Evangelical Lutheran Church building in the afternoon; the congregation who owns the church worships there in the morning. The Hmong congregation does not pay rent. Instead, it contributes a small amount toward the church building's operating expenses. Despite the relatively small population, a Hmong community organization also exists to host a New Year celebration.

Why do those who remain in Mohnton stay when most of their friends and relatives have moved away? Have they ever considered moving and to where? Chai Lue Kue and May Houa Vang, a couple in their mid-fifties, remember their contentious situation over the years. May Houa explains:

> In the early 1990s, there were a series of crimes in the northwest part of Philadelphia where we lived. The perpetrators were Vietnamese and African Americans. What happened to the Hmong houses was that when we were away at work and the kids were at school, they would break into our homes. One day we came home from work and our door was jolted open. We were so afraid and so were the other Hmong people whose homes were broken into. They would also enter through windows. Most of us eventually had to have metal bars on our windows. It was at this time that we actually found an apartment in Rhode Island where some of our relatives lived. We sent the kids and my in-laws there first. We were going to try to find jobs there before moving permanently. We were never able to find jobs so, in fact, we lived in Philadelphia while my in-laws and the kids lived there for about a year. We finally brought them back because of our jobs.[56]

In 2003, five of their friends and relatives decided to make the Philadelphia area their permanent home. They set out to find a place to build homes. After searching for building sites for some time, they settled on a new development in Mohnton, which is an hour northwest of Philadelphia. The rural environment was appealing to the elders. There, they invested their life savings accumulated over the previous twenty years. They sold their homes during the good housing market in 2002 and built new homes on six lots, five of which are on three-acre lots and one slightly less than three acres on the lower side of the main street. Those with three acres all raise chickens. Early in the morning, the roosters crow simultaneously.

When asked how they think others in the development view the concentration of Hmong houses, Kao Nhia, in her mid-twenties and Chai

Lue's and May Houa's daughter, comments, "Some of the white neighbors had sold their homes and moved away. I don't know if it is because they don't like all the Hmong people or because there are other reasons. It's pretty scary sometimes because there are a lot of white supremacist groups in Philadelphia, and they are out in the open about their hate messages."[57] May Houa further describes their relationships with her white neighbors as complex:

> The neighbors to our right and back are pretty nice. When they have special food or other items, they bring me some. I do the same for them, especially food items from my garden. I plant "Hmong" cucumber every year and give some to the neighbors. The ones in the back said they love the Hmong cucumbers because they are so much sweeter than the ones from the store. My next-door neighbor has a parakeet who loves peas. I either take some to my neighbor to feed his bird, or I invite him to come and pick them whenever he needs them. He's also very helpful in that he teaches us about how to keep our lawn green. We don't know much about landscaping, and he shares his knowledge with us. As for the neighbor across the street, they never talk to us or acknowledge our existence. We don't know if he just doesn't like us or that he's indifferent. One trend I see is that many of the neighbors also moved here from Philadelphia so they are used to seeing people like us. Some of them actually still work in the city.[58]

As a mother, May Houa has struggled emotionally with moving to the rural area while her adult children have mostly chosen to live in the city. May Houa Vang and Chai Lue Kue's relationships with their Hmong American children, white neighbors, and Hmong relatives and neighbors tell a great deal about the intricacy of immigrant life in America. While the younger generation welcomes the vast opportunities in large cities, many of the immigrant generation yearn for a quiet life away from urban centers.

DANVILLE, ARKANSAS

The desire for "village" life along with their hard-work ethic drove some Hmong to the southern states. The phenomenon of purchasing poultry and breeder farms in high numbers beginning during the mid- to late 1990s led to a dramatic increase in Hmong population in the south. Paging through the classified advertisements in ethnic newspapers such as *Hmong Times,* which is the oldest community newspaper still in circulation and *Hmong Today* in St. Paul during the late 1990s through the early 2000s, one sees numerous ads for poultry and breeder farms for sale in Arkansas and other southern states such as Missouri, Oklahoma, Georgia, and North Carolina. Not only do these ethnic newspapers provide news to their majority Hmong American readers but also they serve as an entrance into the Hmong community. Real-estate brokers, such as Jack Elder with Tall Star Realty in Gentry, Arkansas (see fig. 7), sought Hmong American buyers in 2005 for European American–owned farms.[59] Having worked for years in manufacturing and service-sector jobs, many families had accumulated some wealth by the late 1990s. Drawn by the prospect of financial gains and independence, and the nostalgia of farm life, some invested all or significant portions of their assets on these businesses. The stories of success by a few Hmong American farmers and the appeal of being able to work for themselves described by real estate agents and farm owners lured others, possibly without adequate savings, to borrow the down payment from relatives and friends. This led to an estimated six hundred Hmong families owning and operating poultry farms in Arkansas, Missouri, Oklahoma, and North Carolina.[60]

The experiences of most, however, were not as described by sellers and real estate brokers. In addition to being surprised by complicating factors, such as the required intense labor with minimal returns after expenses are paid, few prospective buyers were savvy enough to examine

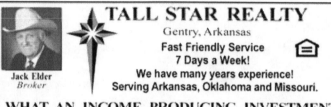

Figure 7. Poultry Farm Ad attempts to attract Hmong Americans to southern states. Advertisement courtesy of Hmong Today, 2005.

business records and thereby determine cash flow. The thrill of independence led countless individuals to purchase failing poultry businesses.
Like Mee Thao and Pao Thao (not their real names),[61] most were drawn
to the idea of "being your own boss" and owning many acres of land.
Mee and Pao had invested heavily in real estate in the Twin Cities during the 1980s and 1990s. They had a cousin and friends from a church
they previously attended who had purchased poultry farms in Danville,
located in west central Arkansas, approximately seventy miles east of
Fort Smith. With a population of 2,392, Danville had seen an increase in
Asian American farmers who were exclusively of Hmong ethnicity. From
2000 to 2005, vanloads of Hmong Americans from around the country
traveled to places like Danville to make offers on poultry farms.[62] Mee
and Pao purchased a poultry farm for $1.2 million and used the cash from
the sale of their properties in the Twin Cities for the 20 percent down
payment. After less than a year, they lost their contract due to their inability to find money to make the required upgrades to the facility. They
also learned that the farm did not generate the income that the sellers
had presented. Mee and Pao were reduced to shutting down their operation. Like many others who made similar investments in this industry,
they subsequently returned to the Twin Cities bankrupt. Other families,
while still having possession of their farms, are working long hours for
what is calculated to be less than minimum wage. Their desire to return
to the land has forced many to the impoverished situation in which most
began their lives in America.

3   Re-creation of Social Structures

> While ethnicity implies that a group shares a real or
> mythological common past and cultural focus, the central
> defining characteristic of ethnic groups is the belief in
> their own existence as a group.
>
> —Philip Kasinitz, *Caribbean New York*

Migrating across the globe requires flexibility and a willing-
ness to confront inevitable disruption to existing social structures. When
Hmong refugees settled into their daily lives in the United States, many
no longer had access to the kinship system to support them and provide
continuity. They were required to explore and utilize available resources
in the host communities to create new, meaningful support systems. The
ways in which they developed formal organizations, whether secular or
religious, reflects previous social and cultural practices brought from the
homeland. In doing so, Hmong in America invested a great deal of time
and resources in creating new identities. Although the primary purpose
for establishing formal organizations was to pool and obtain resources
for community members, the rise of ethnic, community-based organizations and churches reflects clan identity politics and the politics of ethnic
representation to the larger community. Leaders of these formal institutions frequently speak for "the Hmong community"; however, diverse
community interests suggest that many represent only some aspects of
the different layers of "the Hmong community."

Even prior to their migration to the United States, the conversion of
Hmong to Christianity had begun to alter Hmong social organization.
Although respect for elders was maintained due to the contained envi-
ronments in which Hmong lived, converts in the village context began to

seek help from pastors and church leaders outside of the clan or subclan. Family conflicts were then brought to the church for resolution. Some Christians began to distance themselves from members of their clan and extended family members. Some non-Christians regarded the converts as strange and treated them as outsiders. The promotion of Hmong youth to positions of leadership due to formal education during the war years also transformed Hmong social organization from that period up to the present and subsequently altered the role of elders in the diaspora dramatically.

For the first Hmong refugee arrivals, their ethnicity served as an organizing force. Even traditionally divisive clan affiliation did not prevent them from coming together to reduce isolation and support one another. When the refugee population was small, interclan community interactions were common. As more people arrived, clan and kinship affiliations increased in importance, and refugees began to establish informal support groups based on these relationships, thereby excluding some. When populations in particular locations increased due to resettlement from refugee camps and secondary migration from other areas, some subclan communities further developed and excluded others. Clans further divided into subclan communities based on religious differences. Though some are largely dominated by particular segments of the above "communities," two new structures created in the United States have, to some extent, transcended such Hmong social organization criteria: Christian churches and mutual assistance associations (MAAs or also generally referred to as nonprofit and/or community-based organizations). Consequently, the term "the Hmong community" became even more problematic, as those using this expression may indeed be referring to only a small segment of the larger population.

Formalizing Community

Migrant associations have been shown to play three important roles in facilitating integration into host societies.[1] First, they provide information and assistance with the problems of housing and employment, occasionally offering limited financial aid during related crises. Second, by providing a context for "ethnic" activity, they serve as a central place where the cultural and status hierarchies of the home country can be maintained. Third, voluntary associations connect the migrant to the home society and influence the politics and culture of those societies.[2] Associations of the first two types dominate the Hmong American experience. Several organizations focusing on homeland politics have also emerged to fulfill the third role.

MUTUAL ASSISTANCE ASSOCIATIONS

Hmong Americans' multilayered community practices are similar to the core immigrant traditions of establishing permanent communities, obtaining security, gaining citizenship, and seeking economic, familial, and personal betterment.[3] While extended family members frequently moved to form small support groups in certain locations, other Hmong have strategically worked to encourage Hmong unity across the country in order to build larger enclaves capable of having more significant economic, social, cultural, and political influence. One prominent way in which emerging Hmong refugee leaders have consolidated their ethnic power is through the establishment of MAAs.[4]

The genesis of MAAs is part of the *becoming a refugee* process and owes its existence to Southeast Asian refugee-resettlement programs during the late 1970s. Federal, state, and private funding sustained these organizations to help vulnerable refugee populations overcome barriers they faced in American society. Like other refugee and immigrant self-help groups, many MAAs began as informal gatherings for social, cultural, and spiritual purposes and offered newcomers opportunities to celebrate their traditions and find comfort in a common language and culture.[5] Though funded to provide basic-needs support and to help integrate the refugees into American society, in reality, they often become a means of political expression. They also foster competition between subgroups over leadership, funds, and representation. Their funding sources are diverse, with a significant portion coming from government contracts, private foundations, and corporations.[6] From 1975 to 1980, only a few MAAs were directly funded by the federal government to provide social services to new arrivals. Following the dramatic increase in the number of arrivals in the United States in 1980, however, MAAs were singled out for special consideration and support by the newly formed Office of Refugee Resettlement (ORR) as part of the Refugee Act of 1980.[7] Since then, federal programs have provided special assistance to these ethnic organizations in an effort to encourage their participation in the refugee-resettlement service-delivery system.

The impetus for funding ethnic-based organizations was that mainstream organizations often lacked language and cultural knowledge to adequately address the complex needs of refugees. The rationale for the development of these organizations was framed as a deficiency in the traditional resettlement agencies. Emerging Hmong leaders advocated for the hiring of bilingual staff within service agencies in the larger community that lacked language-appropriate services. Many agencies understood the advantages of recruiting respected members of the client community to help solve problems, but some agency directors viewed this as an attempt by the formerly powerful people or emerging refugee leaders to selfishly promote themselves and their supporters.[8] However, the general agreement among those involved was that the Hmong were not being helped sufficiently by resettlement programs designed to aid Indochinese refugees with different cultural and religious backgrounds; this insufficient help, therefore, justified the need for such ethnic organizations.

The loss of immediate- and extended-family support systems due to migration encouraged the early refugees to utilize various strategies to create a sense of community. Although they do not receive new sponsor support if they relocate, refugee families often become eligible for social-service programs available to low-income community members. Friends and relatives helped new arrivals access the services and assisted them in registering children for school and locating the nearest hospitals and grocery stores.

Shortly after their arrival in the Twin Cities, Hmong refugees attempted to collaborate with Lao ethnics because they shared a home country. Xang Vang describes this attempt: "In the early year, when we first started, there was an organization *Lao Loom Phau* (United Lao Race Association) that the Hmong and Lao joined together. But since the Lao weren't active in the organization's affairs and business, we decided that if the Lao didn't want the organization to be the focus point, then we needed to start another. During the time that the Hmong Association was being created, I arrived from Missoula."[9] Hmong interviewed for this book perceived that few Lao refugees became involved in the organization due to their indifference to social-services needs. Tong Vang, one of the first few refugees to settle in Minnesota in June of 1976 and a former board president of the Lao Family organization, explained that the main obstacle impeding successful interethnic collaboration was the inability of participants to agree on priority issues; however, he speculates that this early Lao lack of interest may actually reflect some historical interethnic tension, in which Lao ethnics viewed Hmong as inferior. He states, "The Hmong wanted to make sure there is social services available for our people. The Lao were not interested in developing such services because they didn't feel that they needed them. Our people had many problems adjusting. That is why we wanted to have a Hmong organization."[10]

These emerging Hmong refugee leaders took strategic actions to create their own self-help organization. On July 16, 1977, Hmong families living in the Twin Cities area held a meeting to discuss their common problems and to make plans to establish a formal organization. In September 1977, the Association of Hmong in Minnesota (AHM) was incorporated as a nonprofit organization with several objectives, including: (1) to encourage mutual assistance among the Hmong when a need should arise, (2) to establish communication networks for all the Hmong, (3) to advise Americans on the culture of the Hmong ethnic, (4) to advise Hmong ethnic on the facets of American culture and history, and (5) to develop elementary educational materials for the Hmong.[11]

The association worked in a volunteer capacity "closely with refugee sponsoring agencies, individual sponsors, local and state government, the schools, human service providers, and other segments of society in promoting the welfare of Hmong refugees and in facilitating greater cultural understanding between the Hmong people and their American friends."[12] Her Dang, an association cofounder, remembers encountering many challenges: "We didn't have any experience with management of an organization. Tou Fue Vang had come to the United States as a student so he spoke English. He had come to Montana with General Vang Pao. He came to Minnesota and helped us to form the Hmong Association. He told us that forming an organization was the only way we could help other refugees that were arriving. I think Leng Vang was the first board chair, then Ya Yang and then on to Ly Teng."[13]

The association operated under this name until June 28, 1980, when its membership voted to affiliate with Lao Family Community Inc., a private nonprofit organization founded in March of 1977 by a group of Lao and Hmong refugees in Santa Ana, California. The group included former General Vang Pao.[14] In an effort to collaborate across ethnic lines, this California group agreed to embrace the Lao Family name and envisioned formal organizations serving all people from Laos. The Hmong association's name change into Lao Family was in recognition of the immigrant generation's affinity with its Lao identity, as well as a representation of General Vang Pao's influence during the early years in America. As Xang Vang, a former executive director, remembers, "General Vang Pao came to town to talk about Lao Family. He said that since we are citizens of Laos, we should include services for the Lao. It's important that the Hmong and Lao are still brothers. In summer of 1980, we turned Hmong Association to Lao Family."[15] Today, about a half dozen Lao Family organizations exist in various locations throughout the United States; however, they served primarily Hmong clients, with services ranging from youth and families to employment, English education, cultural training, and health promotion. The size of Lao Family organizations varies significantly across the different locations. While a few operate with budgets in excess of one million dollars, most face funding challenges. The Lao

Family organization in Minnesota is the largest, with several service sites.[16] Acceptance of the Lao Family name suggests that the diaspora context—removed as it was from the historical Lao physical space where Hmong were deemed inferior—allowed the Hmong to make an ideological shift in seeing themselves as former Lao citizens. Hmong inclusion as citizens of Laos in the 1947 constitution insinuates Hmong identity as Lao, in particular those like Vang Pao who had worked for the Royal Lao Army.

What is significant about the name change is that some preferred their Hmong ethnic identity over a Lao identity. As explained by Her Dang, opposing voices were in the minority regarding the change: "At that time, General Vang Pao was also creating the Lao Family organization in Santa Ana, California. It was during Ly Teng's term as board president that we changed the name to Lao Family. Many of us wanted strongly to keep our name Hmong Association, but as Hmong people, whether it's right or wrong, we just follow our leaders. Also, Ly Teng was very close to General Vang Pao. He was president of the board, so they changed it. Because we wanted to serve Hmong, we wanted to keep the name Hmong Association. General Vang Pao's purpose was to involve the Lao. I suppose the leaders thought that if we were to be able to return to Laos, being inclusive would be better. He encouraged us to change the name, so it was changed."[17] Her Dang's statement suggests that the leaders in Minnesota did not openly protest the name change even if they were not in favor of it. The close ties between Vang Pao and some in leadership positions dictated the organization's direction.

In the beginning, the organization was established based on a common interest in facilitating refugee families' adjustment to American society. As the Hmong refugee population increased and other segments of the population felt excluded or unable to enter the leadership structure, other organizations were established to meet the changing needs.[18] Although the association responded to and addressed many family issues, its leaders were primarily men. Few Hmong women were involved in its board of directors.[19] Consequently, two Hmong women's organizations were established in 1979, one in Minneapolis and the other in St. Paul. The Association for the Advancement of Hmong Women in Minnesota (AAHWM) began in Minneapolis.[20] Cofounder May Ia Lee explains what led to AAHWM's creation:

> When we began the Hmong women's organization, I felt like it was my fault. I came up with the idea and then shared it with other women, and they wanted to move forward to start the organization. At the time, I

felt that Hmong women didn't have much peace, and many had been abused by their spouses. We wanted to have equal rights, education opportunities, and support system as well as supporting in building good relationships with our spouses. I told my ex-husband these ideas. He was completely supportive of the idea. Hmong women needed the support. We wanted to elevate women's status. So, Mrs. Lee Tou and I started to brainstorm about it. I don't know how we did it. We didn't have much knowledge. But, we were able to talk to other supportive people in the larger community who guided us. . . . We did have one American woman, I can't remember her name, who helped us. She was there, but we came up with all the ideas.[21]

Similar to Her Dang's reflection, May Ia Lee concedes the limited knowledge she and other refugee Hmong women had about forming such an organization. They worked for a couple of years with the help of their American friends, and AAHWM obtained its nonprofit status in 1981.

On the St. Paul side, a group of progressive Hmong refugee women founded the Women's Association of Hmong and Lao (WAHL). Although both entities focused on issues affecting Hmong women, WAHL's leaders, similar to the Lao Family process, remained partially committed to their Lao identity until the organization's demise in 2003. Cofounder Gaoly Yang recalls the tensions during WAHL's creation:

Three, four years after we got here, we started the [WAHL] because those involved worked in various organizations, and we saw an opportunity to advance Hmong women. That's why we created the organization. It was a big learning curve. We had no idea what we were doing. Well, we knew that there was this thing called nonprofit organization, and if we create it, we could employ people. Those people would work to help refugees. We wanted to give women an edge. I mean, we were pretty radical to take that on. Interestingly though, because the men already had the Hmong Association, Xang Vang and the others were complaining that if we created one, we were disrespecting Hmong men. They said, why don't you just join us. You can do what you want to do. We can help each other. But their board members were mostly men, just one or two women. They said that if we joined, then they would let us run programs that teach girls to dance, food preparations for events, etc. We said, NO. We wanted a woman director and create programs that empower women. . . . They complained, tried to *ntxias* [trick us with kind words], but when they couldn't convince us to stop, they complained more. They said we weren't obedient. What do we do? The first thing we started was a domestic-abuse project![22]

Gender issues as well as challenges imposed by the larger community placed many of its women leaders in difficult positions. Furthermore,

WAHL leaders had continually debated the relevance of the *Lao* part of the organization's name to young Hmong American women, many of whom identified themselves only as Hmong. While WAHL eventually refused to sponsor the Hmong New Year celebrations, AAHWM, on the contrary, continues to play a large role in cosponsoring the celebration to the present. Ly Vang, AAHWM executive director, has served as emcee and lead organizer of many program activities. She believes that it is important to continue to support the event, even though she does not agree with some of its practices.[23]

The desire to achieve gender equality and nurture women's leadership skills served as the driving force for the establishment of the two Hmong women's organizations. Why, then, have many other ethnic organizations been established? How are they different from or similar to Lao Family? As long as all the kin groups were struggling to survive in the United States, the appeal of a national mutual-assistance association was strong, and divisions based on kinship, regional loyalty, dialect, and political alliance could be bridged by a coalition of leaders headed by General Vang Pao.[24] However, as the situation improved for some groups, the perceived need for a single national organization became less important. Although Lao Family organizations have been established in California, Minnesota, and Wisconsin, to date no national organization exists. The organizations are separate entities within those states and serve local constituents.

Interestingly, apart from the first Lao Family and the two women's organizations, other Hmong ethnic organizations in Minnesota began to emerge only in 1990. This practice also took place in the Chicago area, where the Association of Hmong in Illinois (AHI), formed in 1978, broke into two organizations in 1981 to form the Chicago Hmong Community Services (CHCS) due to clan divisions and organizational disagreements.[25] With the founding of Hmong American Partnership (HAP), Southeast Asian Community Council (SEACC), and Hmong National Organization Inc. (HNO) in 1990, new competition emerged for funding sources. The Hmong American Mutual Assistance Association (HAMAA) was formed in 1991, Hmong Minnesota Pacific Association in 1992, Lauj Youth Society (currently known as Hmong Youth Education Services) and Hmong Cultural Center in 1993, Center for Hmong Arts and Talent (CHAT) in 1994, Hmong 18 Clan Council in 1996, Hmong American New Year in 1998, Hmong American Family Inc. in 2003, Hmong Nationality Archives in 1999, and Hmong American Institute for Learning (HAIL) in 2003.[26]

By the 1990s, community needs had evolved considerably. Some Hmong Americans in the Twin Cities wanted to focus exclusively on local level concerns and/or Hmong American issues. In contrast, most of the organizations established since that time are small and have a particular focus, such as a specific clan or subgroup, for instance, youth. Some receive limited federal refugee-resettlement funds, but, generally, most depend on local foundations focusing on various priority issues. Of the organizations established during the 1990s, Hmong American Partnership is the only organization to have grown significantly. Its founders asserted an interest in integrating into American society by reducing homeland politics. Since its establishment, the agency has grown from a small community-based organization focusing on basic refugee-resettlement issues to an established provider of comprehensive, culturally appropriate services.[27] Its programs include English classes, computer training, youth activities, support for parents, job placement, and volunteer opportunities. After being located in several spaces throughout the 1990s, HAP purchased an old YMCA building on the east side of St. Paul in 2001. Since then, its leaders have obtained funding to demolish it and build a new facility on this location.

HAP has not, however, been without problems. A different level of community politics emerged in 2006 when its board of directors fired a long-time executive director for undisclosed reasons. Community members accused the board of gender and racial bias because members of the board of directors were primarily Hmong American women, including the chair, and European Americans.[28] The organization's decision to hire its first Hmong American woman executive director in 2007 was also criticized by some community members as a biased preference by its female-dominated board of directors.[29] It appeared that Hmong American women were accepted in leadership positions in Hmong women's organizations and in the larger community, but they do not necessarily receive the same treatment in an organization trying to represent all Hmong. Although census data show higher educational attainment levels among men compared to women nationally, the rapid increase of Hmong American women obtaining higher education has resulted in those serving as elected officials, executive directors of national organizations serving Southeast Asian Americans, managers at the state and county levels as well as the private sector, education administrators, educators from elementary school to college and university, and news reporters. As more women achieved higher education, they also created new support networks such as the Professional Hmong Women's group based in St. Paul.

While most community organizations emphasize social services, the Hmong Cultural Center's Resource Center in St. Paul has both a community and a scholarly focus. The resource center contains one of the most, if not the most, comprehensive collections of Hmong studies scholarship in the entire United States. The collection includes books, academic articles, and newspaper articles related to the Hmong people and the Hmong experience in Minneapolis–St. Paul and across the world.[30] The Hmong Nationality Archives in St. Paul was established as a Hmong repository and contains a distinct collection of Hmong-related historical items and out-of-print books. When Concordia University in St. Paul established the Center for Hmong Studies, the collection moved there. In combining resources, both entities assumed the responsibility of documenting and making available more information about Hmong history and culture.[31] Differences in priorities have resulted in the archive relocating to a new location in St. Paul in 2008. In 1994, the literary-arts journal *Paj Ntaub Voice* began as a youth project with HAP and then transitioned to form the Center for Hmong Arts and Talent (CHAT) to nurture and promote new and emerging Hmong American artists and writers. Leaders of this organization are primarily members of the one-and-a-half- and second-generation Hmong Americans who are engaged in dialogues about difficult issues in the Hmong American community. This grassroots literary movement was originally led by Mai Neng Moua, who, in 2003, left CHAT to form HAIL to "promote and preserve Hmong expressive culture."[32]

At the national level, the Indochinese Refugee Action Center (IRAC) was established in 1979 "to guard the human rights of Southeast Asian refugees entering the United States, and to foster the development of nonprofit organizations led by and for Southeast Asian Americans."[33] In 1993, a mostly younger, American-educated group established the Hmong National Development (HND) in an attempt to form a national organization with broader appeal. Based in Washington, D.C., HND serves as a national resource and works with more than eighty local MAAs.[34] HND has provided advocacy at the national level by tracking various legislation and congressional activities that affect the Hmong community. In addition, it has hosted fourteen national conferences in different locations throughout the United States that draw, on average, five hundred participants from the community as well as many students and scholars from colleges and universities. In 2009, both Southeast Asia Resource Action Center and HND executive directors were Hmong American women.

Like MAAs operated by other Southeast Asians and recently by newer refugee groups from Africa, the size, types of services offered, and number of organizations vary considerably across states. Whereas states with larger populations often have numerous organizations competing with one another, smaller communities usually focus their energy and resources collectively on a single organization for that population. For example, by nature of the number of Hmong Americans in California, more than thirty organizations operate in that state. The overlap of services across organizations sometimes creates tension. Various attempts are made to encourage collaboration among MAAs, but genuine collaboration often does not materialize because of competition for the same financial resources and the proximity of the organizations. This is particularly true in Minnesota, where the overwhelming majority of the Hmong population lives in the Twin Cities. Due to philanthropic institutions' geographic limitations and funding priorities, organizations here often struggle with the need to demonstrate what "community" they are serving when other ethnic organizations also target the same population. The situation differs somewhat for MAAs in Wisconsin, due to the dispersal of the Hmong population throughout the state. The Wisconsin United Coalition of Mutual Assistance Associations (WUCMAA), an umbrella entity to provide leadership and technical support to enhance the operations of MAAs in Wisconsin, consists of the fourteen organizations serving Hmong Americans.[35] In addition to seeking resources and advocating for its members, WUCMAA also holds an annual conference where its members can interact with and learn from each other. The Wisconsin MAAs seem to be more collaborative because their members are dispersed throughout the state. However, some MAAs in cities with small populations struggle to justify their need for financial resources. In addition, many may feel more comfortable integrating into the larger community rather than isolating themselves in ethnocentric organizations.

CHRISTIAN CHURCHES

How does religion facilitate or hinder integration into the host society? How do Hmong conceptualize their ethnic community within their new faith? Simultaneous with the development of mutual-assistance associations was the rise of Hmong Christian churches serving many socioeconomic needs along with meeting the religious needs of their members. Much of the social-science research during the 1980s and 1990s highlighted the experiences of impoverished Hmong lives and concluded that they were not "becoming American," when, in fact, Hmong people were acculturating at multiple levels, including through the Christian churches. One explanation for this disconnect is that most researchers examined the most vulnerable Hmong populations since these individuals were most accessible as clients of formal mutual-assistance associations struggling to meet their basic needs. Because of this, the experiences of a large percentage of the Hmong American population have been overlooked by social-science studies scholars who traditionally study problems. Such inattentiveness to the intersection of religion and immigration in research studies of both historical and social science has resulted in a limited understanding of the role that religious communities play in immigrant lives. The ways in which community building has manifested within the Christian Hmong American population complicates and contradicts "essentialist" narratives about Hmong. The few studies conducted on Hmong Christianity were by Hmong American seminary students.[36] As Christians themselves and members of Christian and Missionary Alliance (C&MA) churches, the authors tend to focus primarily on the history of the Hmong C&MA movement. Therefore, little is known about other denominations or religions.

Because animist traditions require support from shamans and extended family members, religion served as a pull factor prevalent in the secondary migration described in chapter 2. Hmong conversion to Christianity has also been, and continues to be, a complex process. Some individuals have made personal decisions to leave the old beliefs in favor of the new, but the conversion process for many often involved the influence of others, frequently immediate and extended family members and sometimes Christian sponsors, whether intentionally or unintentionally. Furthermore, some Christians moved to areas where Hmong Christians were concentrated in order to join Hmong-only congregations.

The idea that a stateless people such as the Hmong must have been chosen by God to come to America is often heard in sermons by Hmong American pastors trying to make sense of their members' lives in America. How else can one explain the migration of villagers from one of the most isolated areas of the world to one of the world's most developed countries? Although Hmong conversion in the diaspora is often viewed as a consequence of living in a predominantly Christian society, this perception is inaccurate. People of Hmong ethnicity in Asia were targets for European and American missionaries before migrating to Western societies. Prior to the Hmong people's migration to the Indochinese peninsula, Christian missionaries (in particular missionary Samuel Pollard, who arrived in China in 1882) had attempted to convert people of Hmong ethnicity. In Laos, four different groups of missionaries invested time and effort to reach the Lao (and Hmong) people.[37] Despite the first Catholic missionary, Jerret Von Wusthoff, arriving in Vientiane in 1641 with the Dutch East India Company, the Roman Catholics' efforts were not successful due to strong opposition by Buddhist monks. Only by the late 1800s were Catholic missionaries finally making progress in converting Lao people from the southern part of the country.[38] Other missionaries to Laos were the Presbyterians in 1880, the Swiss Brethren in 1902, and the Christian and Missionary Alliance (C&MA) in 1929.[39]

Although Catholic missionaries were present in Laos first, the first Hmong conversion to Catholicism did not occur until 1954.[40] The first documented conversion to Christianity took place in 1950 in Xieng Khouang Province in the presence of C&MA missionaries Ted and Ruth Andrianoff.[41] The Andrianoffs arrived in Xieng Khouang with their assistant Nai Kheng, who was a member of the Khammu ethnic minority, to distribute literature to the people. They rented a house across the street from Hmong religious leader Boua Ya Thao. The house was widely professed to be haunted. The shaman had heard about the missionaries and waited to see if their God would be able to deal with ghosts. Shortly after their arrival, Boua Ya encountered a dilemma. His cousin's wife was very ill, and all his efforts as a shaman could not drive away the evil spirits. Since he could not heal her, he suggested that his cousin invite Nai Kheng and the Andrianoffs to tell them more about God. While the missionaries presented the gospel, Boua Ya Thao and his family converted. It has been said that Boua Ya Thao's status as a shaman influenced other people's conversion. Some felt that, as a shaman, he would be in the best position to understand both worlds. Following this conversion, Nai Kheng and Boua Ya Thao traveled to many Hmong villages throughout the province to spread the word about God. Consequently, families and even whole villages converted to Christianity and began to establish churches, which was characterized as a "people's movement."[42]

Reasons for Hmong conversion in the village context were indeed diverse. According to Timothy T. Vang, factors for conversion in Laos include (1) the social, political, and economic hardships that Hmong faced during and after the war; (2) the similarity between the Hmong traditional belief system and Christianity; and (3) the idea of establishing a homogenous unit within Hmong Christian churches. One of the most common motivations was the potential to be cured from illnesses and/or be rid of evil spirits, as Chou Vang, one of the first arrivals in 1976, corroborates concerning her family's conversion: "As my brother traveled to conduct business, he had met some Christians. One of the problems was that where we lived in *Dong Dok*, my brother had purchased these big Vietnamese-built homes, which were haunted. Before we became Christians, I lost one younger sister. An older sister also died suddenly. So, when my brother heard from the missionaries, he became a Christian. Our whole family converted."[43] Because her family had converted, Chou's mother eventually decided to send her to Bible school to become a missionary. She became one of the few female Bible-school students in

Vientiane during the early 1960s. Upon completion around 1966, however, she changed her mind about becoming a missionary. She explains her anxiety, "When I finished Bible school in Vientiane, I decided that I didn't want to do missionary work. As a woman, I didn't want to go out there all by myself." Similar to other Hmong women who had some formal education, she joined the nursing program at Sam Thong hospital.

Following the first conversion, missionaries implemented several methods to reach more villagers: providing leadership training by setting up Bible schools; organizing the local churches to form a national church organization, the Lao Evangelical Church; assisting with the development of a written script for the Hmong language so that Hmong can learn in their own language; translating the Bible into the Hmong language; C&MA purchasing and using an airplane to reach remote villages; establishing a youth group for Bible study, fellowship, worship, and evangelistic activities (by the mid-1960s); recording and sending messages to Hmong Christians via radio (around 1970); producing and distributing Sunday-school materials; and building and operating hostels for Hmong students who came from the highlands to study in Vientiane.[44]

Hmong oral history confirms that members of the Thao clan were the first to convert as a result of Boua Ya Thao's efforts, followed by the Moua and Her clans due to the proximity of their villages to that of the Thao's. In addition, the Green Hmong (*Moob Ntsuab/Moob Leeg*) were the first believers. As pastor PaMang Her explains:

> The Green Hmong were the people the spirits were around more and were harsher on them than the White Hmong. The spirits were really harsh and mean to the Thaos. This is why they were so scared. For example, like us Hers, if we went gardening, and we carried food in our back-basket, and we saw fruits around and picked them and put them in our baskets, when we got to the garden and later tried to find our lunch, there would be snakes there. So there were many things that the Hmong people tended not to do. The Hers had many of these things to prevent any horrible situations. If you didn't do this well, the spirits would make you sick and die. The Hers had what they called a curse, and they were what people were so afraid of—for example, sin. If you have many children, and you are addicted to opium, and you cannot provide [for them], or if you are rich but have no children or if you have children and money, then you'll die soon. The Hers were really scared so when they heard that if you became a believer that you'd be OK, they started to believe, and God helped them, and they escaped the curse. The Green Hmong became believers because the very first one was Green Hmong.[45]

The first White Hmong to convert was Chai Pao Vang. His conversion story is also one of the missionaries freeing someone from possession by an evil spirit.[46] During the 1960s, as war progressed and large concentrations of displaced Hmong formed in certain locations, it became easier for Hmong Christians to assist in spreading the gospel.[47]

Like military personnel who came to Laos in the 1960s, missionaries often arrived in the country with no local language skills. The development of the Hmong language using the Romanized Popular Alphabet (RPA) in 1953 by American missionary linguist William Smalley, Reverend G. Linwood Barney, and French missionary Father Yves Bertrais was intended to help convert the Hmong to Christianity in northern Laos. Although each had initially developed his own method for learning the Hmong language, these missionaries agreed to work collaboratively to develop a Hmong written script. Bertrais recalls, "We wanted something simple, without marks. We wanted to make sure we could capture the tones. At the time, I knew that Hmong had seven sounds. I had different marks from Smalley's numbers that he used to indicate the tones. We decided and agreed that once constructed, we would not change it. It only took us five days together to construct the Hmong RPA script. I was very happy, and we began to teach the script right away. The two young men with me were among the first to learn. Others heard, and seven to eight people would come to my house every evening to learn how to write in Hmong language."[48]

Writing in the Hmong language began to spread, and as more people learned, it became a communication tool for villagers. As word spread that the missionaries' God was able to get rid of ghosts and evil spirits and that they had created a written script for Hmong language, conversions, sometimes of whole villages, increased. At this juncture, the appeal of this writing was their interest in literacy. Australian anthropologist Nicholas Tapp best summarizes the relationship between Hmong and missionaries: "Christian mission work among the Hmong has had a long and well-established ancestry. It seems often to have carried with it something of a mass appeal, particularly in situations of severe economic stress, and to have achieved much of its success through the prospects of education, and above all, literacy, which it promised."[49] While others, such as missionary Pollard, who had worked with Miao in southern China and translated the New Testament into a Romanized version of Hmong, had developed various Hmong scripts, these scripts did not become widespread. According to Hmong in Thailand, the original loss of Hmong literacy is attributed to the original loss of territory and flight out of China. Significantly, Hmong legends speak of a lost book; perhaps this influenced Hmong curiosity about the Bible and conversion.

These various efforts by missionaries throughout the 1960s increased the number of Hmong Christians to an estimated fourteen thousand by 1975.[50] At Namphong where the airlifted refugees were placed in May 1975, they were confronted with a new dilemma when the Thai authorities informed them that they would be resettled in a valley. Sai Lee explained that the valley was thought to have ghosts. Rumors spread that people who pass through that location would have bloody noses and then die, which created a great deal of fear among the refugees. According to Sai Lee, the group made a decision to send the Christians first:

> Colonel Xay Dang and Pastor Nou Toua said that the Christians would go ahead. When we got to the valley, which didn't have a name yet, we set up camp. We would keep the lights on all night long. Christian songs were sung. My wife was one of the ones who sang a lot. The Thai then asked us what we wanted to call this valley. We didn't answer them. But, when the Thai officials said that every refugee who comes to this valley needs to *coj lavbiaj vibnais* (follow the rules). So we thought about calling the place *xoon lavbiaj Vibnais*. [Vibnais] means to stay under control. Like soldiers who have to stay *lavbiaj vibnais* and follow their leaders. After the Christians had been in the valley for about a month, others followed when it seemed safe. Nothing bad happened. Few illnesses and deaths took place. When more people arrived, then such things began to emerge.[51]

Sai Lee's recollection suggests that Christianity had become a significant part of life for a segment of the population. The concentration of Hmong in refugee camps further opened up new opportunities for those who had been trained in Laos to minister to others who were in dire need. The continued arrival of Western camp workers from Christian-based relief agencies further facilitated conversions.

While Hmong and other Southeast Asian refugees awaited their fate in refugee camps, thousands of church members across the United States contemplated lending a hand to those in need. As previously discussed, the decisions that American church members made in subsequent years greatly impacted refugee lives. Family social-science scholar Daniel F. Detzner describes a call for Americans to help displaced refugees: "Postwar feelings of guilt generated a sense of obligation in many Americans to those whose lives had been most directly affected by the decade-long intrusion. There was an unprecedented call for Americans to commit to the financial and social obligations of sponsorship for individuals and families they had never seen before."[52] Tension arose within some American churches over the refugee issue. Some members advocated sponsorship and were successful in convincing their congregation to "help those in need," while others who were supportive of refugee resettlement were marginalized by their fellow parishioners. As discussed in chapter 2 about Wausau, Wisconsin, resentment toward the Hmong refugees increased as Hmong began to encourage others to relocate to this city from around the country. Furthermore, the animosity was not solely toward the Hmong refugees themselves but also toward those who had first invited them. It appears that those angered by the continuous flow of refugees viewed the refugees as outsiders who did not have the right to invite others to places where they themselves were newcomers. And because many refugees became dependent on public resources, some townspeople felt that sponsors should not have brought the burden to their local community.

Outright resentment was present in some areas, but generally, most American communities were supportive of the refugees. The motivation and interests of particular sponsors would significantly impact refugee lives. Mai Yer Her described her sponsorship situation. She and her husband were sponsored by a Chinese American businessman in Hawaii. In comparing her experience to that of her friends and relatives who were sponsored by churches, she argues, "For those of us who came in the early days, it is clear that those who were sponsored by churches received greater support. They were much better off. They had people who helped them."[53] Mai Yer's assessment is representative of many others who were welcomed into the homes of church members. In this case, members took turns to assist the refugees in obtaining various services, thus spreading the burden to many in the congregation.

Even though they are affiliated with religious organizations and inspired to help those in need based on their faith, resettlement agencies encouraged sponsors to refrain from imposing their religious beliefs directly on the refugees. Information was provided to sponsors about the different religious backgrounds of the people to be welcomed into their homes and congregations. However, faith-based resettlement organizations inevitably expressed their religious beliefs in their organizational rhetoric and networks.[54] PaMang Her recalls his experience of starting a church in Kentucky: "Pastor Chang [Xiong], who was the first man to translate the Bible into White Hmong in Laos, and I got together and formed a . . . Christian Missionary and Alliance church, because Pastor Chang's sponsor was a Christian Missionary and Alliance pastor and sponsored him to come into the US. So we were the first Hmong Christian Missionary and Alliance Church in [Kentucky]. I came here to the U.S. in 1976, and we were able to get all the Hmong refugees to become believers in Kentucky. At that time we told them to be believers because there was no other way they could worship their spirits anymore."[55] Pastor Her's comments suggest that although the C&MA sponsors may not have imposed their religion on all refugees they sponsored, Hmong Christians exercising influence over Hmong nonbelievers encouraged their conversion. Some non-Christians may have converted out of convenience and as a means of survival due to the sponsors' role in providing basic needs support.

Xao Vue arrived in Chicago with her husband in late 1979. With no formal education, she was primarily confined to their small apartment while her husband attended English as a Second Language (ESL) classes.[56] When they learned of other relatives who had been sponsored by a church in Sheboygan, Wisconsin, they asked the relatives to see if their church would help them move to Sheboygan. The congregation was receptive, and when they arrived in Sheboygan in 1982, they received furniture and other household items. To show their appreciation, they attended church regularly, even though they did not understand the sermons. When her newborn son cried constantly, she sought help from a Hmong pastor. When the child stopped crying after the pastor's prayer, they became believers. The following year, her mother-in-law, Shoua Vue, who was a shaman, became very ill. They all thought she would die. At particular moments, it did appear as though she had passed away. Miraculously, Shoua woke up and felt well enough to leave the hospital a few days later. According to Shoua, "The computers were shaking and the lights were blinking in my hospital room. I could see angels in white uniforms coming down to tell me that I would be saved if I believed. When we came home, I threw away all of my shaman equipments and never looked back. I am so blessed. As a shaman, I know how dark the other world is. I know the difference, and I would not want to go to that world when I leave this one."[57] Testimonies of miraculous healing often inspired Hmong to convert to Christianity. In the American context, some other reasons for conversion include the lack of shamans in a particular location, the inability to perform religious rituals that require beating on gongs and animal sacrifice in urban communities, desire for community and a social-support network, and the lack of elders who understand animist traditions.

In her study about Taiwanese immigration and this group's religious experience, sociologist Carolyn Chen argues that in their efforts to become American, many Taiwanese immigrants become more religious in America than they ever were in their home country.[58] Hmong refugees frequently convert to Christianity after immigrating because Christianity is a part of the Americanization process in which some early refugees feel they must take part. But as they live in this country longer, and their congregations are almost exclusively a Hmong version of Christianity, the issue of whether going to church represents becoming American becomes blurred. When attending a Hmong Christian church on Sundays, it is difficult to determine whether members feel more American in any particular way. While many Hmong congregations may worship in the same space as a mainstream congregation, they have little interaction. Their relationships are more of a landlord-tenant arrangement than as common believers.

Although no empirical study has been conducted to determine the distribution of Hmong American religious affiliation, it has been estimated that by the year 2000, as many as 50 percent of Hmong Americans were Christian.[59] Some large congregations are formed and led by pastors who have received the highest training in theology available from American institutions. Many congregations, however, are led by individuals who received only basic pastoral training. It was not uncommon throughout the 1980s and 1990s to have Hmong pastors with limited English proficiency leading all-Hmong congregations. Similar to the status held by executive directors of MAAs, pastors were also held in high regard, often despite the fact that many have little formal education. What occurred in the development of MAAs with respect to gender did not emerge in the church movement. Although women may play key roles within the church, they have limited power in the overall operation of congregations. Because all of the existing congregations are led by male pastors, it suggests that the prospects for a Hmong woman to lead an all-Hmong congregation are not likely going to take place soon.[60]

Aside from the phenomenon of faith healing, another factor influencing Hmong conversion is the sense of dependence Hmong experienced upon arrival in this country. In describing Hmong in Philadelphia during the early 1980s, anthropologist Christine Desan argues that the religious disorientation exhibited by Hmong refugees is in strong contrast to centuries-old Hmong behavior in China and Laos: "There is a strong sense of ethnic identity, a reluctance to assimilate, a high mobility, and the isolation of the hill communities [that] insulated and guarded the identity of the Hmong religion. In the United States, however, the sponsoring system of resettlement has consistently stressed adaptation and adjustment rather than enforcing ethnic identity. The dependence of the refugees on sponsors, social agencies, and public aid has drastically reduced their mobility and rendered isolation from Americans virtually impossible."[61] It is no coincidence that large numbers of Hmong converted to Christianity, the most widespread religion in America, and the one most closely aligned with Hmong sponsorship in the country. Such conversions can be attributed to a shared desire for social and community support, rather than doctrine. Hmong like Xao Vue argue that it is easier to be accepted in the United States by being a Christian, due to the fact that, when practicing this religion, one is engaged in activities similar to those of other Americans.

In 1978, CMA field director Xeng Xiong counted 1,525 Hmong Christians in the United States. Throughout 1979, five Hmong CMA churches were organized—in Texas, Minnesota, Colorado, California, and Utah, respectively.[62] From these small efforts, one sees that Christian-based community building mirrors the community building efforts discussed earlier. To better understand the local church building practices of Hmong refugees in the United States, it is helpful to examine the initial efforts. The St. Paul Hmong Alliance church (SPHAC) has its roots in Liberty Plaza, the public-housing complex operated by Dayton Presbyterian Church in St. Paul where many Hmong refugees lived. Under the leadership of Shoua Chai Kong, three families, totaling eleven people, began weekly prayers in 1976.[63] By 1977, SPHAC was still a developing church; in 1979, it became an accredited church with the C&MA district office. In 1980, it was incorporated in Minnesota. Beginning in 1986, SPHAC leaders began a campaign to raise funds toward the development of a permanent home for the congregation and eventually decided to locate in the contiguous St. Paul suburb of Maplewood. Construction began in 1987 on a new building, which opened its doors in 1988. SPHAC's membership increased to 2,895 by 2005.[64] Two services are held on Sundays to accommodate the high number of churchgoers.

The Hmong in America have organized their churches under the following structures: Hmong American National Catholic Association (established 1983 and located in Minnesota), the Hmong District of the Christian and Missionary Alliance (established in 1979 and located in Colorado), the Lao Evangelical Church, the Hmong National Southern Baptist Association (established in 1982 and located in Minnesota), the Association of Hmong Community United Methodist Church (established and located in Wisconsin), the Hmong National Fellowship of the Assemblies of God (in St. Paul), the Hmong Lutheran Church Missouri Synod (in Michigan), and the Hmong Christian Reformed Church (in Wisconsin).[65] According to the Ethnic Christian Church Directory, 148 Hmong congregations existed in twenty-six states by the year 2008.[66] Interestingly, the State of Wisconsin has the third-largest Hmong population but the highest number of Hmong churches at twenty-nine, followed by California with twenty-six, and Minnesota with twenty-five. Churches affiliated with the C&MA are the most numerous, with fully eighty-seven congregations tied to the Hmong District of the Christian

Missionary Alliance.[67] As of 2010, Southern Baptist church data listed forty-three Hmong American congregations.[68]

Although the rise in the number of Christian Hmong organizations parallels that of community-based organizations, it is important to make one distinction. Whereas MAAs rely almost exclusively on funding sources from the larger society, churches rely primarily on tithing and special donations from their members. However, also important is that the success of Hmong churches is influenced by the support they receive from mainstream congregations of the same denomination. Clearly, the C&MA stands out as the most numerous, both in terms of membership totals and the number of congregations around the country. This may be because C&MA missionaries in Laos had been successful in converting the first Hmong. Other denominations, such as the Assembly of God, continue to have a relatively small number of churches, some of which struggle to stay in operation and rent space from mainstream congregations. Of the several congregations, only the First Hmong Assembly of God in St. Paul has its own worship space.

The Politics of Ethnic Representation

Group membership, cultural meaning, social networks of solidarity, mutual support, and reciprocal obligations can provide important coping mechanisms, channels of mobilization, and strategies of adaptation to an alien social environment. Over the years, leaders of MAAs and churches have worked diligently to grow their institutions. In doing so, they often assert that they represent "the Hmong community." In the early days of Hmong emigration, the number of refugees was smaller, and the population was more homogenous—meaning most of the Hmong had first-hand refugee experiences. Under these circumstances, it was easier for community organizations to speak firmly for "the Hmong community." The emerging leaders of the various Hmong organizations were immediately perceived as leaders by the larger community. Though a director of a social-service agency is considered a leader by the larger population, the extent to which he or she is asked to speak for his or her community is small, compared to the leadership roles that directors of Hmong ethnic organizations have had to play—sometimes self-imposed and at other times community imposed. In theory, ethnic organizations represent the ethnic group's culture and its traditions, but what happens when such culture and traditions are in flux and changing? What happens when a dependent constituency no longer exists to demand job-search assistance, language support, letter translation, or spousal-conflict resolution? How do ethnic organizations remain relevant during rapid cultural changes? Political scientist and philosopher Seyla Benhabib argues, "The claims of diverse groups engaged in the name of this or that aspect of their cultural identity have become contestants in the public sphere of capitalist democracies and are embroiled in characteristic struggles for redistribution and recognition."[69] The growing number of community-based organizations has made it difficult for funding institutions to determine which entity represents "the Hmong community." Some funders are confused by the plethora of nonprofit organizations all claiming to serve this community.

Two parallel arguments still prevail in the Hmong refugee politics of representation. First, the established leaders from Laos along with emerging leaders in Minnesota still seek to distinguish themselves from other Southeast Asian refugees; they claimed their uniqueness based on their alliance with Americans during the secret war in Laos. Emerging community leaders appropriate the knowledge produced about Hmong people as illiterate and unskilled yet hardworking, and some worked diligently to promote access to services, placing bilingual/bicultural individuals within various institutions and systems or cultural brokers. Xang Vang describes how the advocacy work was implemented: "Whenever we saw a gap in services in any areas, we would meet with those in decision-making positions to make recommendations. On their own, institutions would not create the various positions for Hmong Americans. We had to educate and fight for them to be created. This was at all levels, from community police officers to county and state levels. Minnesota is very good for the Hmong since the beginning."[70] Shoua Vang also remembers intentionally inviting others with certain skills to the state: "Vang Xang, we recruited him. Vang Chia, we recruited from Indiana because there wasn't anyone to work with the schools. Nowadays, our peoples' lives are significantly better. Many may not know, but I'm pleased that a few of us worked very hard in the beginning to build this community."[71]

Interestingly, Hmong Americans' perspectives vary regarding the future of ethnic social-service nonprofits. Those who are currently involved in the nonprofit sector view them as a necessary component of Hmong American life, while some no longer involved question the motives of those who remain active. Chou Vang was active in AAHWM's initial development but decided to work in corporate America, which has limited her community involvement greatly since the mid-1980s. As she puts it, "If Americans still have resources to support our community organizations, then we will still have a community. If no more financial resources are available to these organizations, then we will not have a community. Even people in community organizations work for a paycheck. They don't always do it for free. Some of the organizations will not survive when the community integrates and new refugee families do not come any more. Community organization workers like titles. But what they don't realize is that these organizations have only been able to help those with little or no education. Only these community members will respect these workers. If the funding sources stop, of course the workers then need to go work somewhere else. They need to feed themselves."[72]

The notion of community-based organizations as people helping others in need out of the goodness of their hearts has been challenged in many Hmong ethnic organizations. These organizations create jobs where community members have to compete with one another. A common issue within Hmong organizations in large populations is that if board members come from a certain layer of "the Hmong community," then certain individuals outside that particular layer are likely to be excluded. The growth in the number of organizations with varying missions and services may further reflect a greater interest in accessing capital from the mainstream, non-Hmong community for different segments of the Hmong population. No one can argue that ethnic-based organizations have been instrumental in Hmong American settlement history. However, lessons from the past suggest that community-based organizations frequently are interested in obtaining resources to meet their constituents' basic needs and preserve their culture and traditions insofar as constituents are dependent on such services. Multilayered community formation through community associations can be a response to surrounding political structures and their tacit bureaucratic expectations. Their existence, however, has depended on the continued efforts of a few individuals and the availability of funds, which can be accessed only through an official organization. The associations, as formal constructions of an ideal, do not always reflect the reality of their members. Furthermore, their existence is dependent upon continued social policy focused on refugee communities.

In *Against the Romance of Community*, feminist scholar Miranda Joseph examines the contradictory history of the nonprofit sector in the United States. On one hand, it has been associated with a narrative of grassroots volunteerism that has origins in diverse colonial religious organizations and the notion of American exceptionalism. On the other hand, narratives of the nonprofit sector detail a story of a contest between private organizations and the state for control of public affairs, in which the agents of private initiatives were not the grassroots but rather capitalists and corporations. Joseph writes, "The history of the nonprofit sector in the United States is widely imagined in both popular and academic literature to be a story of voluntary associations welling up from the grass roots and evidencing the exceptional American character. . . . [The claims] that nonprofits are American and that they are an expression of the grass roots, are of course linked by an ideology that posits the United States as the model of democracy to which the rest of the world should aspire."[73] If grassroots organizations are an example of American identity, then Hmong and other Southeast Asian refugees, in a sense, *became American* shortly after they landed in the United States. This phenomenon is important in that although nongovernmental organizations provided aid of various sorts in Laos and, in particular, in refugee camps, Hmong themselves did not operate any similar organizations. Although they gathered in groups based on clan, kinship, and other interests, they did not create formal entities with the types of public and private funding that MAAs have received in the American context.

What is problematic is that nonprofit organizations mean something different for Hmong Americans/refugees. In the earlier years, Hmong refugees primarily viewed nonprofit organizations as a new form of leadership that would advocate on their behalf, in particular if they did not possess any formal education and required literate, bilingual individuals to help them maneuver through the various American social-service systems. This new leadership structure, which placed young, literate individuals in positions of power, contradicts traditional Hmong social organization, which promoted a reverence for elders. In addition, the systems of clan and kinship meant that some community members who did not have representatives within the MAAs felt disenfranchised; this created divisions, as explained by Detzner: "Each cultural group used its mutual assistance associations to obtain funding to teach about and negotiate the American system, to train emerging community leaders, and to provide social and financial support to its constituents. There were numerous internal political squabbles within and between groups, and struggles for power and leadership as well. Although internal dissension is not a wise survival strategy for new immigrant groups, it is a sign of vitality and ethnic development within emerging new communities."[74]

Political squabbles may be the best description of the evolution of Hmong ethnic organizations, as tensions based on clan affiliation, gender, and perspectives on homeland politics have divided community members. For example, if individuals were dissatisfied with certain aspects of an organization, they would frequently move on to start another agency. Consequently, the idea that community-based organizations represent "the Hmong community" is blurred with clan, gender, political perspective, and generation politics. Although the existence of these organizations does not depend on preexisting organizations in Hmong society, their practices reflect preexisting categories in Hmong culture.

Identities are subject to ongoing negotiations and are shaped by experiences and memories of migration and settlement and by racial marginalization, exclusion, and discrimination, as well as by group-internal struggles over definitions of self, role compliance, and cultural change.[75] Although differences in religious rituals have been an integral part of Hmong social organization, the conversion of Hmong to Christianity, both in Laos and in the United States, has affected cultural practices and kinship ties while further dividing the community. The division is multidimensional; both Christians and non-Christian Hmong hold varying perspectives about one another. For example, fearing that others will question their faith in the new religion, some Hmong American Christians no longer participate in animist and ancestral worship ceremonies held by their families and relatives. Some non-Christian Hmong often point to the frequency of required church attendance and tithing and suggest that Christians merely want to collect funds from their members. For still others, limited and/or no interactions remain once family members choose their faith, as Xao Vue describes: "My sister-in-law and her husband still practice Hmong religion. I sometimes don't mind visiting them, but not when they have a shaman ceremony. All the alcoholic drinking and the long hours of just sitting around waiting for the shaman to finish just don't appeal to me anymore. Because of this, I don't really have a close relationship with my only sister-in-law."[76]

The extent to which relatives congregate now depends in part on their religious beliefs. In the village context, it is a tradition for extended family members to help each other. In the American context, many who practice the same religion frequently gather to support each other's religious events. On one hand, an unspoken conflict exists where Christians view themselves as more modern due to their Christian faith.[77] Because Christianity is everywhere in America, some Hmong Christians see themselves as more integrated into American society than those who continue to practice ancestral worship. On the other hand, Hmongness is frequently intimately associated with Hmong religion. Those who practice ancestral worship often see Christians as selling out and no longer being authentic Hmong since they no longer value animist traditions.

Contradictions often arise during particular moments of Hmong family life, such as New Year celebrations, births, and deaths. In the American context, Hmong New Year celebrations are attended by thousands of all religious backgrounds due to the commercialization and entertainment components. For example, some church groups frequently use the New Year celebration to fundraise by selling food and drinks on behalf of the church. In addition to the large community celebrations, individual Christian Hmong congregations or groups of churches frequently celebrate the New Year by hosting events at church, and members wear Hmong costumes. Rather than folk songs, participants sing Christian songs, which often have cleansing themes but do not include animist rituals. When asked whether such practices were still Hmong, some individuals made clear distinctions between culture and its traditions and religious. Mao Heu Thao comments, "I don't know. I think it is still Hmong. It's not one or the other. The clothes are Hmong. It doesn't matter if they are Christian or not. The only difference is that Christians don't *lwm qab* [cleansing ceremony with chicken sacrifice]. Even in Laos, Christian children wore Hmong clothes to the New Year. Those who knew how to sing folksongs still do, especially the young. There was a huge celebration at church. They would set up the food around the church. When it was Christmas, they would have skits. I have seen that done in Laos. After singing many special songs, they would prepare the food."[78]

In this case, Christian Hmong wear Hmong costumes to church-sponsored New Year celebrations. The clothing did not seem problematic; however, what is unclear about this characterization is that in the village context, villagers had limited clothing options. In the United States, community members have many choices. Regardless, some Hmong Christians adamantly argue that costumes are not religious, as Dang Her suggests: "Personally, I believe that God created all of us. Hmong clothes, language, and folksongs are given to our people. If you wear these clothes or speak the language, that doesn't offend the Creator. It's part of the natural process. It doesn't matter. It's only material things."[79] To Christians like Dang Her, material culture should not be confused with religion.

As public spaces, Hmong New Year celebrations are contested sites because community members have to negotiate their varied identities. What happens in private spaces for such events as births and funerals? In the former, Christian families no longer hold the ceremony (*nqees plig*) to officially name the child and thank the ancestors for the blessing. In animist tradition, a small feast is prepared for close immediate and extended family members. Instead, many plan a feast that may not occur exactly three days after the child's birth, as in animist tradition. Despite the fact that it is not called *nqees plig*, the Christian feast to *ua Vaajtswv tsaug/ua Vajtswv tsaug* (thank God) has a similar meaning. As for the latter, funeral components are different, but the process is similar. Until the last few years, only two Hmong-owned funeral homes existed in the Twin Cities: Hmong Funeral Home Services Inc. and Metro Funeral Home. "Traditional" funeral services involve intricate rituals over several days to guide the deceased to the other world. In the American context, Hmong funerals frequently begin on Friday and remain open twenty-four hours over the weekend, followed by the burial on Monday. Ritualistic components involving immediate and extended family members take place along with the beating of the drums and playing of the instrument *qeej*. Friends and relatives come to pay respect, and many make financial contributions to help offset the family's costs.

Hmong Christians frequently criticize the lengthy funeral process, but due to their interest in also holding Christian funerals for several days, they nonetheless use the same funeral homes. Again, Hmong Christian funeral practices are a specific Hmong version with elements of Christianity and Hmong traditions. While one does not hear drum beats and the *qeej* playing, sermons are sometimes given, and songs accompanied by pianists are often sung. Friends, relatives, and church members come to pay respect, and many also make financial contributions. In their attempts to distinguish themselves from the non-Christians, most Christian funerals no longer remain open at night. Family members and guests frequently leave around midnight and return the following day to continue with the funeral services. This illustrates a middle ground in their acculturation process, which still has features of traditional Hmong funerals.

There is no doubt that Christian churches formed by immigrants are often a nexus of their negotiation between the old and the new.[80] While Christians have abandoned strict Hmong religious practices, they maintain certain elements and reinvent new traditions that differ from that of the former beliefs—and yet remain familiar to them—such as allowing the funeral services to occur for the same number of days as non-Christians in order for friends and relatives from a distance to attend. Non-Christians frequently argue that such practices are not significantly different from the "traditional" practices and insist that if Christians embrace a new religion, then they should completely change their funeral practices to clearly articulate the differences.

The Hmong church in America as an integral part of Hmong American identity formation has evolved so that missionaries of Hmong ethnicity are now sent to Thailand and, to a lesser extent, Laos. A sense of competition exists within and across denominations in the area of missions abroad. Although these transnational migrants are not the cosmopolitans, due to the lack of high levels of capital, whom Aiwha Ong discusses, Hmong Americans, both Christians and non-Christians, indeed hold a hegemonic position in their particular transnational practices.[81] With respect to churches, those outside of the United States, due to their political and economic status, in particular those living in Asia, look to Hmong American churches for support. Along with the increase in the number of Hmong American Christians is the emergence of divisive, competitive elements among and between denominations and congregations. Often, disputes of various natures result in the disintegration of existing congregations. If the dispute is between members, some leave the congregation to join another. If the tensions are between leaders of the congregation, it is common for the congregation to split into two or more groups, thereby establishing many small congregations.

Unlike animist traditions where certain lines delineate religious practices within clans and subclans, the Hmong Christian churches do offer an inclusive space. In theory, clan membership is not a prerequisite to joining a particular congregation. In practice, however, some congregations consist primarily of a particular clan and/or families who share a common lineage, as observed by Maile Vue: "Before he passed away, my uncle's congregation consisted primarily of his sons, their wives, and grandchildren. They were so small, but they preferred to isolate themselves rather than merge with another congregation. It was truly a family church where the father was the pastor and the members were his children. Of course, a few members were not a part of the family, but they were definitely not the majority."[82] Maile's description of her uncle's church is the norm rather than the exception, particularly in smaller congregations. Divisive issues and factors affecting congregational development result in subgroups within clans to establish separate churches based on kinship ties and/ or friendship. Whereas many immediate and extended family members work collaboratively to grow their congregations, some make personal decisions to follow others. Family members who previously worshiped in the same household establish new families via their congregations and limit their ties with relatives who either continue to practice ancestral worship or have joined a different Christian denomination.

Although Hmong language classes are sometimes offered at community-based organizations, it is more common to see these organizations invest their resources in English as a Second Language (ESL) classes. It has been within the Hmong American Christian community that the maintenance of the Hmong language has been most prevalent. Some of the immigrant generation may speak Hmong, but few may have learned how to write it. Hmong language and literacy classes are frequently offered to youth as an attempt by the immigrant generation to reproduce ethnicity. In their study of immigrant congregations in the Houston area, Helen Rose Ebaugh and Janet Saltzman Chafetz found such practice to be universal: "[Although] eager for their offspring to achieve educationally and occupationally, and grateful for the opportunities provided in this country for them to do so, a large number of immigrants worried about the potentially harmful effects on their offspring of what they define as pernicious cultural influences in American society. Congregations respond to adult members' desire to reproduce ethnicity by organizing ethno-religious classes for children."[83] Such classes contribute to Christian Hmong children's ability to maintain the Hmong language. While this may be an important language-maintenance strategy, some congregations have worked hard to not mix English and Hmong languages during church activities. Instead, they attempt to offer options for their members. Large congregations such as the St. Paul Hmong Alliance church hold separate services, one in Hmong and the other for members who speak English. For example, a service in the Hmong language geared toward members with limited English would be held in the morning; an English service, which tends to attract a predominantly younger population, is given in the afternoon.[84] In his reflections on what a Hmong is, anthropologist Gary Yia Lee suggests that Hmongness includes observing Hmong culture and its traditions in addition to language maintenance. He further argues that what characterizes a person as a Hmong includes being born Hmong, having a Hmong name, speaking the Hmong language, belonging to a Hmong clan, and observing Hmong rituals. If a factor such as language is a core component of Hmongness, then one can argue that Hmong Christians have not become less Hmong. What remains to be seen is whether this pattern will continue to the second generation and beyond. Overall, it is clear that in Hmong attempts to become American, new social organizations specifically pursue cultural balance by maintaining some continuity with the past while integrating into the larger society.

4 *Continuity and Reinvention of Traditions*

> How do strategies of representation or empowerment
> come to be formulated in the competing claims
> of communities where, despite shared histories of
> deprivation and discrimination, the exchange of values,
> meanings and priorities may not always be collaborative
> and dialogical, but may be profoundly antagonistic,
> conflictual and even incommensurable?
> —Homi K. Bhabha, *Location of Culture*

When the strangeness of new faces, language, and environment had subsided, the early refugees began to wonder about their future. Through social interactions, they accumulated meanings essential to their self-awareness. Refugees arriving in multicultural urban communities immediately learned about social and racial hierarchies as they struggled for scarce social-service resources with others living disenfranchised lives. In more homogenous areas, particularly small towns, they felt isolated and yearned for familiar faces—eventually utilizing existing cultural resources to connect with one another and locating other Hmong throughout the United States. In particular, the attempt to maintain some continuity across time and place prompted new arrivals to assemble to celebrate the Hmong New Year. Since then, such celebrations have served as a site for community building in the United States, both sustaining old and fostering the invention new traditions and thereby prompting questions of the celebration's authenticity.

Intergenerational conflicts emerged, as second-generation Hmong introduced new traditions within the American context and thus challenged their parents' attempts to maintain the historic integrity and familiarity of long-established Hmong cultural practices amidst alien surroundings. These challenges have been further augmented by a transnational dimension in which "authentic" Hmong culture brought from Laos has become infused with elements from Hmong in other countries, in particular China. Today's Hmong New Year celebrations offer a collage of cultural items and diasporic music genres alongside "traditional" art from Asia, offering attendees a uniquely Hmong American experience that is globally informed. It is American in the sense that commercialization, politics, art, and culture are allowed to be displayed in the same space. Performers and vendors have the freedom to express themselves in uncensored ways. Because of this, New Year celebration organizers frequently face discomfort due to both the content and quality of performances presented to thousands of onlookers, including distinguished guests. Vendors selling videos and music albums compete for sales by turning up the volume on their television sets and stereos. For some, the fierce competition in a confined space produces excitement, but some Hmong Americans bemoan the sense of chaos this fosters.

In the diaspora, other large gatherings, such as soccer festivals and conferences, attract hundreds of participants from near and far, but only the New Year celebration can be claimed as unique to Hmong culture. The other gatherings are rooted in Western traditions that many Hmong have come to embrace. Regardless of whether one is a member of the Hmong American community, entrance into the Hmong New Year celebration can be dazzling. I argue that as a cultural practice brought from the homeland and sustained across space and time, the New Year celebration serves as a site for affirming established Hmong cultural identities and creating new ones. Furthermore, these public events are spaces that manifest changes in gender relations, identity formation, citizenship, and belonging.

Role of New Year Celebrations

New Year celebrations have long held an important place in Hmong society, both at the individual household and community levels. In villages and towns throughout China and Southeast Asia, New Year celebrations have served as central community gatherings for centuries and continue to this day. The celebrations usually occur for one to two weeks in December after the harvest season, with specific rituals performed to drive away evil spirits and to ask for blessings from the ancestors for the upcoming year. In these traditions, men and women of all ages follow spiritual leaders to receive blessings. Individual households sacrifice animals to the ancestors for guidance in the new year. Explaining the celebration's special place in Hmong culture, Hmong scholar Dao Yang relates, "Depending on the size of each village, Hmong New Year lasts from four to five days to more than ten days. Everyone gathers to share feasts, bless one another, and work together to build a better future for the community. These are times for Hmong people to remember and respect Hmong religious and cultural practices. That is why regardless of what country, state, or city Hmong people reside in, we continue to celebrate our New Year. . . . Because each family has prepared a pig (feast), each village enjoys on-going feasts for 4–5 days. People from all walks of life who come to Hmong villages are invited to eat and drink with the villagers."[1]

Clearly, the New Year serves social, cultural, and religious purposes. Kou Yang, another Hmong American scholar, describes the Hmong New Year as consisting of three main events: the feast (*noj tsab/noj tsiab*),[2] the ritual ceremony of transitioning from the old to the new year (*lwm sub*), and the celebration.[3] It provides an opportunity for family and community bonding. As a holiday celebration, it is also a time of courtship and marriage.[4] In the village context in Asia where Hmong lived in isolated villages, few opportunities existed for young people to interact with prospective mates. During the celebration, young people wore their best costumes and prepared to sing their original folksongs to impress members of the opposite sex as well as the parents who often accompanied their teenagers, especially the girls. Shoua Vang, a former secretary in the clandestine army and community leader involved with refugee resettlement for many years, shared his recollection of New Year practices in Laos: "There weren't many opportunities to spend time together. We relied on the New Year to reconnect with our friends and relatives. A time to bring our young people together and toss balls. Elders would gather around to listen to folk songs sung by their sons and daughters. It was a festive time. Before the celebration, you prepared enough food and other reserves to last throughout the celebration. It was a time to rest. No work is allowed. No gathering of fire woods or food for our animals."[5]

The celebration took place at multiple levels, and the festivities were divided into private and public celebrations. In peaceful times, each family worked hard to raise a hog (*npua tsab/npua tsiab*), and during the celebration, individual families butchered their animals to share with friends and relatives. Families who were not successful in raising the *npua tsab* were viewed negatively. Wealth and prosperity were partially measured by the size of a family's *npua tsab* and the meal they prepared.

The public celebrations that people from near and far attend consist of such activities as ball tossing, singing of folk songs, and bullfighting. However, as noted by Kou Yang, the common practice of ball tossing is not performed by Hmong in China today during their New Year celebrations, indicating that the activity was added following migration to Southeast Asia.[6] Its origin is unknown, but its purpose of enabling courtship between single people is common knowledge.[7] The act of tossing a ball back and forth allows men and women to focus attention on one another. Frequently, male individuals observe female New Year attendees before approaching them. Once a man identifies a woman to whom he is attracted, he approaches the woman and requests her participation in ball tossing with him. Single women often carry to the celebration cloth balls carefully sewn either by themselves or their mothers, so that if they are approached by a man, they can readily accept the invitation.

Continuity and Contestations

The New Year's cultural importance has been sustained through migration, as evidenced by the organizing of celebrations at varying levels regardless of the location and size of Hmong populations throughout the diaspora. Exploring the practices and performances at diasporic New Year celebrations is useful in understanding the continuity and contestations embedded in Hmong American cultural production and community-building initiatives. The particular activities at these events tell a great deal about Hmong American values, old traditions, new traditions invented in Laos and refugee camps, and those created in diasporic locations. An examination of these cultural sites provides greater insight into the cultural influences behind the works of today's young Hmong American artists. Despite attempts to introduce new practices into traditional festivities, some artists from successive generations of Hmong do value continuity and pursue connections with their fellow Hmong and their traditional Hmong heritage, in their lifestyles, life choices, and life decisions.

PRACTICES AND PERFORMANCES

In the diaspora where Hmong religious rituals often contradict Western rules and regulations, New Year celebrations have compromised some religious elements. Large celebrations in urban settings have become "cultural goods" produced by a segment of the population to be consumed by an almost exclusively Hmong American population. What is produced by event organizers reflects their *taste* and may contradict the preferences of spectators and participants. The role of organizers as cultural producers dictates what is included or excluded at these events. As Pierre Bourdieu argues, the "cultural goods" produced indeed reflect a demand for those goods, which essentially supports the reproduction of such goods over time. He asserts, "The consumption of the most legitimate cultural goods is a particular case of competition for rare goods and practices, whose particularity no doubt owes more to the logic of supply, i.e., the specific form of competition between the producers, than to the logic of demand and tastes, i.e., the logic of competition between the consumers. One only has to remove the magical barrier which makes legitimate culture into a separate universe, in order to see intelligible relationships between choices as seemingly incommensurable as preferences in music or cooking, sport or politics, literature or hairstyle."[8] Attendees may disagree with the various cultural representations. Some may eventually refuse to attend in protest, arguing that the celebrations are no longer authentic, while others will attend the events mainly as a community festival where they can meet new people and possibly reconnect with old friends.

In the late 1970s, when few Hmong families lived in Minnesota, the New Year celebration was a small event but one with great significance for its participants. As part of the first family to arrive in Minnesota in December 1975, Dang Her remembers yearning for opportunities to connect with other people from his ethnic group. He explains the driving force behind the initial diasporic New Year celebrations: "We missed our friends and families so much that when we learned about other Hmong families in Minnesota, we immediately tried to contact them. The New Year celebration was quite different from what you see today. Each family contributed some food. It was a potluck. We were all just happy to be with other Hmong families."[9]

Similar to other ethnic festivals, New Year celebrations helped to affirm Hmong cultural continuity.[10] Shoua Vang also remembers how the New Year gatherings helped him to reduce loneliness: "In those early years, we were all isolated with our own sponsors. We didn't have many opportunities to come together. So, [the New Year celebration] was a gathering to reduce isolation."[11] As a cultural event, the New Year celebration legitimized participants' desire to congregate and connect with one another. Social support gained from the initial gatherings encouraged some of the early refugees to organize future events. The continued flow of Hmong refugees throughout the last quarter of the twentieth century permitted the celebrations to increase in size, scope, and frequency.

Although New Year celebrations were celebrated during slightly different times in Laos, a shared country of origin inspired Hmong and ethnic Lao refugees in Minnesota to create interethnic solidarity by co-hosting a celebration. Tong Vang, a former board president of Lao Family Community of Minnesota Inc., recalls, "When we first got here, we actually started an organization with the Lao refugees because we [all came] from the same country. . . . We had one New Year celebration together, then when we started the Hmong Association, we began to have our own celebrations. It was small. We did wear our traditional clothes and ate great Hmong food."[12] The Lao New Year is celebrated in April, so perhaps the time difference influenced the decision to no longer collaborate. A closer examination, however, suggests that ethnicity and religion may have further divided the two ethnic groups. Although some of the early refugees from both ethnic groups had converted to Christianity in Laos, many Hmong practiced ancestral worship, which differed greatly from most Lao following Buddhist traditions. One can further speculate that because the growth of the Hmong population in Minnesota surpassed that of the Lao, Hmong community leaders no longer needed to collaborate since their population was large enough to allow them to hold events specifically for their own ethnic group.

The process by which the Hmong in Minnesota expanded their celebrations would reflect their population increase in the state. As the demand for activities beyond tossing ball and singing folk songs increased, organizers developed additional ways to attract attendees of all ages. Music and dance competitions provided an avenue for musicians and artists to exhibit their skills. Beauty pageants permitted young Hmong women to display their beauty and talents. Vendors set up booths in the hope of making a profit. Ly Vang, a Hmong American woman and community leader who had been involved with New Year event planning since the late 1970s, reminisces about the evolution of diasporic New Year celebrations: "In 1977, we gathered a lot because we were all still dealing with loss of our own family support. I think 1978 was the bigger New Year celebration. I think there were about twenty-five families. Then we started to move to churches in St. Paul, then International Institute [of Minnesota]. The first big New Year was 1983, and 1984 we had the first beauty pageant."[13]

When the population was very small, families would gather at individual homes. As the number of people grew, so did the spaces from private homes to church banquet rooms to community centers to hold the celebrations. The events eventually moved to large convention centers. In 1980 with the largest arrival of Hmong refugees to the United States, the critical mass enabled Hmong Minnesotans to expand their New Year celebrations to the civic center, as a staff member for the *Association of Hmong* newsletter reveals: "It has been many long days plan for the Hmong New Year 1980–81. Many Hmong and their leaders in the Twin Cities did not have enough time to sleep and enjoy their families as usual. They put a lot of effort to make the New Year possible for the Hmong people to chase away bad luck and ugly thoughts that they have in mind and heart during the past twelve months, and to welcome the New Year with new hope, new spirit, best luck and good opportunities for the incoming year. . . . Over 6,000 (six thousands) Hmong were gathering at the St. Paul Civic Center to cheer each other as a traditional celebration."[14]

The passage shows that at the outset, the event was as much a community-building effort as it was a means for cultural preservation. The event is envisioned as a display of Hmong unity where attendees come and "cheer each other": "To share their happiness, Mr. Ly Teng, the President of the Lao Family Community in Minnesota, and the Hmong also invited the Honor of Mrs. and Mr. Latimer, the Mayor of the City of Saint Paul and many other high rank officers from various departments in the State of Minnesota as well as many Americans in the area along with General Vang Pao, the International Chairperson of the Lao Family Community Inc. from California and many other fellow Hmong from other neighboring states of Minnesota to share the happiness together. To open the New Year Celebration, Mr. Ly Teng briefly expressed that the Hmong New Year cannot be celebrated on the exact date of the traditional calendar because we have to wait for the weekend and the availability of spaces to get together for a long time."[15] This practice of inviting elected and appointed officials and General Vang Pao to deliver speeches has continued to the present.[16] The distance from which the New Year celebrations drew their participants over the years has increased significantly with the change in Hmong American economic status. In the early years, most attendees were residents of the state or from neighboring Midwestern locations. Today, it is common to see participants from all parts of the United States and from other countries of resettlement. Occasionally, some Hmong from Laos attend if they visit family members in the state.

An ongoing question about New Year celebrations is whether transformations occurred only in the United States or were there changes prior to migration out of Laos. Many in the general immigrant population assign blame partially to American society for the lack of understanding and the devaluing of Hmong traditions. However, a closer historical analysis reveals that changes in New Year traditions, in large part, stem from the relocation of displaced Hmong during the war years and from Hmong exposure to Lao cultural practices. Ly Vang shares her observation, "I saw the changes. Back then [in Laos], we do a lot of things based on traditions. In rural areas, your frame of reference is very narrow. So, you have bullfights, folk songs, *qeej*. No dance. Those are the traditions they learned from agricultural way of life. Not much room for incorporation of others. After 1970, changes began to emerge. In Long Cheng, the urban settlement allowed for beauty pageants to be added. I think there were two or three pageants that were held. In that historical moment, we began to add dance performances to the New Year. But, they did classical Lao dance."[17] Ly Vang's statement reveals that the New Year as celebrated in isolated village contexts before the Vietnam War era changed when Hmong became exposed to other forms of entertainment. As time progressed and new additions became common practices, people then began to appropriate them as Hmong traditions.

The practice of borrowing from other cultures seems to have been an integral part of Hmong history as the Hmong migrated from one area to another. The process of becoming a refugee and the displacing effects of refugee camps further facilitated the transformation of old and the invention of new traditions. Critiquing the claim that the "traditional" dance commonly used to entertain Americans was a Hmong tradition, former Hmong artist and entertainer Yia Lee comments, "I was one of the first Hmong to learn *laavong* [classical Lao dance]. There is no Hmong *laavong*. But, there was dancing prior to migration. What we call Hmong traditional dance is in fact not Hmong. We learned from the Lao. I don't mind the use of all kinds of popular art at the Hmong New Year. It's natural. I know this. All these new art forms are fine. What troubles me a lot is that artists don't know how to compose their own music. They would write the lyrics and then use other peoples' tunes. This is sad."[18] Yia Lee, known for taking risks in art and entertainment, elaborates, "In Laos when we first started to sing modern songs, I was criticized. In the refugee camp, people laughed at our Western-style music." Ly Vang agrees that modern Hmong music and dance expanded in the refugee camps. Amidst the significant boredom of camp life emerged new cultural expressions. The refugee state of confinement, loss, and uncertainty ironically energized camp inhabitants to create new meanings for themselves through art.

Shong Yang, who is a prominent businessman and former chairman of the Hmong American New Year (HANY) in Minneapolis, believes that differences in New Year celebration practices between the United States and Laos are due to rules and regulations in American society that prevent certain religious rituals from occurring in public spaces: "[In Laos, there] were no contests, either beauty pageants or music. Part of this has to do with the fact that few people were educated. In this country, one of the activities missing is the bullfights because we can't do that here. We still *lwm qaib* [conduct chicken ceremony], ball toss, sing folk songs. We have added new activities that are available to us because of technology, such as music and beauty pageants like other people. Additionally, we have added sports competitions at the Minneapolis New Year. All of these activities are new."[19]

Hmong Americanization has come to signify increasing American cultural and economic influence.[20] Technology, education, and capital all seem to contradict tradition. Many Hmong Americans contend that New Year celebrations have become too commercialized. They negatively view charging money because it takes away the fun elements of New Year celebrations that are free for all and because they believe that the event organizers tend to be more concerned with making money than with preserving culture. Other community members require higher-quality performances and activities because they pay a fee to enter. Many call for greater accountability by New Year organizers in addition to using proceeds to better the community.

There appear to be two competing perspectives about performances at New Year celebrations. One is that the current performances have abandoned Hmong culture and its traditions, attributed both to the borrowing of other cultures' arts and to the lack of interest in traditional activities. The other perspective is that a balance needs to be kept between culture and entertainment. In the former, a lack of control over the content and types of performances frequently places organizers in uncomfortable positions. As Ly Vang explains, "You can't really turn performers away but you don't have a way to determine the content of their performances. It's sometimes frustrating because we have a lot of political leaders who attend and some things may not be appropriate, but we don't know how to control that."[21] Here, inappropriateness refers to the poor-quality performances of both genders and to young women dressing in provocative clothing. Often, the performances would be more appropriate in a nightclub scene than in a cultural event with a diverse audience of small children, elderly grandparents, and distinguished guests from the larger community. Shong Yang cautions against the incorporation of other cultural forms: "In terms of traditions, I want to see young people maintain as much Hmong cultural practices as possible. If they are going to sing, sing in Hmong. I can't control what people prefer to use as examples of their skills, but I hope that they do not replace Hmong culture."[22] His suggestion privileges Hmong language as the true Hmong culture. It seems that, to him, artistic style is less important than the need to ensure that Hmong language is used in the performances.

With respect to the perspective of balancing culture and entertainment, many interviewees are open to change. Chou Vang believes that the performance of dances borrowed from Bollywood and China is inevitable: "How can you stop the kids? They live here. They grow up here. That's what they like. Soon after we all die, they will not know much anymore. You can't stop them from doing whatever they like."[23] As one of the women who had received an education in Laos and was active in organizing diasporic New Year celebrations during her early years in the United States, Chou argues that the younger generation will become less interested and knowledgeable about Hmong traditions. She indicates that they should create something that is meaningful to them. Daobay Ly, former chair of the St. Paul New Year committee, adds, "That's part of encouraging the youth to be expressive in whatever they like. . . . What is amazing is that some youth are appreciating Hmong culture and traditions, except that they have different ways of expressing them. While we do have young people who just don't want anything to do with the 'old ways,' there are others who amaze the elders by learning folksongs and being confident enough to perform in front of thousands."[24] Daobay Ly is a member of the one-and-a-half generation Hmong Americans. He has observed a difference in how young people are perceived by their peers and by the immigrant generation. Although some youth regard their peers who embrace Hmong traditions as old-fashioned, the young people who follow tradition are highly regarded by the older generation, who see such an act as evidence of their Hmongness.

What can one expect to experience at the large New Year celebrations? It is common to see Hmong American women wear costumes from their Hmong coethnics throughout Asia alongside those wearing prom dresses, business suits, and torn blue jeans. The ethnic costumes include coins dangling from all sides of the body, silver necklaces, turbans, and high heels. Women and girls wrapped in shawls walk through the parking lot in cold weather, because their heavy costumes prevent them from wearing winter coats. The dress of men and boys varies from jeans to casual shirts with slacks to business suits. Those who wear Hmong costumes, however, usually do so with a Western-style shirt worn underneath a vest covered all over with coins. After standing in line to purchase tickets, attendees are expected to pass through the security station. Then, they may proceed toward the auditorium. Entrepreneurial elderly women spread their important, dried herbal medicines, jewelry, and handicrafts throughout the hallway. The new arrivals are soon consumed by the smell of homemade sausages, compounded with those of papaya salad and fried chicken. Vendors sell items ranging from amateur videos, clothing, music albums, and toys to photography booths with the latest technology to ensure that attendees are able to preserve memories of having attended the celebration. Although attendees are overwhelmingly Hmong Americans, non-Hmong people are present at these celebrations. Often, they are individuals who work with and/or are friends with Hmong individuals. Occasionally, one will encounter others who attend out of curiosity.

In the main auditorium, elected and appointed officials focus on "cultural performances" by youth of all ages. Performers enter and exit the stage. Young women dressed in provocative outfits performing to music by such American artists as Janet Jackson and Madonna can be immediately followed by another group of females, dressed in sweat pants and dancing to Korean hip-hop music. When the group finishes its performance, another troupe, dressed in Asian Indian clothes, dances to a Bollywood tune. The next group, dressed in beautiful Lao clothes, performs a classical Lao dance. The evening may end with a Chinese dance performance, which has become a vibrant component of diasporic New Year celebrations.

CULTURAL IDENTIFICATION

If cultures are formed through complex dialogues and interactions with other cultures, then the boundaries of Hmong culture are fluid, porous, and contested.[25] Although interviewees agree that those in the younger generation should be free to express their artistic talents, they frequently hope that such practices will not completely replace traditional cultural elements. For competitions, contestants are not limited regarding ways to demonstrate their skills. Long-time celebration organizer Ly Vang shared a contradictory insight regarding borrowing from other cultures: "Because Hmong people have very limited music artists that are attractive, many young people turned to Chinese and Indian dance and music. They do it, but it's not a tradition. It's not accepted as Hmong tradition. It's a temporary borrowing of others' forms of traditions. It's just an experience, and it will be let go gradually. When youth borrow from other cultures, it's not permanent. It goes away because it's not accepted. Look at the use of rock music. From 1983 to 1999, a lot of rock music [was] used in dance contests. But now, you don't see that anymore, very few groups. When those people enter contests, they never win. Those who usually win first place are those who do traditional Hmong dance. Indian dance, they win. Chinese dance, they can win, too."[26] Why is rock music, which is an American art, not a means to winning a contest, while *traditional* Hmong, Indian, and Chinese dances provide winning opportunities for contestants? I contend that an element of pan-Asian identity formation exists on the part of young people, where they identify Hmong heritage as Asian. Although the interviewees did not mention hip-hop, video analyses and celebration observations reveal many performing to this American popular art. These contestants also do not win.

An exploration of competition judges reveals that their "taste" often differs from that of performers. Are competition judges instructed to place higher value on certain styles over others? One explanation is that New Year organizers rely solely on volunteers to serve as judges. Organizers frequently recruit community members they know to assist in this daunting task, often regardless of the fact that some individuals possess little or no expertise in the particular area. Since most organizers and volunteers tend to represent the immigrant generation, a possible conclusion can be drawn that they value art forms that most closely mirror what they personally prefer. The acceptance of Bollywood dance may be the result of the popularity of Bollywood films in the Hmong American community, in particular the common practice of entrepreneurs dubbing Bollywood films into Hmong language. Although Hmong American dancers have used Chinese music in their "traditional" dance for a long time, dance ensembles performing Chinese-style dances at Hmong New Year celebrations were popularized by the controversial sponsorship of a Hmong Chinese woman who gave instruction in Chinese dance to the Twin Cities in the mid-1990s.[27] The acceptance of these dances by some Hmong Americans suggests that they view China as the original homeland. Some may further see embracing Chinese-style dances as a way to sustain Hmong culture across time and space.

Although Chinese-style dances are welcomed, some members of the immigrant generation fear a loss of Hmong traditions. However, what they often indicate as tradition is problematic. In discussing what constitutes Hmong tradition, they seem to be referring to language, costumes, ball tossing, folk songs, "traditional" dance, and religious rituals. Due to U.S. laws, the religious ritual requiring the sacrifice of a chicken is not carried out in the public spaces where Minnesota's New Year celebrations have occurred. Many participants spend more time shopping than as spectators of performances on the main stage. Folk songs are rarely heard on the ball-tossing field because fewer people know how to sing them. Frequently, individual singers are now invited to sing the songs through microphones, sending the messages throughout the auditorium. Although attendees may hear the songs through loud speakers, few people listen thoroughly to the words. The folk songs then become a backdrop to the conversations and television and radio noises. As a consequence, folk songs have lost their meaning in Hmong New Year celebrations.

While some are adamant about maintaining cultural practices, Toua Thao believes that cultural change has always been an integral part of Hmong history. He has worked in the private sector since he arrived in Minnesota in 1976. Although he attended celebrations over the years, he has kept a distance. He comments, "From a cultural perspective, having it helps, but even [so], Hmong people adapt to many societies and many customs. Our clothes have changed a lot. We sing Hmong songs, Lao songs, Thai songs, Indian songs, et cetera. So, it's hard to really trace what is authentic Hmong culture. It's hard to judge the celebrations because I haven't been in charge of organizing them, so perhaps it's not fair for me to criticize. As an observer, I would like to see higher-quality activities, but I don't know if I could do any better. There are so many borrowings of other cultures that, again, make it difficult to get a handle on the real traditions."[28] Toua Thao considers the incorporation of other groups' traditions into Hmong culture a natural product of living among other cultures. Although he openly critiques New Year organizers' practices, he is quick to admit that it is a difficult task; therefore, perhaps the best approach is to allow things to continue to evolve rather than trying to grapple with what are "real traditions."

POLITICS AND ECONOMICS

Critics of diasporic New Year celebrations often question the authenticity of the various elements now referred to as Hmong tradition. Determining celebration components' authenticity is further complicated because of the commercialization and political activities embedded in diasporic celebrations. Regarding larger community politics, candidates seeking office in the urban districts, both St. Paul and Minneapolis, and in state and federal offices often attend Hmong New Year events. Some have booths and distribute literature, while others attend either to deliver speeches or to be recognized for their status as politicians, regardless of their rank within government entities.

The presence of non-Hmong individuals suggests that race plays a contradictory role in this semipublic context. Because the event is attended predominantly by Hmong Americans, non-Hmong, in particular those of European descent, sometimes regardless of their socioeconomic status, are honored by organizers. They are treated as distinguished guests, while Hmong Americans of similar or higher status are not honored in the same manner. Organizers seem to go out of their way to display Hmong culture in honoring these non-Hmong individuals. From the outset, New Year celebrations were used as a forum to acknowledge Hmong Americans' alliance with Americans during the Vietnam War, as evidenced by the frequent appearance of men dressed in military uniforms. One political candidate and/or elected official after another has publicly thanked the Hmong people for their contributions to America before they even set foot in the United States. While elected and appointed officials from the larger community consistently praise the Hmong American community publicly during their speeches at New Year celebrations, these praises are heard only by those who physically attend—almost all of whom are Hmong Americans. Although these politically inspired words of thanks may serve to gain Hmong support, they do not, in fact, bolster mainstream public sentiment toward Hmong people because these sentiments are rarely heard by the American public. Mainstream-media coverage of the celebrations almost always zooms in on the exotic elements of Hmong culture and its traditions, in particular the colorful clothing worn by women.

In addition to the contradictions above, organizers are frequently questioned about their business practices and accountability. A perception of organizers receiving personal financial kickbacks has plagued those involved in celebration planning, despite the fact that many others profit from the existence of these events. Organizers do charge an entrance fee, but they suggest that the fees help to pay for costs associated with holding the event. Renting space, paying for law enforcement to help with security, and paying for staff time are all required expenses. The hundreds of vendors at these events are required to pay a larger fee. Individuals and/or families obtain booths to sell a variety of items. Many groups ranging from high school and college clubs to nonprofit organizations and religious entities use New Year events to raise funds for many different purposes. Although the profit that individuals and/or groups make varies depending on the products sold, many benefit from the ability to reach thousands throughout the two-to-three-day celebrations.

GENDER INEQUALITY

Community politics and controversies over both the process and outcome of New Year celebrations have become more evident as the size of the events has increased. The first sign of dissatisfaction came from the leaders within the Women's Association of Hmong and Lao (WAHL), which was established in 1979 to support Hmong women and give them voice. Discussing the ways in which she and other progressive Hmong women leaders tried to influence New Year celebration practices, Gaoly Yang, a former WAHL executive director, states, "From the very beginning, Lao Family was pretty open. We partnered. Our board members helped to volunteer, and the organization benefited from participation. But, all along, we had an issue. Again, it's about radical feminist thoughts. We just didn't agree with the pageant. They said it was just entertainment. We've always known that Hmong men have abused Hmong women, and this is something that we would be perpetuating by supporting the celebrations." Early New Year celebration planning attempted to operate in a democratic fashion. The celebration chair position rotated annually among the half-dozen sponsoring organizations. The disagreements intensified one year in the mid-1980s, when WAHL chaired and attempted to reorder the celebration program. In addition to contradicting the religious order, WAHL's leaders also opened the door to Christian groups to sing songs. Gaoly Yang further explains the contentious situation, "When we chaired, we did let everything happen. Because we changed the order of events, they didn't like that. They wanted to have the New Year rituals before anything else. They said you have to *lwm taws qaib* (chicken-sacrifice ritual) before you celebrate the New Year. We actually celebrated the New Year before we had the rituals. In retrospect, I think we probably overdid it. We crossed the line because it was religion. We probably should have stayed out of it altogether."[29] Still, these missteps were not central to WAHL ceasing its cosponsorship of the St. Paul celebrations. The primary reason for this action was in protest to the Miss Hmong Minnesota pageant, which WAHL members believed to be demeaning of Hmong women and girls.

As previously mentioned, beauty pageants were not completely new to Hmong. As many displaced people relocated to areas in and around Long Cheng before emigrating to the United States, they began to have some exposure to Lao culture; this was primarily due to Hmong student attendance of schools in Vientiane and the relocation of some families to the capital city during the 1960s. Lao culture had incorporated Western concepts of beauty pageants, which ethnic Lao Americans and those in other diasporic communities continue to host. Prior to their emigration, Hmong in Long Cheng had held a couple of beauty pageants (*xaiv ntxhais nkauj ntsuab*), thereby familiarizing local Hmong with this concept. In fact, only young women from wealthy families were able to participate in those earlier pageants, thereby rendering the event a marker of social class. Although beauty pageants were not completely new diasporic cultural inventions, progressive Hmong women criticized the objectification of women.

The women were also concerned with other issues. For instance, in a clan-based ethnic community, where there has historically been competition to be the most powerful, it is difficult to ensure fairness in any arena. Skeptics were concerned that judges would vote along clan lines rather than scoring according to measures of talent and beauty. Others wondered how gender equality could be achieved within the context of a male-dominated culture that insists on women playing only supportive roles. Throughout the 1990s, the winner of the St. Paul New Year pageant received a donated, new Toyota Camry. Young women contestants were required to speak the Hmong language, and the winner was validated by former General Vang Pao and surrounded by his entourage.

One of the tasks of the winner was to serve as a role model for other young women. This responsibility was not what those affiliated with WAHL contested. Rather, progressive Hmong American women were against practices they perceived as devaluing the contestants, as illustrated in the following lyrics sung just before announcement of the winner during one of the pageants:[30]

> Noj tsiab peb caug kaum ob hli dua
> Peb tuaj xaiv tug nkauj Hmoob zoo nkauj.
> Leej twg zoo txaus thiaj yuav ua tau
> Ua peb tug nkauj Hmoob zoo nkauj.
> Noj tsiab peb caug kaum ob hli dua
> Ua ntxhais nkauj ntsuab zoo tsis txawj tag.
> [A new year celebration after twelve months
> We are here to choose the Hmong beauty queen.
> Whoever is the most beautiful will serve that role
> To be our beauty queen.
> A new year celebration after twelve months
> To be the most beautiful queen of all time.]

> Muaj tug tua teg tuaj qhaib los tsis tau
> Ua tsaug cov muam nkauj Hmoob zoo nkauj.
> Xaiv nej los zaum ua nkauj thawj xyoo
> Ua cov ntxhais zoo kom nyob ruaj ntseg.
> Tau ua niam tsev kom nyob kaj lug.
> [Is there a beau who's asked for your hand yet?
> Thank you, our beautiful Hmong sisters.
> We've chosen you this year
> Be strong-minded young women.
> Become a housewife and live peacefully.]

Although the song praises Hmong women's beauty and encourages them to be strong-minded, it ends by telling them to become housewives, which supposedly will lead to a life without worries. The ending implies that women are destined to be dependent.

In addition to this portrayal of Hmong women, Ly Vang recalls women's designated peripheral role in organizing diasporic New Year celebrations during the earlier years in America: "When we first got involved in 1983, I think we got kicked out a lot. We were denied a lot. The men didn't think we had the capability, the vision, and strength to put everything in place for the New Year. Women volunteered a lot, and when they see the value of women, then we got invited to participate. When they saw that women had a lot of skills, and their participation benefited the community, they then let us join. It was not open. It was tight. It took a lot of time for those men to realize our contributions."[31] She remembers negotiating with Lao Family's board president: "We said that if Lao Family was not open for the whole community to enjoy the New Year, then we would have one in Minneapolis, too." As the negotiations proceeded, those involved decided that they did not want the community to be divided and that it was important for everyone to work together. It was agreed upon that as a community event, the New Year planning process would become more inclusive. Additionally, a decision was made to rotate the celebration between St. Paul and Minneapolis. However, an unforeseen problem emerged from this. The building expansion of the Minneapolis Convention Center preventing its use by organizers resulted in the lack of a comparable space in Minneapolis. Thus, the Minnesota Hmong New Year celebration continued to be held in St. Paul.

Although gender-inequality criticisms and community politics had emerged early on, no one stepped up to challenge the Thanksgiving weekend New Year celebration. Small, clan-based celebrations were held, but no other celebrations of its scale were hosted. From 1980 to 1997, Lao Family and its cosponsors enjoyed a monopoly over the New Year celebration planning, implementation, and proceeds. The year 1998 brought about new dimensions to the celebration as another group of community leaders prepared a separate event held a couple of weeks after the St. Paul celebration. What transpired was intense criticism from many community members who considered such actions as political posturing.

EXPANSION OR DIVISION

Shong Yang, cofounder of HANY, argues—as many others have—that Hmong New Years are traditionally celebrated in multiple places where all are invited. In 1998, HANY members approached the board of the Hubert H. Humphrey Metrodome regarding the possibility of hosting a Hmong American New Year celebration in this location.[32] As previously discussed, having a large New Year celebration in Minneapolis was not a new concept; it had been done before. But the difference in 1998 was that the organizers were no longer the group who had controlled the celebration in St. Paul. Made up of mostly younger entrepreneurs, this group attempted to organize a New Year celebration that solely reflected their Hmong American identity, as illustrated by the name of the organization: Hmong American New Year (HANY).

The first Minneapolis Hmong American New Year was held at the Metrodome in December 1998, within weeks of the St. Paul event. This led both to perceptions about community division and to confusion in the larger community regarding the importance of Hmong New Year celebrations. On one hand, it can be explained as community expansion, but on the other hand, hosting a second celebration on a similar scale less than one month after the St. Paul celebration reflected community division. To some Hmong community observers, heterogeneity has always existed in the Hmong American community so the event was not a surprise. A range of factors influenced community members to promote such parallel activities.[33]

When asked whether they felt hosting two large celebrations is expansive or divisive, interviewees offered mixed opinions. Some saw having two events as providing people with more choices, so that if they were not available to attend one, they could participate in the other. In addition, they saw two events of similar scale as Hmong American progress. Xang Vang comments, "This is America. Anything is possible. If they can do it, great. Competition is good for all businesses. . . . To some extent, it is fine. Competition is good for the betterment of civilization."[34] Ly Vang, as do other Hmong Americans, considers having two large events as an even more authentic New Year celebration practice and make reference to its practice in Laos:

> I think it's expansion, it's not division. I think it's OK to have one in Minneapolis and one in St. Paul. Our community has grown to Brooklyn Park and other areas. It just makes people feel better. They do that in California. There's one in Sacramento, then Merced, and Fresno. Each community has its own, but people still come together and share. When there is the St. Paul New Year, the Minneapolis people come, and everybody goes to Minneapolis New Year. Some people may misjudge and think that it's division. But in a very narrow mind. The community has grown. It's time for expansion. In Laos, it's part of the tradition to have many celebrations. I think we have decreased our traditions a lot. In Laos, small villages would have their own celebration. Like, for ex-

ample, Frogtown could hold its own New Year celebration. When there are small clans, they may join another village.[35]

Mao Heu Thao concurs with Ly Vang's view: "I think it's fine to have two celebrations. In Laos, we did that. One village would have its celebration this week and invite other villages to join them. The next week, another village may choose to have its New Year. That's the real tradition."[36]

Conversely, other interviewees adamantly argue that separate celebrations were evidence of a divided Hmong community. Given the proximity of the two cities, these individuals did not feel resources should be spent to host two similar events. Neng Va Lo, a former St. Paul New Year committee chair, does not think it is a good use of resources: "It's definitely a division because everyone thinks they're more educated. Why create two separate events? I am saddened by this division. The Minneapolis New Year is just a big party. It has declined the value of our New Year. The consequence has been that more than $200,000 of our community money is being paid to others not in the community. Why are we doing this to ourselves? Having two large New Year celebrations has clearly ruined our people's reputation."[37] Txong Pao Lee, executive director of the Hmong Cultural Center, thinks the cities are geographically too close to have two large celebrations: "It's definitely division. Yes, in Laos we would have small celebrations in the villages. But this is a different situation. Minneapolis and St. Paul [are] basically one city. Why do you need to have two celebrations? I would understand if the cities were farther apart. It's all politics."[38] Shoua Moua offers similar perspectives: "You see, the St. Paul one is so big already. . . . Americans are confused. It's not even outsiders who don't understand. Our own Hmong people don't even understand. Hmong are so inconsistent. For example, whether it's New Year time or not, communities all over are having New Year celebrations at anytime they feel like."[39]

A few others could not decide and cautioned against jumping to conclusions about organizers' intentions. Bauz L. Nengchu articulated it best: "I think it's 50-50. The perception is that we are divided. As for the other 50 percent, I remember being so glad as a young girl that several New Years took place in different villages. It was so exciting to do that. So, in a sense, it is part of the traditions. In Laos, people didn't all come together to join one large celebration. The New Year is not just about going outside and participating in the celebration. It's also what families had to do together to prepare for the celebration."[40] From Bauz's perspective, the large celebration is a Hmong American invention. In the village context, individual families contributed to the celebration, while in the American context, a planning committee dictates what constitutes Hmong culture. Diasporic attendees become passive rather than active producers of the cultural celebrations.

Most interviewees have been involved in one way or another in planning one of the two large events. The contradictory perspectives reveal community differences. At the onset of the Minneapolis Hmong American New Year celebration in 1998, a discontented community member wrote, "As usual the Hmong New Year will be celebrated with Hmong beauty pageant contests along with traditional ball tossing. Other entertainment programs also include talent shows and drama. Some of the program events symbolize part of our New Year tradition, but others seem strange and odd, which are not a part of the New Year at all. For instance, the New Year is supposedly a time to quit spending for three days, a time to rest, a time to socialize, a time to receive fortune blessing and a time for young to seek engagement and courting. . . . [T]he New Year event is full with business booths. . . . The New Year only benefits business folks and the organizers. . . . This is not Hmong New Year! [It's a] shopping fair. Why can't we celebrate the New Year like other people on the face of this earth do? What a shame!"[41]

The writer argues against the commodification of New Year celebrations and distinguishes acceptable traditions from new forms of entertainment infused into New Year activities as a result of living in America, that is, beauty pageants, talent shows, and drama, all of which originated with other cultural groups and which continue in both large celebrations. The above writer is most critical of lucrative profits made by businesses and organizers during the celebrations. Hmong American New Year Committee member Koua Yang makes a similar argument: "[T]he New Year celebration has in the past been used by a few organizations with no accountability to the Hmong community. . . . Hmong *American* New Year celebration will give back to *the community* the spirit of the Hmong New Year—as a beacon of hope to the Hmong community, fostering success, unity, peace, and pride back into the community . . . empowering its people to become productive citizens in America."[42] It is not clear how the Hmong American New Year organization in Minneapolis intends to give back to the community.

Former St. Paul Hmong New Year committee chair Daobay Ly states, "[The] New Year celebration should be inclusive, and it should be for everyone to enjoy. It shouldn't be about peoples' personal politics." He describes his efforts as chair during 2005 to give back to the community: "Last year we created a scholarship because in the past people have complained about how the New Year doesn't benefit anyone. I took the opportunity to give back to the community by creating the scholarship. I don't know if they're continuing. I heard that it would be, but since they didn't want to reelect me as chair again, I don't know."[43] Both groups promote unity and peace. Both groups also argue that they are operating on behalf of the Hmong community. Each claims to be representing the Hmong community and doing good for the Hmong community. The distinctive difference is the articulation of the new group on Hmong *American* identity as opposed to the first group's sustained identification with Hmong and Lao identities. It appears that supporters of the St. Paul celebration, by nature of its ties to General Vang Pao, maintained loyalty to Laos as the homeland, whereas the new group emphasizes Hmong as "productive citizens in America." While many community leaders and politicians are invited to the Hmong American New Year each year, Vang Pao is not one of them. He, however, had consistently been at the center of the Hmong New Year in St. Paul for years.

While beauty pageants, folk songs, vendor booths, costumes of all sorts from various Asian Hmong groups, and singing and dancing competitions present in the St. Paul celebration are also found during the Minneapolis event, HANY organizers have incorporated new elements into the Minneapolis celebration that differ from St. Paul's event. These key components include a Prince Charming competition and a sports tournament (volleyball, *kato* [takraw], top spin [carved wooden tops], and similar sports). Unlike the Xcel Energy Center in St. Paul, where separate spaces hold particular events, the Metrodome provides one large, open space, where attendees can observe all of the above activities at once. Minneapolis organizers call the beauty pageant the "Miss Hmong American" pageant (see fig. 8); the St. Paul event is called "Miss Hmong Minnesota" (see fig. 9).

In the end, what is the difference between the Minneapolis and St. Paul celebrations? On the surface, one may note that the only *real* difference is that on the east side of the Mississippi River, the beauty queen stands in a Hmong costume next to former General Vang Pao, and on the west side of the Mississippi River, she stands in a Western evening gown next to Prince Charming. However, unpacking these two particular practices reveals substantive differences. The St. Paul celebration represents the immigrant generation's attempts to hold on to Hmong tradition, as signified by the traditional dress, whereas the Minneapolis celebration illustrates the fluidity of Hmong culture, as well as processes of Americanization, as represented by the evening gown and Prince Charming. Perhaps a more appropriate synopsis of the situation is the role that cul-

Figure 8. In Minneapolis in 2006, Alicia Yang captured the beauty queen title, and Her Thao was chosen as Prince Charming. Photo courtesy of Hmong Times.

Figure 9. NaSee Lor is crowned Miss Hmong Minnesota in St. Paul for 2006. General Vang Pao is to Lor's right. Photo courtesy of Hmong Times.

ture plays in reproducing and contesting social relations. Depending on who is representing Hmong culture, certain aspects will be projected and others marginalized. It appears that organizers are engaging in cultural politics, and each group argues that it is legitimately representing Hmong culture and its traditions.

EVOLVING MEANINGS

It is clear that New Year celebrations have evolved to have diverse meanings for different Hmong community members. In describing the busy Thanksgiving weekend for Hmong Americans in Minnesota, Daniel F. Detzner observes, "[The] Hmong mutual assistance associations and other affiliated groups rent the downtown St. Paul Xcel Energy Center, formerly the Civic Center, to celebrate Hmong life and culture. Hmong people from all over the country, especially Wisconsin and California, flock to St. Paul for the biggest celebration in the nation. The celebration is as much about the presence of a large community of Hmong people in such an unlikely place as it is about the New Year."[44] Detzner suggests that while diasporic New Year celebrations promote cultural maintenance, they also contribute to greater exposure of the Hmong American population. Regardless of one's opinion about the two events, as a concept, New Year celebrations remain a meaningful gathering for people of Hmong ethnicity who desire to be in the company of other Hmong. As one of a few transnational migrants of Hmong ethnicity who does not have the refugee experience, Bauz L. Nengchu recalls her first experience with Hmong New Year in the United States while visiting from France: "It's one of the most important events in our community. In 1978, I saw a New Year celebration in California. It shocked me, but it made me proud that our people is united. Some people don't go because they do see the same things every year. Sure, the activities are the same. But generally, I think all Hmong are pleased to see the New Year celebrations continuing. Basically, when I go, I want to see friends and family members. I want to see what the latest items vendors are selling."[45]

The pleasure of being around other people of her ethnicity appears to be more important than the availability of *traditional* practices. Some other interviewees described New Year celebrations merely as habits difficult to break but indicated that they preferred to spend the time doing other things. Chou Vang passionately argues, "I think the New Year is just a habit. It's not important to us. But it is a peaceful thing for the elderly. They have it every year to go through a cleansing process for new blessings. It's a time for them to take their children to experience Hmong culture. But everywhere the activities are the same. You go and you just fight through the crowd. Same performances and beauty pageants. Nothing new and interesting. That's why we don't go any more. We'd rather go fishing or camping instead. I think people can try to keep these traditions, but in terms of the culture and traditions, these young people don't have any frame of reference. They rather spend their time with other things like fashion and technology."[46] As a devoted Christian woman, perhaps the religious rituals no longer have meaning for Chou. Perhaps the fatigue that attendees encounter as they "fight through the crowd" does contribute to the perception of "sameness," despite the actual dynamic elements presented each year.

In random interviews with New Year attendees, the concept of a social gathering emerged as a major theme across generations. Younger individuals tended to perceive the New Year as a source of entertainment. A young female in her twenties said, "Yesterday was more fun for me. There were more people. More people wore Hmong clothes. I'm not wearing it today because I'm tired." A female teenager adds, "This is the first day I'm here. I was working the last two days. We just got here and started tossing ball. The best part is just being here, and it makes me realize who I am. I like being here and learning about the Hmong culture." Due to limited cultural education opportunities for the younger generation, other participants view New Year celebrations as a time to teach Hmong American children about Hmong culture. Other participants expressed hope for this to take place. A middle-age man states, "Our leaders have done a lot to prepare this celebration for us. It's a tradition from our country. We need to continue to have them so that our children will remember. We have it inside a building, but we must not let this tradition go." A woman in her forties comments, "Our children come to the New Year to have fun and also learn about our culture. Those here have different ways now. Some don't listen to parents so they don't practice things like ball tossing. I don't know about the future." Another man in his thirties states with much excitement, "The New Year celebration is great. It is *vaam meej* [prosperity]. There are people from all over, no matter how cold it is. There are many New Year celebrations, but I think the more the better, especially if it helps our businesses. Business is very important to the Hmong. We need to support them."[47]

New Year celebrations with similar goals are now prevalent from Alaska to Michigan, North Carolina, Arkansas, and California. In addition to community centers, large arenas, and county fairgrounds, college campuses and high schools across the nation host this cultural celebration. Celebrations of a similar nature also occur in Canada, France, and Australia. Hmong beauty pageants select young women to wear crowns across these diasporic locations, with names such as "Miss Hmong International," "Miss Hmong California," "Miss Hmong Minnesota," "Miss Hmong France," "Miss Hmong American," "Miss Hmong San Diego," and "Miss Hmong Michigan."[48] This practice suggests an evolving significance of the beauty-queen competition that is culturally Hmong but locally informed.

Just as important as the meaning of these New Year celebrations to Hmong in the diaspora is how Hmong transcend national borders. Hmong singers from Laos have toured Hmong American communities, and Hmong Americans have frequently journeyed to participate in celebrations in Laos and Thailand. Crossing national borders to "sell, buy, participate and observe" culture are new transnational practices in which people of Hmong ethnicity engage. In light of globalization, these practices do not seem problematic. Yet, the selection of Gao Nou Vue, a Hmong from Yunnan Province, China, for the 2007 "Miss Hmong American" beauty-pageant title in Minneapolis presented a contradiction to HANY goals. HANY organizers have worked hard to distinguish its focus on *Hmong American* identity from the St. Paul organizers. Permitting a non-Hmong American to represent Hmong Americans seems to discredit their previous emphasis on Hmong Americaness. Some may interpret this as a sign that culture is fluid; however, such practice could be viewed as this group placing higher value on ethnic affiliation than American citizenship.

5 *Political Activism*

Our reading of political history in the Americas leads us
to hypothesize as well a recursive, dialectical process, in
which subordinate populations, by engaging in varieties
of resistance and opposition, may transform social and
political outcomes.

—Tony Affigne and Pei-te Lien, "Peoples of Asian
Descent in the Americas"

How does the articulation of Hmong service and loyalty impede or transform Hmong American politics in ways that are different from other immigrant groups? In what ways does that then interject into Hmong community politics an enduring cold-war logic? Many in the immigrant generation readily point to their dislike of communism, which, they argue, contributed to their flight to refugee camps and eventually to the United States. I argue that Hmong Americans have been partially responsible for the maintenance of their perpetual refugee[1] identity as an organizing tool to obtain resources, to combat discrimination, and to attain social and political justice for their community.

Hmong people's adjustment to life in America has been quite public. Bad or unfortunate news of this ethnic group is often covered by mainstream television and print media. During the last three decades, negative news has also served as a motivation for them to organize. They have chosen when it is useful to highlight their commitment to the United States (by utilizing American political participation strategies) and when it is advantageous to point to their unique Hmong culture. Members of the refugee generation have used their distinctive history as allies of the U.S. personnel during the Vietnam War era to exhibit their commitment to freedom and democracy. They have also done so in order to present a contrasting image to that of the perpetual-foreigner label, with which Asian Americans have often been saddled.[2] Hmong have used media accounts and have continued political efforts to garner recognition of themselves as loyal Americans *before* they even set foot on American soil.

Building Alliances for Resources

In *Caribbean New York: Black Immigrants and the Politics of Race*, political scientist Philip Kasinitz asked why an immigrant group would play down its separate identity and merge with a larger category at one point in its American experience, only to later emphasize its cultural distinctiveness.[3] Hmong in America have sporadically engaged in this selective identification process and have chosen, or, more accurately, a subset of the population has chosen, to focus on their ethnic identity in particular ways to obtain resources for their community rather than embracing a pan-Asian identity. This decision was partly influenced by the fact that when Hmong refugees arrived in the United States, other Asian Americans, such as Chinese, Japanese, and Koreans, had become the model minority. As a consequence, some in these model communities viewed Hmong acceptance of public resources as something shameful. Hmong leaders also resisted being referred to as Asian Americans since their community was in dire need of social services for survival and thus did not fit neatly into the model minority category.

Although they may not have clearly understood American institutions, the emerging Hmong leaders in the mid-1970s took strategic actions to build alliances with mainstream organizations and government entities to obtain support for the growing Hmong refugee population. In addition to establishing their MAAs, they participated in many activities at the neighborhood, city, county, state, and federal levels. As previously discussed, traditional resettlement agencies and state-government entities had limited knowledge and/or guidance in the difficult task of resettling refugees with little or no formal education. They frequently relied on community leaders, who were often assigned positions as board members and executive directors of nonprofit organizations, to educate them about effective and culturally responsive strategies to assist refugee families. These community leaders learned that such roles were not so cumbersome but provided opportunities to help their people as well as placing them in visible leadership roles. Whenever issues arose within systems and institutions involving Hmong refugees, emerging Hmong community leaders were called upon by mainstream leaders to speak for their community, and most willingly responded. As a consequence, community members began to perceive employees and board members at MAAs as powerful leaders.

Significant parallels exist between leaders in the West Indian community in New York, as examined by Kasinitz, and the evolution of Hmong ethnic leaders. Kasinitz found that prospective leaders may differ greatly in both ideology and ability but are united by two fundamental beliefs. First, they agree that there is a community to be led; thus, they need to emphasize the group's cultural distinctiveness. Second, these individuals recognize the personal gain to be had as leaders of that community. They believe in and seek out a community, and, therefore, these leaders are at least partially responsible for inventing it.[4] As a result of these dynamics within the Hmong community, many members believed that MAAs had more power than they possessed.

In the 1980s, mainstream organizations serving refugees often worked collaboratively with ethnic organizations to resolve issues. Frequently, they hired bilingual staff to serve as cultural brokers. These staff members then represented their ethnic group to the larger society and regularly spoke on their behalf. Choua Thao, the only Lao Family woman board member during the early 1980s, recalls with much pride, "In 1985, President [Ronald] Reagan invited some refugees from the various states to talk about the many refugee issues, so I went as a staff at Lutheran Social Services. We were given opportunities to talk about what needs we saw in the community and make recommendations. The one issue that I spoke about was the one-hundred-hour rule for those on welfare. I asked them to fix it so that people are not punished for trying to work and support their families. It took seven years for this rule to change, but I felt like it was a contribution."[5] Even though the community is not always well defined, ethnic representatives often provide input to policy makers as a service on behalf of the community. Xang Vang describes his own involvement as follows: "I was asked to go to Washington, D.C., to help educate the U.S. Congress as well as the executive staff about Hmong circumstances, situations in 1992, 1993, and 1994. I went to educate on Capitol Hill every day about the forced repatriation of Hmong refugees to Communist Laos."[6] Individuals like him willingly represent Hmong people in different contexts to ensure that Hmong voices are heard, but at the same time, it is difficult to decipher whether the positions they take truly represent the interests of people in the community or merely the opinions of individual advocates.

The practice of demanding the creation of positions within state, county, and city and larger community service organizations has been a general strategy for leaders in America. These ethnic representatives came to be thought of as opportunists by some, both in the larger community and within the ethnic community, because they sometimes recommended those with whom they have familial or personal ties for such positions. Although the positions often only amounted to community liaisons or bilingual customer-service representatives, they were again viewed by Hmong community members as positions of power.

In addition to these types of activities, various initiatives and government entities have specifically appointed Hmong Americans to take part in committees and task forces. For example, when the administration of Bill Clinton began its President's Initiative on Race in 1997, Lee Pao Xiong was appointed to serve on the committee. As an activist and visible, emerging community leader from the one-and-a-half generation, Lee Pao Xiong had previously served as the executive director of Hmong American Partnership and executive director of the Council on Asian Pacific Minnesotans (CAPM), the state agency to advise the governor on issues pertaining to Asian Americans in Minnesota. He was appointed to the Metropolitan Council in 1998 by Governor Jesse Ventura. After Xiong's term ended, Song Lo Fawcett, an attorney and also Hmong American, was appointed in 2003 by Governor Timothy Pawlenty. Some local, state, and federal elected officials have also hired and/or appointed Hmong Americans to work in their offices as liaisons to the Hmong and/or Asian American communities. In doing so, the officials not only hope to gain Hmong American votes but also ensure that information from their office is disseminated to this community.

Hmong Americans in Minnesota have a history of ties with both Democratic and Republican policymakers.[7] In the early days, Governor Rudolph George (Rudy) Perpich and others frequently consulted the emerging leaders on many refugee issues. Most of St. Paul's mayors since the mid-1980s have involved Southeast Asians in various roles within their administrations. The city of St. Paul initially hired a Southeast Asian liaison who was Vietnamese American. Beginning with Norman Bertram (Norm) Coleman Jr.'s administration when he was St. Paul mayor, at least one Hmong American has served in a similar capacity in the mayor's office.

With the advent of federal welfare reform during the last half of the 1990s and its impact on immigrant and refugee communities, the Hmong American community actively lobbied officials to ensure that the public safety net in their community was not eliminated. The federal legislation signed into law by President Clinton on August 22, 1996, denied food support to legal immigrants. Hmong elders who were disabled were affected by the legislation. Hundreds participated in hearings, and many

were brought to the state capital to share their struggles with elected officials.[8] Through their testimonies as America's loyal allies and the efforts
of many community groups, Minnesota was one of fourteen states in the
nation that, prior to federal restoration for legal immigrants, developed a
food-assistance program of its own in response to the federal cuts.

Mobilizing for Recognition of Past Contributions

The organizing strategies implemented by early refugees to bring friends
and relatives to Minnesota and to create formal organizations were also
used by some to seek recognition for the role that Hmong in Laos played
during the Vietnam conflict. It is common to see groups of Hmong who
were once members of special guerrilla units (SGUs) in Laos dressed in
military uniforms at public events, such as New Year celebrations and
sports tournaments. Officer uniforms are often decorated with various
medals given by former General Vang Pao. Some men in uniform appear
young and clearly are not old enough to have served with SGUs. Although
appearing to detract from the respect paid to those who did serve, this
public display of the group's military service exemplifies pride in past
Hmong sacrifices.

If people of Asian descent in America have generally struggled to
gain recognition for their role as soldiers in America's many wars, especially when fighting on foreign soil in American uniforms, how then
have Hmong refugees positioned themselves to gain recognition for their
involvement in Laos? What have Hmong Americans gained from being
America's loyal allies? Although other U.S. veterans of Asian descent
were not opposed to Hmong efforts to gain recognition, no pan-Asian
veterans' alliances developed.[9] The lack of direct Asian American support
of Hmong veterans is likely not due to any particular animosity; rather,
other Asian Americans who had or have been in the United States for
significantly longer did not themselves obtain adequate recognition until
recently. A very few Asian Americans fought in America's nineteenth
century wars, and a larger but still very small number served in World
War I. Only beginning with World War II have there been relatively large
numbers of Asian American soldiers serving in the U.S. military.

Hmong veterans and their American supporters, largely Americans
who were involved as military advisers and/or knowledgeable about U.S.
involvement in Laos, have worked hard to ensure that their efforts in
Laos do not go unnoticed. The initial impetus behind this effort was the
California-based Lao Veterans of America (LVOA) Inc. during the mid-
1980s. Since then, local chapters in many cities with Hmong populations

have been established throughout the country. LVOA was intimately tied to General Vang Pao until 2004, when some members split from him, due partially to differing opinions regarding normalization of U.S. trade relations with Laos. Unlike other Hmong-focused organizations, Phil Smith, LVOA's executive director, is not of Hmong ethnicity but played a critical role in representing Hmong veterans in Congress. For a long time, Smith worked effectively to create opportunities for Vang Pao and other Hmong to apprise Congressional members of their past military services.

Hmong Americans and their supporters lobbied elected officials and struggled on many fronts to raise awareness of their involvement with U.S. military personnel in Laos. Their efforts, in particular those of Hmong ethnic minorities, gained momentum following the publication of several books detailing U.S. involvement in Laos during the Vietnam War era.[10] In addition, former CIA director William E. Colby appeared before Congress in 1994 and validated the Hmong's claims of their sacrifice on behalf of the U.S. war effort in Southeast Asia. Following Colby's formal acknowledgment, LVOA worked with former military advisers, CIA station chiefs, Vietnam War veterans, and members of Congress to seek a permanent memorial at Arlington Cemetery to publicly honor those involved in the so-called secret army in Laos.[11]

The multilayered efforts resulted in a formal recognition at the federal level. On May 14 and 15, 1997, the "Washington, D.C., Commencement" was held near the Vietnam Veterans Memorial to honor Hmong soldiers who served in Laos from 1961 to 1973, their families, and their American advisers. In the outdoor ceremony, one politician after another praised the Hmong peoples' sacrifices on behalf of the United States, and former General Vang Pao presented several elected officials with plaques from the LVOA. Most of the former soldiers wore military uniforms, and many of the women were dressed in traditional Hmong clothes.[12] Although it is likely that the speeches were forgotten soon after the event, the simultaneous placement of a granite plaque at Arlington National Cemetery serves as a permanent reminder of Hmong service to the United States. The memorial monument's dedication includes the following statement: "Dedicated to the U.S. Secret Army in the Kingdom of Laos 1961–1973 in memory of the Hmong and Lao combat veterans and their American advisors who served Freedom's cause in Southeast Asia. Their patriotic valor and loyalty in the defense of liberty and democracy will never be forgotten. Yov tshua txog nej mus ib txhis [You will never be forgotten]. Lao Veterans of America May 15, 1997."[13] Another recognition celebration was held on May 13 through 15, 1998 in Washington,

D.C., but it was not of the same nature nor as well attended as the event in 1997.

Interestingly, a new group emerged in the mid-1990s to work towards obtaining Lao-Hmong and American veterans' recognition. In 1995, the Lao-Hmong American Coalition (LHAC) formed "to formally acknowledge the Lao-Hmong Special Guerrilla Units (SGUs) veterans as America's staunchest and most loyal allies."[14] This led to the establishment of more than a dozen LHAC chapters around the country. The collaborative nature of LHAC between Lao-Hmong and their former American military allies resulted in a number of recognition ceremonies in various locations. Though working towards the same goal, tensions exist between LVOA and LHAC, resulting in debates in communities, as well as in cyberspace. For example, Dennis X. McCormack of LHAC writes to a young Hmong encouraging LVOA and LHAC to join forces on November 11, 2003, "True, it would be good if the two groups would come together, but the desire of the various Hmong groups to be 'first' seems to impede any meaningful chance of reconciliation. LVOA's first loyalty is to VP [Vang Pao], and VP decides who the group will support. And VP does not like LHAC. He views them as an upstart competitor for the Hmong's attention, and that is something VP definitely doesn't like, the Hmong having opinions other than his. So, I don't think we'll be seeing any group hugs between the two organizations in the future." McCormack's comment reveals a prevalent dimension of Hmong community politics. Collaboration seems to be something that only develops when funders require groups to work together. Each group's desire to be first created a complicated situation, where different groups and/or individuals make claims of being the first Hmong(s) to achieve certain things, sometimes due to their own ignorance that someone else has already obtained the title elsewhere.

To compete with LVOA, LHAC held a ceremony in Golden, Colorado, on July 18, 1998, that included speeches by U.S. Ambassador Wendy Chamberlain; Sam Zakhem, former U.S. Ambassador to Bahrain, retired CIA agent, and former senior U.S. official in Laos until 1968; James W. (Bill) Lair, former CIA agent; and retired Brigadier General Harry "Heinie" Aderholt of the U.S. Air Force. Each praised the Lao-Hmong SGU forces from a podium in front of a large sign, "American's Loyal Allies."[15] In addition to remembering the past, the event also celebrated nine Hmong residents of Colorado who had obtained U.S. citizenship. This display complicates the notion that Hmong refugees are not assimilating. Highlighting of the Hmong as America's most loyal allies followed by the showcase of their citizenship status was the refugees' attempt to assert

Hmong American identity. The focus on Hmong as American citizens in such public displays seems to close down other constructions of identity. The status of citizen erases the notion that Hmong are aliens. While these public displays are to remember past contributions Hmong made to American war efforts in Southeast Asia, former U.S. military advisers also seem to enjoy their revered status.

Associated with the efforts for recognition was the Hmong Veterans Naturalization Act, which the Lao Veterans of America had pursued for many years. The act was the result of bipartisan support, as well as the work of veterans, Hmong American community members and organizations, members of Congress, and former American military advisers in Laos. To the Hmong in Minnesota, however, U.S. Representative Bruce Vento was the leading figure in this fight and had first worked with the LVOA to introduce the original bill.[16] After many years of advocacy efforts, the Hmong Veterans' Naturalization Act of 2000 became law on May 26, 2000.[17] An important milestone in Hmong Americans' fight for recognition, the act provides an exemption from the English-language requirement and gives special consideration for civics testing for certain refugees from Laos who apply for naturalization. In his signing statement, President Clinton proclaims, "Today I signed H.R. 371, the Hmong Veterans Naturalization Act of 2000. This legislation is a tribute to the service, courage, and sacrifice of the Hmong people who were our allies in Laos during the Vietnam War. After the Vietnam War, many Hmong soldiers and their families came to the United States and have become part of the social fabric of American society. They work, pay taxes, and have raised families and made America their home. . . . This new law is a small step but an important one in honoring the immense sacrifices that the Hmong people made in supporting our efforts in Southeast Asia."[18]

In early November 2001, U.S. Representative Thomas Tancredo of Colorado introduced House Concurrent Resolution 88 to officially designate July 22 as National Lao-Hmong Recognition Day. The House passed the resolution on November 13, 2001. Outlining the Hmong's "warrior tradition, loyalty, and bravery," as well as the role of SGUs in engaging North Vietnamese troops, the loss of more than thirty-five thousand Hmong lives, and their experience as "victims of acts of retribution and atrocities," the resolution asked President George W. Bush to issue a proclamation supporting the goals of Lao-Hmong Recognition Day and calling on the people of the United States to recognize the service and sacrifice of the men and women of the Lao-Hmong with appropriate ceremonies and activities.[19]

Lao-Hmong national recognition celebrations subsequently took place in cities with large Hmong populations. Although the first Lao-Hmong Recognition Day was officially organized in Minnesota in 2004, a more significant event organized by the Minnesota chapter of the LHAC occurred on July 22, 2006, in St. Paul. This event was a celebration of several former SGU soldiers who received citations and Purple Hearts for their gallant efforts in fighting communism and in support of U.S. forces during the Vietnam War more than thirty years ago.[20] Many elected and appointed officials attended as St. Paul Mayor Chris Coleman declared July 22 as the official National Lao/Hmong Veterans Day.[21]

On July 15, 2006, the Lao, Hmong, and American Memorial Dedication took place in Sheboygan, Wisconsin, population fifty thousand, of whom four thousand are Hmong. In this relatively small city, this memorial was built due to the many local Hmong Americans who worked tirelessly on the project. The memorial also materialized because of some key individuals in the larger community—for instance, Steve R. Schofield, retired major and a member of the U.S. Special Forces, who served in Laos—interested in raising awareness about Hmong wartime service, both in society generally and among the younger Hmong American generation.[22] The *Sheboygan Press* reports the long struggle for the memorial, "The dedication of the Lao, Hmong and American Veterans Memorial at Deland Park on Sheboygan's lakefront is the successful culmination of an arduous, six-year effort by community leaders who worked tirelessly to raise the money, locate a suitable location and get the memorial built. The $140,000 memorial honors all veterans, including those Lao and Hmong soldiers who fought the communists and assisted U.S. troops in Southeast Asia as part of the Secret War."[23] In a heartfelt speech at the city-donated, Lake Michigan site, Wisconsin Governor James Edward (Jim) Doyle proclaimed July 15 Lao/Hmong American Veterans Day.

Hmong Americans have clearly welcomed the gestures of elected officials in different cities declaring various dates as Lao-Hmong recognition day. However, lack of a consistent or coordinated effort to designate one agreed-upon date is problematic. That local communities have different recognition days, compounded with divisions among veterans groups and their supporters, may contribute to these days evolving into something with little meaning in the long run. At the federal level, formal recognition of their unique ties to American military personnel in Laos was achieved through the May 1997 Lao-Hmong veterans memorial in Arlington National Cemetery, the Hmong Veterans Naturalization Act of 2000, and House Concurrent Resolution 88. While the many recognition ceremonies in various parts of the country may have achieved the desired outcome, once the speeches are delivered and the individuals involved—in particular elderly veterans—pass away, only such permanent structures as the memorials in Sheboygan and Arlington will remain.

Mobilizing in Electoral Politics

As Hmong refugees gain citizenship, one manifestation of their desire to reinvent themselves according to prevalent notions of authentic U.S. citizenship is their exercise of voting rights. These rights are not available to all persons who are Hmong and living in the United States because although the overwhelming majority of Hmong enter the United States as refugees or legal immigrants through regular U.S. immigration programs, some individuals resettle here from other Western nations. They come to the United States legally to visit friends and relatives. After spending some time here, they decide not to return to their country of legal residence. Some may eventually be able to adjust their immigration status, but others who overstay their visas exist on the fringe of society as illegal immigrants. May Joseph describes "the expressive staging of citizenship in the culture of new immigrants" and immigrants' pervasive "need to reinvent community in the interstices of political visibility," further asserting that "such staging [often would] coalesce around former histories, current allegiances, and future possibilities, accentuating the arenas of national minorities."[24]

The initial catalyst for political activism in the Minnesota Hmong community was the landmark election in 1992 of Choua Lee to the St. Paul Board of Education. Her election set in motion Hmong political activism. A decade later, in January 2002, attorney and community activist Mee Moua ran as the Democratic Farm Labor (DFL)–endorsed candidate and won during a special election for a seat in the Minnesota Senate. Senator Moua was reelected on November 5, 2002, becoming the first Hmong American to be elected to a state legislative office. The November 5, 2002, election was also memorable for Hmong Americans and Asian Americans in Minnesota due to the election of Cy Thao, community activist and artist, to the Minnesota House of Representatives. Thao was unsuccessful as an independent candidate in the previous election but won the November 2002 election with 81 percent of the votes.

The year 2003 was also unprecedented for Hmong American political participation. Six Hmong Americans sought elected office in St. Paul: four for city council and two for school board. Although neither won, Bao Vang and Toumoua Lee ran against each other in a hotly contested battle for ward 1, changing the landscape of Hmong politics, where Hmong candidates had previously run solely in contests against mainstream incumbents.[25] As Paul Demko writes, "Bao Vang and Toumoua Lee are just candidates in a freewheeling contest that features at least five legitimate contenders, but their presence has created some unusual discussions and disputes among Hmong citizens."[26] Ward 1 is St. Paul's most diverse neighborhood, with a strong African American presence. During this election, tensions arose not only across racial lines but within the Hmong American community. Another twist to this contentious race was that this ward received the highest precinct caucus participation in thirty years.[27] With contenders mirroring the demographics of the ward, democracy appeared to have functioned along racial lines, as evidenced by the following description: "This divisiveness flared up at the party caucuses. Kerri Allen, another City Council candidate, who currently works for the city on education issues, alleges that one of her supporters was unable to secure a delegate slot because the proceedings in his precinct were conducted entirely in Hmong. 'He was shut out of the process because he didn't know what was going on,' she maintains."[28]

Of the two Hmong American candidates, Bao Vang ran on a largely progressive platform and garnered the support of many advocacy and labor groups. She viewed younger Hmong American voters as a primary source of support. Toumoua Lee, on the other hand, courted the business sector and Hmong American Christians, suggesting that religious practices influence political decisions. He also sought support from the heads of the eighteen Hmong clans, who were traditionally the leaders of the community. The other two city-council races included Pao Yang, who ran for a seat on St. Paul's East Side, and Christopher Moua, who ran as a Republican against the ward 7 incumbent, Kathy Lantry.[29] Christopher Moua was the first Hmong American candidate to run as a Republican. Neither Pao Yang nor Christopher Moua was successful. Kazoua Kong-Thao and Michael Yang sought two of the four vacant St. Paul school-board positions. Michael Yang dropped out early in the race, but Kazoua Kong-Thao went on to win one of the seats.[30]

For a long time, Hmong Americans have tended to align themselves more closely with DFL candidates, as witnessed by their close relationships with the late U.S. Representative Bruce Vento and the late Senator Paul Wellstone. Non-Hmong political candidates also frequently seek support from Hmong American community leaders. For example, when Jesse Ventura ran in the Minnesota gubernatorial election of 1998, he visited the Frogtown area of St. Paul and met with Hmong American activists and community leaders. During their campaigns in 2000, Congresswoman Betty McCollum and Senator Mark Dayton both engaged Hmong community members and have been committed to appointing Hmong

Americans to their staff. The emergence of a Republican Hmong contingent became apparent during the 2002 election. Multiple reasons exist for this shift, but it is partially explained by the strong ties that Hmong Americans had established with Norm Coleman, then mayor of St. Paul. After the formerly DFL-endorsed Mayor Coleman changed political parties to become a Republican in 1996, he maintained close ties to the Hmong community, in particular General Vang Pao and his supporters.

The critical mass of Hmong Americans in the Twin Cities is a key factor in Hmong American candidates' success in politics at all levels. Although not all Hmong Americans voted for candidates from their ethnic group, I would contend that without the large concentration, Hmong American candidates would not have the necessary support base. In a presentation regarding her experience in running for office, St. Paul school board member Kazoua Kong-Thao states, "I thought that the [Hmong] professionals out there would be the ones I could count on for my campaign. Certainly, many did lend their support, but in the end, it was really a lot of the younger people and the elders that really came out to support me."[31] Whereas the strategy of seeking the elders' support may not have worked for Toumoua Lee, it affected Kazoua Kong-Thao's candidacy positively. It is, however, inaccurate to credit the success of Hmong American candidates in St. Paul solely to the Hmong vote. All candidates have, to varying degrees, received support from many in the broader community. What is true regarding the Hmong vote is that all successful Hmong American, elected officials represent communities and districts within the city of St. Paul, which is home to the largest number of Hmong Minnesotans.

Hmongs' status as political refugees meant that many were eligible for naturalization. Partially due to the passage of the federal welfare-reform law in August 1996, which made legal immigrants ineligible for federal benefits, such as Supplemental Security Income (SSI) for the elderly and disabled, many elderly individuals were motivated to obtain citizenship. The federal government provided special funding to many community-based organizations to provide citizenship classes. Upon naturalization, people were then expected to become politically active through voting in elections.

Candidates running for office frequently seek support from community members at New Year celebrations and the annual summer sports festival, also held in St. Paul, as these are opportunities for them to reach many people. As previously stated, New Year celebrations are spaces for candidates to obtain greater exposure. When community activist and attorney Mee Moua decided to run for the Minnesota Senate in 2001, she distributed literature at the November Hmong New Year celebration in downtown St. Paul and informed community members that she was seeking office. She made the decision to run for office after working with other community activists to identify prospective candidates after Senator Randy Kelly became mayor of St. Paul. Having assisted other candidates in their campaigns, she understood what it took to run one. As she greeted curious New Year attendees, Senator Wellstone walked by and congratulated her for her decision.[32] For Moua herself and for many other Hmong Americans, the candidacy is a crowning moment in her quest for full participation in American society.

The increased qualifications and skills of Hmong American candidates who are educated in American society allow them to appeal to the larger community. These candidates' professional experiences mean that they can respond to the needs and interests of all constituents in their respective districts and beyond. What is also significant, though, is that all of the candidates also speak the Hmong language fluently and can appeal to the older Hmong generation. To these elders, speaking the Hmong language indicates that the young person values Hmong culture and is thus worthy of their support.

Today's new, younger generation of Hmong leaders differs significantly from former generations, when elder, male clan leaders served as the voice of authority. However, it is important to understand that even with this growing knowledge of maneuvering through the American political system, campaign strategies continue to include the major involvement of the older generation, in particular, during election time. One strategy implemented by both Senator Moua and Representative Thao included providing transportation and interpretation support for older Hmong Americans. Both candidates utilized the highly active volunteerism of high school and college students to distribute literature at events and throughout their respective districts. Most important, bilingual volunteers telephoned households on Election Day to remind them to vote and to investigate any potential barriers to voting, such as transportation, that campaign volunteers could assist in overcoming. Such practices increased Hmong American voting generally while specifically increasing votes for both candidates.[33] In 2007, candidate Pakou Hang was unsuccessful in her bid to defeat incumbent Dan Bostrom for the city-council seat representing St. Paul's ward 6, otherwise known as the East Side. A graduate of Yale University with a bachelor's degree in political science and a doctoral student in political science at the University of Minnesota, Pakou Hang was not only knowledgeable about political and social issues but also had prior campaign experience. She had served as a deputy political director for Wellstone's reelection campaign in 2002 and had managed Mee Moua's campaign to victory in 2001. Pakou Hang ran "an intensive, bilingual field campaign [that] brought more than one hundred delegates to the convention, many of them first-time participants in the DFL endorsing process. For the first time in ward history, the DFL provided simultaneous translation for Hmong-speaking delegates, who heard convention proceedings over wireless headphones."[34] On one hand, this unsuccessful community mobilization occurred because she ran against a long-time incumbent with very strong ties to the St. Paul community. On the other hand, as reflected in one St. Paul resident's letter to the editor, three Hmong American elected officials was one too many.

Regarding the school board, members are at-large and do not represent specific geographic areas within the city. One may wonder why there continued to be only one "position" for a Hmong American on the St. Paul school board. Following Choua Lee's successful election in 1992, one Hmong American community member has continually served on the school board. When she did not seek reelection, Neal Thao was elected in 1995 and served two terms. When Thao announced that he would not seek another term, Kazoua Kong-Thao then filled the position.

Of the 38,500 students in St. Paul's public schools, 75 percent are students of color. Thirty percent of the total student population is Asian American, with the vast majority of these Hmong American. Twenty-five percent of the district's students speak Hmong as a home language.[35] Since this demographic characteristic suggests that Hmong American participation on the school board is essential, it is difficult to decipher why there is consistently only one position. Whether or not the St. Paul community will embrace the presence of more than one Hmong American member remains to be seen. Bao Vang and Toumou Lee's contest for the ward 1 city-council position indicated that Hmong American candidates might be more likely to succeed if they are not running against other Hmong Americans. Furthermore, Hmong American candidates also benefit from clan affiliation and family ties since those who have been successful tended to have large kinship bases in Minnesota. Though they did not win solely due to the Hmong American vote, they received support in many forms from Hmong Americans across the generations.

Organizing Long-Distance Nationalism

Obtaining resources in the United States has helped Hmong families to thrive in numerous ways and become active participants in the American political process. Despite some success in rebuilding their lives in this country, a segment of the Hmong American population continues to participate in advocacy efforts relating to their coethnics in Laos. This kind of nationalism expressed by Hmong in the U.S. diaspora is the result of print media that brought the issues facing those in Laos in touch with those in the United States, thus creating an "imagined community," as discussed by historian Benedict Anderson.[36] Anderson explains the transnational link he refers to as "long-distance nationalism," in which migrants or their descendants organize their presence in their adopted countries according to a relationship to the country of origin. These actors try to influence the host country's policies in favor of the people to which they feel connected.[37] Hmong long-distance nationalism has manifested itself through individual and organizational attempts in the United States to turn U.S. foreign policy makers against the Lao People's Democratic Republic (Lao PDR) government.

Hmong influence on both American foreign-policy makers and the U.S. relationship with Laos has changed over time due to different U.S. and Lao PDR priorities. The longer those in exile are in the United States, creating a distance between Hmong in America and those in Laos, the more difficult it is to maintain strong ties. Stéphane Dufoix argues, "The success of an exopolitical group also depends on its capacity to not lose contact with the real country, because its goal is always to return. But as more years of exile go by without political changes in the home country, the divergence between the two grows and the likelihood of their being aligned shrinks."[38] As soon as Hmong refugees arrived in the United States, they immediately forged alliances with their sponsors and American policy makers to advocate for their coethnics remaining in refugee camps as well as those left behind in Laos. This alliance determines a cold-war legacy in which Hmong "long-distance nationalism" has taken two different forms: support for resistance fighters within the home country and advocacy for the well-being of coethnics remaining in refugee camps and/or in the homeland.

THE POLITICS OF RESISTANCE

When the former military leaders went into exile in 1975, most thought it would be temporary and that they would soon return to rebuild the country. After more than five years in the United States, these leaders increased their criticism of Vietnam's strong presence in Laos and of the new government. In 1981, Vang Pao and other exiled Lao military leaders founded the United Lao National Liberation Front (ULNLF), also known as the *Neo Hom*, to organize and raise funds in support of the resistance fighters opposing the Lao PDR regime and Hanoi's strong influence in

Laos.[39] *Neo Hom* leaders argued that the Lao PDR was controlled by Vietnam and thus was not a legitimate government.

Vang Pao outlined ULNLF's objectives in a speech delivered at the Heritage Foundation, which included: mobilizing all Laotian people, inside and outside of Laos, to overthrow the puppet regime imposed on the Laotian people by the Socialist Republic of Vietnam; fighting the expansionist policy of Socialist Vietnam and its territorial ambition in Laos and in Southeast Asia; mobilizing support of world public opinion in favor of a democratic and peaceful Laos, protected by solid international guarantees; and combating Hanoi's regional expansionism by promoting a new structure of stability and peace in Indochina. This last objective was based on the tenet of absolute respect for the fundamental national rights of all people living in the region, as stipulated by the 1954 Geneva Agreement on Indochina, the 1962 Geneva Agreement on Laos, the 1973 Paris Agreement on Vietnam, and the 1973 agreement in Vientiane on Laos.[40]

Publicly, *Neo Hom* was presented as an organization promoting peace and self-determination for Laos without Vietnamese interference. Its opposition to Vietnamese presence suited American foreign interests well during the cold war. To some Hmong elders in the immigrant generation, *Neo Hom* represented hope of returning to their birthplace.[41] In speeches across the United States to Hmong communities, Vang Pao expressed hope for returning to Laos as he highlighted the importance of nation and land. He often emphasized the need to be prepared to return and participate in a new government. His opponents have suggested he influenced some of the Hmong remaining in the Lao jungles to stay and continue the fight. They would receive support from the exiled community.

Due to factionalism and intra-ethnic tensions among the exiled leaders and community members, it remains unclear whether *Neo Hom* made a difference in the resistance movement within Laos. Throughout the late 1970s and the 1980s, the resistance fighters allegedly waged sporadic war activities against and responded to attacks by the Lao PDR regime, but the amount of aid they received was never determined. It was discovered that *Neo Hom* served as a front for fundraising more than actually providing financial support to resistance fighters. Additionally, Neo Hom leaders were discovered to have exaggerated the strength of the resistance forces, which was necessary to continue to appeal for support from the immigrant generation.[42]

Complaints from former members and younger Hmong Americans provoked journalist Ruth Hammond to investigate in 1989, exposing the contentious situation in the Hmong American community. Exploring the inner workings of *Neo Hom*, she found that its leaders often exaggerated the support it provided to resistance fighters in Laos and claimed false American support for their activities.[43] An increasingly skeptical American Hmong community questioned claims of anticommunist activities, which were described as "fragmented, weak and ineffective."[44] Hammond also discovered that Vang Pao and the other displaced leaders promised ranks and titles to supporters who were willing to provide financial support to the organization. Concerned about *Neo Hom*'s questionable fundraising tactics, a disillusioned insider went to the police in 1997 and claimed that the organization raised money "through fraud and intimidation."[45] Increasing questions regarding *Neo Hom*'s use of funds collected from supporters diminished the organization's prestige among some, particularly with refugees who had grown old and had given up on the desire to return home.

As U.S. relations with Laos improved in 2001, Vang Pao began to publicly advocate for normalization of U.S.-Laos relations, assuming that the Laotian government would address remaining human-rights concerns. In response to this change of heart, a wave of violence broke out in Minnesota's Hmong community.[46] By late 2003, a public political split between Vang Pao and some of his former soldiers intensified. A number of violent incidents followed this change in the Minnesota Hmong community: a demonstration, shootings, firebombings, and the arson and destruction of Vang Pao's son's home, where the father frequently stayed.[47] These incidents together suggest that as long as Vang Pao remained an anticommunist, he was revered. Once he entertained the idea of improving U.S. and Lao relations, he was viewed as a problem to be dealt with by those who preferred to continue the rhetoric of fighting communism.

On July 17, 2004, as *Neo Hom*'s appeal dwindled, some of the same exiled leaders moved on to create a new entity called United Lao Council for Peace, Freedom, and Reconstruction (ULCPFR).[48] Fueled by the 2004 British Broadcasting Corporation (BBC) investigative film "One Day of War," which highlighted the "hunting" of Hmong men, women, and children in the Saysombun–Special Zone (the area where former CIA headquarters was based) inside Laos, a segment of the Hmong American population grew anxious.[49] The visual images of crippled young men, starving children, and sick elderly men and women angered some in the community. Even those who were not politically engaged, including young college students, could not believe that such tragic incidents were occurring.

ULCPFR urged exiled leaders in the United States, Canada, European Union, Australia, and New Zealand to work collectively across ethnic lines to support the Lao People's Movement for Democracy, which documents indicated was formed on May 4, 2003, by freedom fighters inside Laos. Appealing to "all Laotians in the free world to advocate for the freedom fighters and help promote peace, justice, freedom and affect democratic changes to the Laotian people," ULCPFR founders sought international attention to highlight alleged oppression inside Laos. It listed its leaders as Dr. Khamphay Abhay and General Vang Pao and the council as the Lao People's Movement for Democracy and the exiled Laotians worldwide. The organization is charged with working towards addressing the "ongoing conflicts in Laos regarding freedom advocates, human rights violations, humanitarian crisis and government corruption against innocent Laotian civilians, Lao ethnic minorities, in particular the Lao-Hmong and Lao-Khmu." To demonstrate its legitimacy, ULCPFR documents stated that it is a registrant under the Foreign Agents Registration Act of 1938 of the U.S. Department of Justice and with the U.S. Congress under the Legislative Act of 1995. Its international conference, held November 27 and 28, 2004, in St. Paul, Minnesota, brought together 439 registered delegates from Australia, Canada, France, Laos, and the United States. Participants proposed a new national policy for the future governing of Laos, which included items ranging from government structure to domestic and foreign affairs. Furthermore, the document revealed specific intelligence and strategies, which not only assessed existing equipment in resistance groups' possession but also strategies inspiring uprising by resistance fighters.[50] Most people in Southeast Asian diasporic communities pay little attention to these activities. Some regard them as merely the nostalgic imagination of the old military leaders who remain focused on the great era in Laos, when American support gave them unchallenged power.

Although anticommunist activities by military leaders in the diaspora had been tolerated during the cold war, most American foreign-policy makers today no longer tolerate guerrillas in American's midst in the post-9/11 era.[51] Hmong veterans' label as *America's most loyal allies* suddenly transformed into *terrorists* when Congress enacted the USA Patriot Act and the REAL ID Act in 2005, which defines "terrorists" as those who provided "material support" (e.g., providing food, water, shelter, and the like). Consequently, the United States banned Hmong and thousands of other refugees from entering the country or prevented those already in the country legally from adjusting their immigration status. In response to this, through the combined efforts of community advocates around the country and in Washington, D.C., Hmong and other affected groups convinced President Bush to sign into law a provision exempting nine groups from the new terrorist statutes, which states that these groups "shall not be considered to be a terrorist organization on the basis of any act or event occurring before [December 26, 2007]." Even so, any activities that occur after this date qualifying as terrorist activity may still fall under the material-support bans within the anti-terrorist laws.[52]

As stated earlier, exiled leaders' anti-Lao PDR government activities were largely viewed as important to American's global cold-war struggle, particularly when U.S. relations with Laos and Vietnam were contentious following the American war in Vietnam. The 9/11 tragedy introduced new methods for addressing suspicious activities in the United States. In part because of this, after a six-month undercover investigation by an agent of the U.S. Bureau of Alcohol, Tobacco, Firearms, and Explosives (ATF) and by the Federal Bureau of Investigation's (FBI) Joint Terrorism Task Force, Vang Pao and his coconspirators were arrested in California for an alleged plot to overthrow the Lao government.[53] They were detained for committing offenses against the United States "[in violation of] the Neutrality Act, Title 18 of United States Code, Section 960, by providing and preparing a means for and furnishing the money for and taking part in a military expedition or enterprise to be carried on against the territory and dominion of the foreign and sovereign nation of Laos, with which the United States is at peace."[54] Prior to the arrest, the ATF agent had posed as an arms dealer communicating directly with the only non-Hmong individual arrested, Harrison U. Jack (1947–), a Vietnam veteran and former California National Guard officer, who told many he owed his life to the Hmong. The agent and Jack arranged locations where Vang Pao and his group could view various weapons, in a pattern similar to other CIA operations throughout the world where CIA agents train and direct local counterinsurgency groups against various leaders with whom the United States disagrees.[55]

Considering Vang Pao to be a flight risk and a danger, U.S. Magistrate Judge Edmund Brennan denied bail to the group on June 11, 2007. The decision ignited an uproar among a segment of the population throughout Hmong communities across the United States and France, which supported him.[56] "Free Vang Pao" demonstrations took place in various communities throughout the United States, including Sacramento, California; St. Paul, Minnesota; Madison and Milwaukee, Wisconsin, and Detroit, Michigan. In cyberspace, debates regarding his being a victim of certain U.S. officials became controversial. For some, it seemed as though Vang Pao was once again being lured by U.S. agents, with supporters adamant that the event was nothing more than a trap by certain U.S. government officials. This incident and the 1961 encounter between Bill Lair and

Vang Pao seemed similar, supporters said. Others passionately argued that Vang Pao and his supporters were not above the law and that they should have known better.

Following the arrest, dialogues and debates in cyberspace energized many in the population to reflect about what they stood for. The debates highlighted a certain level of indifference by those in the Hmong community who argued that Vang Pao's leadership was irrelevant to them. Some others cautioned community members to think thoroughly about the implications of Hmong Americans' actions and words when the spotlight is on the Hmong community.[57] The debates are an illustration of a Hmong American population with diverse viewpoints, but they cannot be generalized to the entire population because they merely represent the perspectives of the primarily younger and more Internet-savvy segment of the literate Hmong population. The reactions from others in the Hmong American community suggest that even though Vang Pao is no longer the military leader he was during the war, he represents an important part of recent Hmong history. At the time, some Hmong American Christians prayed. Others e-mailed Bible verses. Still, those who practice animism burned incense and asked for the ancestors to help the Hmong people overcome this dark hour. They saw the issue not only as Vang Pao's personal problem but also one that affected all Hmong communities regardless of whether they supported him.

Diverse perspectives were also captured in newspaper articles across the country. For example, one, "Many Hmong Don't Back the General: 'This is our home now,'" outlined a generational split and presented divided opinions about Vang Pao. Although some in the immigrant generation still felt indebted to Vang Pao's leadership during the Vietnam War and their subsequent resettlement in the United States, many young Hmong Americans did not share this gratitude. Others found "Vang Pao less and less relevant" and worried that the actions of a few individuals in the community would once again place the entire community under scrutiny.[58] These individuals feared hostile response to all Hmong people because prospective perpetrators would not have a way of knowing Vang Pao's opponents from his supporters.

In contrast to these debates following the arrest, many young and older Hmong Americans across the country rallied for Vang Pao's release. Most of the young people had neither personal experiences of war nor a good understanding of Vang Pao and the Hmong's entanglement in American communist-containment policies in Southeast Asia, yet hundreds attended the protests during the summer of 2007. Elderly participants shed tears when looking at photographs of Vang Pao, as one speaker after another reminisced about his glorious past and the debt that America owes the Hmong people.[59] Although Vang Pao and his alleged coconspirators finally posted bail on July 13, 2007, Vang Pao and Harrison Jack were to remain on electronically monitored home detention pending their hearings.[60]

Headlines similar to "Feds Dropped Charges against Hmong Leader Vang Pao" on newspapers across the country on September 18–19, 2009, partially ended the two-year ordeal.[61] Charges were dropped against Vang Pao for insufficient evidence, but two new individuals were arrested, and their fate along with that of Harrison Jack and the other nine Hmong Americans remain in limbo. Vang Pao and supporters across the United States who had rallied in his defense outside the federal courthouse in Sacramento during his court appearances were relieved. Many see the incident as unjust and a deliberate act of betrayal on the part of the U.S. government. Interestingly, some view the case dismissal as a part of a long list of Vang Pao's good fortunes, as illustrated by *Los Angeles Times* articles, including, "The government's decision to drop Vang Pao's prosecution marked another escape for a storied war hero who defied bullets and dodged artillery on the battlefield." Although Vang Pao may have dodged another bullet, his "soldiers" may have a steep hill to climb as they face up to life in prison if found guilty of all charges.

A NEW ERA OF HOMELAND POLITICS

Homeland politics has mainly been associated with the secret-war veteran generation. However, in December 2005, when news spread about the desecration of graves of more than nine hundred Hmong refugees who had resided at the Wat Tham Krabok monastery in Thailand, Hmong Americans once again expressed their concerns. Working with the Human Rights Program at the University of Minnesota, Hmong Americans found that "[contrary] to the claims of the government of Thailand the relatives of the dead were not officially notified but rather the majority of them found [out] from video footage that had been taken by those that remained in the camp."[62] As news traveled around the country, community members became enraged and demanded that something be done to rectify the situation.

Families of the deceased and supporters, such as Minnesota State Senator Mee Moua, wrote letters asking the United Nations to prevent future unearthing and dismemberment of the dead; she also organized town hall meetings in communities around the country with large Hmong American populations.[63] Although a National Hmong Grave Desecration Committee was formed to explore the issues, the city of St. Paul formed its own Hmong graves-desecration committee to simultaneously investigate. In April 2006, St. Paul Mayor Chris Coleman proposed a resolution that the city council unanimously adopted, supporting the Hmong community and urging Minnesota's congressional delegation to work with the State Department in dealing with the Thai government to resolve the issue.[64] Politicians stepping forward to seek solutions angered some Hmong community members, who argued that the issue was cultural and religious, not political.[65] Members of both groups went to the site in September 2007 to explore the options for bringing peace and reconciliation to the affected families.[66] Each group came back with its own interpretation.

How and why did disagreements within the community regarding desecration of the graves emerge? The National Hmong Grave Desecration Committee was made up of Hmong American community members led by activist Michael Yang and former mayoral aide and attorney Sia Lo. Mayor Coleman's group included his policy advocate, Va-Megn Thoj, who is also Hmong American, and Senator Moua. The former group treated the incidents as cultural, while the latter saw the desecrations as human-rights violations. In the *Twin Cities (Minnesota) Daily Planet*, Va-Megn Thoj states, "This is a human rights issue and a justice issue. The desecration is really reflective of the oppression that Hmong people experience in Thailand. The Hmong American people were able to send a delegation over there with a clear message that Hmong people are not to be treated poorly. These graves were not unclaimed—these graves belonged to Hmong people."[67] Like Native American remains, Hmong view the remains of their loved ones an important part of the life cycle. Hmong traditional notions of death are intimately tied to life. Because the health and well-being of the living depend on the blessings of their deceased ancestors, some consider the desecration of the graves a direct attack on Hmong people.

Members of the National Committee protested the involvement of elected officials and argued that the issue should instead be dealt with by advice from cultural experts. Prior to the journey to Thailand, they protested outside a St. Paul City Council meeting, where its leaders further contended it was not a city issue. Michael Yang argued that as a religious issue, the Hmong community should be responsible for solving it: "This is about our culture, the way we bury our loved ones so that their spirits can travel to the next world, and the people in the best position to do that are our Hmong elders." On the contrary, Senator Moua maintained that as an elected official who had received many requests from relatives of those whose graves were affected, it was her job to represent their interests. In addition, her group believed that only international pressure on the Thai government would bring results.[68] Following the fact-finding mission, both groups organized meetings to share the information with community members. The actions of both groups suggest that some in the younger generation are interested in actively engaging in homeland politics in a style that reflects that of the secret-war veterans' generation.

The efforts of Hmong Americans and their supporters to influence U.S. foreign policy continue to increase awareness of the plight of those detained in Thailand. Following the "end" of refugee resettlement in 2006 with the last group from Wat Tham Krabok, more Hmong claiming persecution crossed the Laos-Thailand border. In September 2007, a group of about 150 border crossers was on the verge of being repatriated to Laos; however, promises from Western countries to take them halted the move.[69] This act has once again complicated the prospect for a permanent end to the Hmong flight out of Laos first set in motion in 1975.

Mobilizing around Issues of Injustice in America

The practice of organizing against injustices, both perceived and real, in Laos has long been a part of Hmong life in the diaspora because many refugees have friends and relatives there. However, Hmong Americans have been less unified in fighting against discrimination within the diaspora. As people from Asia, Hmong inherited Asian Americans' long and intense history of being the targets of racial injustice. Because of perceptions about the compliant Asian in American society throughout most of American history, Asian Americans had been seen as marginal to American mainstream society and politics. America today is, however, no longer characterized by a division only between white and black. African Americans, Latinos, Native Americans, whites, and Asian Americans are negotiating new positions and relations among themselves.[70] In the diaspora, Hmong found themselves in the midst of a rapidly evolving and complex contemporary racial environment. By the time people of Hmong ethnicity entered the United States, people of Asian descent had transitioned from the "yellow peril" to the "model minority." Their arrival along with other Southeast Asians has been argued by some to complicate this transformation.

At the beginning of the new millennium, a key feature of Asian American politics is its variety and wide scope, due partially to the dramatic increase in the Asian American population as a result of large-scale immigration from Asia since 1965.[71] As discussed earlier, the immigrant generation successfully advocated for many resources for the Hmong refugee population and acquired some recognition for their sacrifices in Laos. Parallel to helping refugees become naturalized citizens, several key community-based organizations and Minnesota's Councils of Color held many advocacy training sessions for communities of color to increase access to and participation in the legislative process. The skill-building efforts increased the awareness and capacity of Hmong Americans and others to influence laws and policies that might otherwise not be done in their best interest.

The new version of advocacy and organizing resulted largely from the leadership of a younger, formally educated Hmong American population for whom language was no longer a barrier. Like other leaders throughout contemporary Hmong history, many understood the power of forging alliances to build political power. Their savvy organizing skills frequently led to demands for justice and equality; their methods were similar to strategies employed by other disenfranchised groups in American society. Three examples from the Midwest illustrate this.

Shouting "We're not going to stand for racism anymore. No! No more!" during a demonstration on the St. Paul Capitol steps, Hmong American comedian Tou Ger Xiong led the crowd in a chant protesting a popular morning-drive program on radio station KQRS. After the lead host of the show, Tom Barnard, made insensitive comments on June 9, 1998, about Hmong culture, a group of irate Hmong activists formed Community Action against Racism (CAAR) with the goal of raising awareness of the incident and other racist issues in the community. Barnard had discussed the infanticide that a thirteen-year-old Hmong girl in Wisconsin allegedly committed after giving birth in a YMCA bathroom. In addition to comments made directly about the girl, he ridiculed the Hmong way of organizing families by clans and the special diet of boiled chicken that Hmong women eat after childbirth.[72] Indeed, Barnard brought attention to this horrific behavior of one girl of Hmong ethnicity. Although Hmong community members agreed that the incident was tragic and that all should be concerned, the attack on Hmong traditions energized people across generation and gender lines to organize against what they considered to be racist statements.

The leaders organized a protest on August 22, 1998, that brought together about five hundred people. Included in the march were supporters from other nationalities and ethnicities—a diverse group of Hispanics, African Americans, other Asians, and European Americans. Unlike the veteran generation that may have had a few non-Hmong individuals working with them, this younger generation strategically sought to build coalitions with other groups who have experienced similar situations.

Similar to the elder generation, however, the younger generation also sought support from elected officials. In a passionate speech at the rally, Congressman Vento characterized the KQRS action as "inappropriate and outrageous" and called on others in the community to stand up against prejudicial and biased statements. Senator Wellstone stated, "KQ, this is our message and it is a Minnesota message. It is your job to inform, it is your job to enlighten! Tom Barnard and KQ need to understand that the Hmong community is a community of worth and dignity."[73] The fact that Hmong sought the support of elected officials suggests that organizers felt a need to legitimize their cause. If respected officials stood by them, then it would strengthen their case.

The many young community activists involved in CAAR went on to work in subsequent electoral campaigns for Hmong American candidates, in particular, for Senator Mee Moua. The activism inspired by success in the political process was implemented following two hunting incidents in northern Wisconsin. On November 21, 2004, Hmong American Chai Soua Vang killed six white hunters and wounded two others in northern Wisconsin after trespassing on private property. Vang escaped but was arrested the following day. The criminal complaint presented conflicting versions regarding what occurred that day.[74]

The prosecutor argued that Chai Soua Vang intended to kill. His legal defense countered that he had responded in self-defense to being fired upon first. Furthermore, racist remarks by the victims made Vang believe that he was in grave mortal danger. The trial raised national interest and was followed by people all over the world. Witnesses and friends of the dead hunters portrayed the killings as cold-blooded murders by an angry man on a shooting rampage. However, the defendant and his supporters viewed the incident as the result of common racial tensions between white and nonwhite hunters that extended beyond those of Hmong heritage. Furthermore, they argued, when white Americans act as individuals, they are rarely judged as a group, while Asian Americans and nonwhites in general experience collective judgment for individual actions. For example, following the Chai Soua Vang shooting on November 24, 2004, journalist Doug Grow in his article "The Group Effect of One Man's Act" for the Minneapolis *Star Tribune* wrote:

> I am as guilty as any other stereotype, for the first thing I did when arriving at work Monday was start calling Hmong leaders regarding the awful shootings in the Wisconsin woods over the weekend. Had the name of the alleged shooter been Johnson or O'Reilly, I would not have been calling Scandinavian leaders or Irish leaders to ask about one man's actions. But the man suspected of killing five people is Chai Soua Vang. And I

was calling Hmong leaders to talk about the group effect of one man's horrible acts. . . . There are four Johnsons in the Minnesota Legislature. Yet, if the name of the suspect in this nightmare had been Johnson, none of them would have been receiving calls from the media. But moments after reporters learned that the suspect in Sunday's shooting was a St. Paul man named Vang, the phone in State Sen. Mee Moua's St. Paul home started ringing. The first thing Moua said to those who called is that she's terribly sad for the grieving families. The second thing she said to reporters is "why are you calling me?"

Because Senator Moua happens to be one of the more well-known members of this community, reporters intuitively sought her opinions on any and all issues pertaining to her community. This burden, as Grow highlighted, is not something that most in similar positions in the majority group have to shoulder.

The incident sent a wave of confusion and fear throughout the Hmong American community. In trying to encourage others in the larger society to refrain from judging all Hmong by the actions of one man, some community leaders felt compelled to hold a news conference at the Lao Family Community center in St. Paul, where former General Vang Pao attended. Through his son, Cha Vang, Vang Pao and others asked "that [the larger community should] not allow the despicable act of one person to stain the reputation of an entire community of good, hard-working people."[75] In addition, the two national organizations representing Hmong and other Southeast Asian Americans, Hmong National Development Inc. (HND) and Southeast Asia Resource Action Center (SEARAC), issued a joint press release on December 15, 2004, calling for "unity among communities" and not "anger" based on racial intolerance.[76] Interestingly, news coverage frequently focused on Hmong culture as an explanation for the defendant's actions. Still, others pointed to how Hmong have difficulty understanding and abiding by laws such as requirements for fishing and hunting permits because such laws do not exist in their country of origin.[77] In the weeks that followed the incident, hate bumper stickers reading "Save a Deer. Shoot a Mung" appeared in Wisconsin. Hmong Americans in Minnesota and Wisconsin also became victims of hate crimes ranging from having "Killers" spray-painted on homes to receiving death-threat letters to having guns pointed at them. As Aimee J. Badillo recounts about the period:

When a crime is perpetrated by a white person, the press does not call out to a specifically white population for answers. . . . After the shootings, the Hmong American community found itself in a strange position; they had no involvement with the case whatsoever and yet were expected to have an opinion on the case nonetheless. Members of the Hmong American community had to consciously ask the public and the media to keep the actions of Chai Soua Vang separate from a Hmong American community group identity. However, they have experienced what happens when individuals cannot not do just that; a shared ethnicity with a defendant became the basis of senseless, racist acts committed by people who could not distinguish between Chai Vang and a greater group of people who are uninvolved with the case. . . . Now the Hmong American community must bear the burden of the media's decision to craft a collective blame.[78]

The crafting of collective blame cannot simply be directed at the media's biased reports. To some extent, Hmong community leaders' responses perpetuated the collective blame. While some refused to speak on behave of the entire Hmong population about the incident, others willingly do so through such vehicles as the news conference, with the intent of appealing to reporters to cover their perspectives.

Despite the fact that accounts conflict regarding what transpired on that November day, the reality is that six people died. Chai Soua Vang was found guilty and sentenced to life in prison without parole on November 8, 2005. With Court TV coverage, the trial became accessible to many beyond the physical space of the Sawyer County Circuit Court in Wisconsin. A Coalition for Community Relations (CCR) was formed by Hmong Americans to "promote racial justice and civil rights in the Hmong community and foster racial understanding between the Hmong community and other ethnic and religious groups." During the span of Vang's trial, over twenty-eight CCR volunteers traveled to Hayward County, Wisconsin, to observe the trial in order to ensure "that justice was served."[79]

Throughout the trial, Chai Soua Vang was referred to over and over again in news coverage as "a Hmong immigrant" or "a Hmong refugee." The fact that he arrived in the United States only in 1980 received great emphasis, despite that he was a naturalized citizen who spent six years with the California National Guard and was honorably discharged in 1995.[80] Contrary to the earlier discussion of the importance of Hmong military service in constructing Hmong American identity, military service became irrelevant in light of Chai Soua Vang's homicide.

With the Chai Soua Vang shooting still fresh in people's minds, another tragedy occurred on January 5, 2007, when a white hunter, James Nichols, shot and stabbed Hmong hunter Cha Vang and hid the body in Wisconsin's north woods. The racial tension that occurred during the Chai Soua Vang case became dominant in public discourse about this second tragedy. Some saw the latter as retaliation of the "white community" against the "Hmong community." In response to this murder, a candlelight vigil was held in Green Bay to remember Cha Vang; most of Green Bay's Hmong American activists from the one-and-a-half and second generations attended a Hmong town-hall meeting on January 14, 2007, led by the Coalition for Community Relations. Hmong Americans demanding that Nichols be charged with hate crime also held a rally at the state capital in Madison on November 26, 2007. The hate-crime argument was based on published comments that Nichols made about despising the Hmong because they "shoot at anything that moves." Although this argument was not proven during the trial, Nichols was sentenced on November 28, 2008, to sixty-nine years in prison.[81] Even though it is difficult to measure the extent to which Hmong American activists influenced the decisions of the jury and the judge, it appears that their activism made some difference in Cha Vang's case because he was the victim, whereas Chai Soua Vang was the one who survived.

Conclusion

> Anxiety links us to the memory of the past while we
> struggle to choose a path through the ambiguous history
> of the present.
> —Homi K. Bhabha, *The Location of Culture*

Modernity, colonialism, and global history from a Hmong perspective suggest that when colonized people speak, it changes historiography. The history of the Hmong people who came to the United States
as refugees beginning in the mid-1970s is a history of larger, modern-
era political and economic struggles. It is a story of the rise and fall of
Chinese dynasties and their interactions with ethnic minorities, of European colonialism and its disintegration during the twentieth century,
of nation-building in the former Indochinese colonies, and of American
empire-building during the Cold War. Hmong experiences have varied
within their own ethnic group and vis-à-vis the larger societies in which
they find themselves; however, one constant across place and time is
that the Hmong, as a world ethnic minority, have struggled to maintain
their ethnic identity. Although they have never had a nation as we know
nation-states today, Hmong nation-building efforts have been an integral
part of their modern history.[1]

The voices throughout this book have, it is hoped, contributed to
a better understanding of the strategic alliances and ethnic divisions in
contemporary Hmong history. The lived experiences of men and women,
both in Asia and in the United States, reveal some cohesion, but they also
introduce new, contradictory narratives. At first glance, it may seem that
these experiences are unique to their ethnic group, but further examination suggests that they are another chapter in America's larger immigra-

tion story and the U.S. place in the global arena. The immigrant generation may have arrived with limited means and were placed at the bottom of the socioeconomic strata, but through their own social networks and access to resources in American society, they not only survived but also to some extent have slowly achieved the American dream and now have a unique, dynamic role in the global context. Consequently, people of Hmong ethnicity across the globe have mixed views of Hmong America. They see Hmong Americans as becoming less authentic with increased integration into American society. At the same time, many look to the U.S. Hmong population for not only economic support but also as the place where through hard work and dedication, dreams can become reality. Similar to other populations around the world with ties to their coethnics in the United States, the flow of people and ideas through different channels has created a global phenomenon that transcends national borders. To some extent, this phenomenon enables Hmong in America to play an important, yet contradictory role in the world Hmong community.

Hmong migration from southern China to the Indochinese peninsula was inspired by political and economic factors. While tolerated by local populations, they mostly existed on the margins of these societies. French colonization of Cambodia, Laos, and Vietnam during the mid- to late 1800s opened up new opportunities for them to participate in these colonies' larger political economies. Their desire for political involvement would come full circle with decolonization processes following World War II.

Americans on the scene in the aftermath of the First Indochina War presented even more opportunities for marginalized ethnic minorities like the Hmong. With the limited but important experience of political and economic gains through alliances with powerful foreigners during the colonial era, some Hmong leaders welcomed U.S. military personnel in their desire to protect their homeland and way of life. American military advisers enticed these leaders with financial and military support, while U.S. humanitarian workers delivered food and supplies and built schools and hospitals to respond to the needs of civilians and soldiers. Given the United States' military and technological superiority, individuals representing American interests during the early 1960s could not imagine U.S. defeat and thus utilized material and financial aid to encourage the local people to continue the fight for more than a decade.

The end of U.S. military involvement in Southeast Asia impacted both those who fled their homeland and those who remained. For the former who were fortunate to reach refugee camps, most desiring to do so resettled in Western countries. In the United States, thousands of individuals, organizations, and communities opened their homes to what they perceived as a temporary resettlement of Indochinese refugees fleeing communism. They did not foresee at the time that the crisis set in motion in 1975 would continue to the present for the Hmong. After decades of civil war, rebuilding the Lao nation, Hmong, and others required profound changes in all aspects of Lao society. Most civil servants had left Laos or were placed in reeducation camps because they were a threat to the new regime. Those who came to power had indeed longed for the moment when the nation would be allowed to focus on self-determination for its people. They possessed only a framework for how to move their nation forward. The revolutionary leaders had great hopes of building a nation whereby communist ideals of equality among all would come to fruition. However, internal subversive groups brought much fear to the government, fear that was compounded by threats from exiled leaders. The Lao PDR grappled with establishing a new government and developing an infrastructure with which to organize and provide services to its citizens. The factors that hindered the Lao PDR's attainment of such a society may have influenced its decisions to impose severe tactics such as imprisoning and/or targeting those who previously collaborated with the French and the Americans.

For the thousands of Hmong who fled Laos and became refugees, most arrived in the United States with little awareness of what kind of life to expect. Regardless of where they initially settled, most gravitated toward others with whom they shared a common cultural background. Emerging Hmong refugee leaders strategically invited their friends and relatives in other parts of the country to join them or were invited to relocate elsewhere. They established formal organizations to obtain resources for their community. Transcending their ethnic social structures, Hmong Christians sometimes moved to areas to build and grow churches where other Christians resided. The proliferation of both churches and community-based organizations evinces an ever-changing population that welcomes new opportunities and different approaches to resolving community issues and defines their lives at the local, national, and transnational levels. To some extent, these American-Hmong associations differ in terms of legal structures, but their actual practices reflect prerefugee Hmong social relationships. In light of the "end" of the refugee resettlement process in the United States and the decreasing number of non–English speaking clientele, community-based organizations—whose initial primary responsibility was to help new arrivals adjust to life in America—will have to evolve to remain relevant. With respect to religion, Hmong Christians may leave particular ancestral worship practices and animist traditions behind, but the Christianity they practice is a specific Hmong diasporic form, where some congregations are overwhelmingly dominated by particular clans or subclans. In sum, Hmong people have made sense of their lives within their disparate American communities by utilizing traditions from the place they left behind to maintain some continuity and inventing new practices in their new homeland.

This book demonstrates that regardless of the unequal power structures, when cultures come into contact, changes occur for both. New social structures were established to meet Hmong needs in America, but the refugees have only partially adopted certain arrangements that fit within their culture and its traditions. What is new is strategically infused with the traditional in order for it to create some sense of continuity. Throughout the communities established across the country, Hmong refugees compromised their culture and its traditions in order to be tolerated by the host communities. Some converted to Christianity for personal and survival reasons, while others who chose to maintain their religious practices do so within the rules and regulations in American society. Going to church enabled some to feel that they belonged because they behaved "like Americans." Those who hold frequent soul-calling ceremonies and/or shamanistic rituals bring only small animals to be sacrificed in the home; large animals such as pigs, goats, and cows are butchered at local farms and/or butcher shops. Such individuals feel that they belong in the United States because they are able to practice their own religion in America with only minor alterations.

While Hmong Americans have made personal and community sacrifices to fit into the larger fabric of American society, host communities have also become transformed due to their presence. Socioeconomic mobility enabled many people to flee from inner-city neighborhoods. The dying small farms in rural America required some to relocate to cities and towns with greater job opportunities. Although the level of reception was clearly diverse and varied with a multitude of factors, it is clear that numerous small and large cities have worked hard to incorporate Hmong refugees into their way of life. Church buildings, convention centers, and fairgrounds are frequently used by the Hmong population to host a variety of cultural events. Often, local businesses and philanthropic institutions provide significant financial support to enable event organizers to host them. On one hand, crime, poverty, and other community problems do drain some local law-enforcement resources. On the other hand, the decrease in birthrate in the U.S. population would have put many local teachers and administrators out of jobs without the high number of Hmong American children in certain

communities. Social programs employed many in the larger community to serve struggling families. In locations with large Hmong populations, doctors and other hospital staff have responded in varied ways to
Hmong cultural practices. When a person is ill, especially an elder, it is
common to have many visitors. Often, twenty people would be present
at the hospital because they want to make sure their loved ones are not
mistreated. Sometimes, they get in the way of hospital staff performing
their duties and at times "take over" visitor waiting rooms. Frequently,
someone stays overnight with the sick person. If the illness prolongs,
visitors popping in and out will persist.

As bothersome as this could be, doctors and hospital staff have increasingly expressed much concern for Hmong traditions, and many do
go out of their way to meet Hmong cultural needs. One of the most fas-
cinating aspects of this is the training program implemented in 2009 at
Mercy Medical Center in Merced, California, for Hmong shamans. As part
of a national movement to consider patients' cultural beliefs and values
when deciding their medical treatments, the country's first Hmong shaman policy formally recognizes the cultural role of traditional healers. Patients can invite traditional healers to perform nine approved ceremonies
in the hospital. The seven-week training program introduces shamans
to principles of Western medicine to increase understanding for medical procedures and to reduce fear. Certified shamans with their badges
have the same unrestricted access to patients given to clergy members.[2]
Because a policy detailing procedures for accommodating a specific cultural belief is rare, the Mercy Hospital program has received a great deal
of attention. Hmong and non-Hmong populations around the country
are hoping this will be a model for their communities to receive holistic
health care.

With increasing transnational marriages between Hmong Americans
and Lao Hmong, as well as an increased interest in business opportunities and travel adventures, the question arises regarding how enduring
ties between Hmong in the two countries will influence the Lao government's view of Hmong Americans. In thinking about the transnational
ties that have been developed over the course of the last three decades
between these two coethnic populations, I contend that Hmong in the
diaspora influence Lao society in several ways. First, each year thousands
return to visit friends and relatives, in particular during November and
December, when New Year celebrations take place. While there, they
contribute to the Lao economy by spending money. Second, many Hmong
in the diaspora regularly send remittances to support their relatives, who
often have limited or no access to job opportunities. With new technolo-

gies such as cellular phones, family members in isolated villages in Laos regularly call Hmong Americans to request financial support for countless reasons, including illnesses, marriage, home construction, education, business development, and the desire to satisfy their materialist whims and thereby keep up with neighbors receiving similar support from diasporic kin. This practice has created a culture of dependency on Hmong Americans, who often resent the persistent requests, which reflect ignorance of the financial struggles confronting many in the United States. Third, some Hmong American men, primarily from the immigrant generation, journey back to Laos in the hope of using their American-citizenship status to pursue marriage opportunities with unwitting young women and their parents, who hope for a more promising life in the United States. This practice contributes to the breakdown of families because many of these men are already married. Interestingly enough, some divorced and/or widowed Hmong American women have begun to return to Laos to seek younger men as spouses. Similar to young Lao Hmong women, young men also imagine a life of luxury in America and thus look for opportunities to marry older Hmong American women.

Following decades in which Hmong Americans from the immigrant generation returned to take part in New Year celebrations, in 2007 the Lao PDR designated November 27 as the official beginning of the Hmong New Year celebration. November 27, 2008, marked the first formal recognition by the Lao PDR of this prominent aspect of Hmong life.[3] This action suggests that Lao Hmong have gained an important place within the Lao nation. While those who attend these celebrations are primarily Hmong American spectators, in recent years, Hmong American musicians have begun to contribute to the festivities. It appears that economic factors are embedded in this official recognition—vendors and organizers appeal to the exiled community. Allowing them to actively participate rather than merely attend as bystanders encourages the Hmong diasporic visitors to further contribute to the Lao economy. Particularly in Lao Hmong concentrations surrounding the area called Lak Ha Sip Song (also known as Ban 52) in Vientiane Province, hotels, resorts, and markets profit significantly from the economic boom created by Hmong diasporic visitors during the holiday season.

Hmong identity in the United States is negotiated, accommodated, and, ultimately, located in the politically constructed space of the refugee. The refugee is popularly imagined as a permanent victim with a legitimate claim of belonging. At the mercy of host societies who grant permanent resettlement, the refugee is provided with all the rights and privileges that other Americans possess. With these rights and privileges, the refugee may transform into a citizen. If becoming American means exercising their rights as citizens of the nation through voting and other civic engagement initiatives, establishing formal institutions to represent their interests and participating in the social, economic, cultural, and political fabric of American life, then Hmong ethnic minorities who originally entered the United States as political refugees have become Americans. At the same time, their position in the world of Hmong diaspora (e.g., education, capital, and so forth) suggests that Hmong Americans have perhaps become more ethnic than during any other time in their history. In China and in the Indochinese Peninsula, Hmong ethnic identity had been suppressed, meaning that only in Hmong language and in their hearts and minds were they able to call themselves Hmong. However, in the larger national history of these nations, they have been known under other labels and have been forced to use those labels in order to survive.

In the American context, people of Hmong ethnicity entered the country at a critical moment in U.S. history. Prior to their arrival, the long struggle for civil and political rights by people of color had transformed American society. In turn, Hmong refugees were able to enjoy the fruits of the hard work of civil-rights leaders and activists. Although discrimination and institutional racism continued to exist in the streets, factories, schools, and housing, most were not prevented from participating in these settings solely based on their skin color or ethnicity. Hmong were able to live in vibrant communities and achieve social, economic, cultural, and political successes due to shifts in the American landscape occurring before they even set foot on U.S. soil. To their benefit, when they arrived in the United States, America was still fighting communism. Their anticommunist rhetoric was welcomed by policy makers, who pointed to them as freedom fighters and depicted them as victims of evil communism.

Today, the images of displaced, struggling refugees during the mid-1970s have transformed into a partially blurred image of upwardly mobile new Americans plagued by fragmented and disconnected social, economic, cultural, and political representations. In their demands for inclusion, Hmong throughout American cities and towns continue to exercise significant agency in building alliances and seeking resources for their ethnic group. Socioeconomic data reveal that on an aggregate level, Hmong Americans remain one of the most impoverished groups in American society. But at the individual-household level, many families enjoy middle-class lifestyles: they take vacations in Florida or Hawaii, pay for music lessons for their children, send their children to Ivy

League schools, travel abroad to broaden their horizons, and move away from their immediate and extended family to chase the American dream. While a segment of the population is treading on dangerous ground by engaging in crime and drug-related activities, more are pursuing higher education than ever before as illustrated by the increase in enrollment at colleges and universities. Since the first doctor of philosophy degree earned in 1972 at a Western higher-education institution, it is estimated that 375 Hmong Americans have obtained advanced degrees: about 50 percent are health related (from chiropractors to medical doctors), 30 percent are doctor of philosophy (from ministry to psychology) or doctor of education, and 20 percent are attorneys. About 80 of the advanced degrees, or 21 percent, are held by women.[4] Certainly, the impact of educational achievement is felt in certain locations more than others. In large Hmong concentrations such as the Twin Cities and Fresno, Hmong American professionals offer a variety of services, and so language and cultural barriers are nonexistent. For many Hmong Americans in these urban settings, they no longer have to learn how to speak English if they do not wish to do so. Consequently, not learning to speak English has been viewed by some as their refusal to truly become American.

While a large segment of the current Hmong American population is foreign born, the future increase in this ethnic group's population will be largely due to continued high birthrates. Anti-immigrant sentiments compounded with domestic economic challenges and improved U.S.-Laos relations suggest that policymakers will not likely support emigration from this country in the foreseeable future, which will prevent the growth of the foreign population. Community observations are that the increase in education attained by some women and costs of raising children in American society have influenced Hmong women to have fewer children. However, census data reveal that the average number of persons in a Hmong American household in 2000 was significantly higher than in the average U.S. population—6.29 persons compared to 2.59. Over half of the total Hmong American population was under the age of eighteen. As the number of American-born children overtakes that of the foreign-born population, what will home mean to those who are ethnically Hmong when home is no longer referred to as Laos but Detroit, Providence, Philadelphia, Sacramento, Minneapolis, or Milwaukee? I suggest that many in the American-born population have little interest in moving to their parents' homeland. Certainly, despite little or no personal ties, some may develop interest in their homeland, perhaps while in college when presented with opportunities to study abroad. Yet, members of this second generation are truly rooted in their American life, referring to home as the U.S. cities and towns in which they were born or those where their parents reside. Furthermore, the increasing number of Hmong Americans converting to Christianity perhaps reflects a growing discomfort with Hmong religion, particularly among those in the younger generation, who may find church-service attendance easier than mastering the complex, intricate animist rituals of their ancestors. However, these rituals may not easily disappear because many community organizations now hold classes to teach young people. In addition, the rituals and practices are increasingly being documented in books and films, suggesting that they will evolve but remain relevant to a segment of the Hmong American population.

For some Hmong Americans, a fundamental tension exists between their identity as citizens of their new country and their continuing identity as people from their ethnic community who must advocate for those left behind. Increasingly, political, social, and economic transnational practices among Laos, Thailand, and the United States have infiltrated Hmong American lives in various ways. This is not to mention the explosion of Hmong Americans connecting with other Hmong through the Internet, in what entrepreneur Teng Lee calls the "Virtual Universal Hmong Nation." As he explains, even while no Hmong physical nation exists, Hmong ethnic ties and nation-building continue to be developed in cyberspace.[5]

Businesses, nonprofit agencies, and churches across the country continue to include *Hmong* in their titles. Nostalgia may not be able to explain why some prominent businesses throughout the Twin Cities and elsewhere are named after places in Thailand and Laos in which Hmong recently lived. For example, the Hmong American–owned butcher shop in South St. Paul is named Long Cheng.[6] A Hmong American–led charter high school in Minneapolis is called Long Tieng Academy. An office building with several businesses located on Jackson Avenue in St. Paul is named Vinai Office Park. Sam Thong Meat Market serves the Sacramento Hmong American community.[7] How Hmong Americans see themselves then is associated with how they see their place in both the United States and in different Asian locations. Although the younger generation may continue to define and redefine home and belonging, for the generation that arrived in this country as refugees, citizenship does not entail erasing memories of their experiences in Asia. Despite community frictions that have often led to disintegration of social structures and the formation of new rules for living, ethnicity remains an instrumental part of Hmong existence. How they see themselves today and what hopes they have about the future are perhaps best summarized by several interviewees. Chou

Vang leaves open the possibility of a broader identity: "When people see me, they know I'm Asian because of my skin color. When they ask me about my ethnicity, I tell them I'm Hmong. Hmong are from China, so sometimes Hmong and Chinese is the same when you think about nationality."[8] Toua Thao, on the other hand, makes no compromise about his ethnicity: "I always say that I'm Hmong. I always think about my 'Hmongness.' I never say that I'm Lao, Vietnamese, Chinese, or Asian. I believe that if you are a good person, then when you tell people that you're Hmong, it is prideful. If people don't ask, I don't say much. But if they ask me, I tell them that I'm Hmong. Sometimes people are surprised that I'm Hmong. Some even say that they don't think I'm Hmong. That's their issue. I think that if you want our community to thrive, then as individuals, you have to work hard towards building yourself to be a good example."[9] Similar to Toua Thao, Gaoly Yang argues that there is something inherently special about Hmongness:

> For those of us born in Laos, we have experienced much discrimination, so you always feel that you have to stick with your kind. Yes, that can be negative because you have prejudice against other people. No matter how great someone is, they can never be better than another Hmong. When you see someone very successful, you wish they were Hmong. . . . We are changing. But I do see that there is still the support. When you go to a town that you do not know anyone, you can look in the phone book to see if there are any Hmong names. When you call that person, you can be 90 percent confident that that person will say, "Come over and I will help you." So, it's still there. That's something unique about Hmong. By nature of you being Hmong, that element is in you. It's an obligation to help another Hmong person.[10]

The interest in providing mutual support to fellow members of the ethnic group appears to remain a strong part of Hmong Americans' identity.

As people of Asian descent, they have benefited greatly from the progress that Asian Americans and other racial minorities have made. At the same time, they have also inherited all of the stereotypes about Asian Americans and have become targets of racial violence in urban settings as well as in suburban and rural areas. Reflecting the ways in which people of Hmong ethnicity have been included into American life since their arrival is Clint Eastwood's film *Gran Torino*, released in December 2008, about a Korean War veteran's interactions with his family and his new Hmong neighbors. Set in Detroit, the cohesive, extended Hmong family life is juxtaposed against the breakdown of American family values, where the main character's children and grandchildren are only interested in his material possessions. The film highlights the struggles of a poor, disadvantaged, new immigrant group that becomes entangled in the urban "pecking order." The film is about Walt Kowalski, played by Clint Eastwood, who sacrifices himself to save the brother and sister pair Tao and Sue from the Hmong gangbangers.[11]

Hearing Hmong language and seeing people of multiple generations interacting in a Hollywood film alongside one of Hollywood's greatest legends have brought much excitement to Hmong Americans throughout the country. The casting of Hmong Americans with little or no acting experience brought relief to Hmong American community leaders and activists who feared that Hollywood would call on established actors of Asian descent to portray their community. As appalling as the foul language and stereotypes may sound, many Hmong American community members have expressed much satisfaction in seeing people like themselves on the big screen. However, Hmong Americans are concerned that any and all stereotypes developed throughout American history about people of Asian descent are portrayed throughout the film. One scene that caught many Hmong American viewers' attention was the young woman Sue plainly stating to Walt that Hmong boys are thugs. Hmong girls go to college, Hmong boys end up in jail. As illustrated by the discussion earlier on education, the notion that Hmong American women have surpassed men in educational achievement is a perception. The highlighting of a few prominent Hmong American women in state elected office, higher-education institutions, and local government compounded with the high-profile hunting incidents and spousal murders by Hmong American men perpetuates this stereotype. But, in the end, this is Hollywood. The film clearly reflects the views of people who have access to capital and plays upon its audience's interest in the exotic Other. Let us hope that *Gran Torino* does not perpetuate in the minds of its viewers a belief that all young Hmong in urban America are gangsters incapable of helping themselves.

If one looks back to where the Hmong were in 1975 when the first refugees arrived in the United States and compares this with the vibrant community that exists today, one finds that notwithstanding continuing poverty and discrimination, the American Hmong community has made great strides. What it means to be Hmong in small towns compared to large cities entails a consideration of the larger frameworks that facilitate or hinder the maintenance and invention of Hmong culture and its traditions. One indisputable fact is that Hmong experiences have contributed to the re-creating and transforming of societies in which they now live. Not only are they changing their own culture and its traditions in order to exist in American society but also the unlikely places in which they have reconstructed community have undergone much transformation as a result of their presence. Those who knew them prior to their migration to Western nations feared that they would not survive in these techno- logically advanced environments. Some even predicted their extinction.[12] However, if the last quarter of the twentieth century tells anything about Hmong people's ability to adapt and create meaningful communities, those fears may now be put to rest. History suggests that while Hmong refugees may have traveled a slightly different path to reach America's gates, their experiences of both inclusion and exclusion are similar to those of previous immigrants. Given access to similar opportunities, they, too, can achieve the American dream.

NOTES

Preface

1. The term *one-and-a-half generation* (also referred to as the *1.5 generation*) refers to children who immigrate to a new country before or during their early teens. They possess some characteristics of the homeland but assimilate. Their identity includes a combination of old and new traditions.

2. Goldfarb, *Fighters, Refugees, Immigrants*. In this book, Mace Golfarb, who was a pediatrician from Minneapolis, Minnesota, detailed the experiences of refugees at Ban Vinai refugee camp where he volunteered to provide health care in 1979. The book included many photos of a group of refugees who arrived in October 1979. Although the book was published in 1982, it would be in the early 1990s when my younger sister, Mao, discovered it. As a curious college student at St. Thomas University in St. Paul, Minnesota, she found the book cover to be extraordinarily interesting. She was ecstatic to see the photograph of a Hmong mother looking down at her young daughter carrying an infant on her back. That woman is our mother, Pang Thao, and the young girl was Mao. The child on her back is our youngest brother, Cher, who was born in 1978. As she flipped through the different pages, she found pictures of other relatives, including our oldest brother, Teng.

Introduction

1. See Faderman, *I Begin My Life All Over*; Fadiman, *Spirit Catches You and You Fall Down*; Faruque, *Migration of Hmong to the Midwestern States*; Koltyk, *New Pioneers in the Heartland*; Donnelly, *Changing Lives of Hmong Women*; Hamilton-Merritt, *Tragic Mountains*.

2. Hein, *From Vietnam, Laos, and Cambodia*, 10.

3. Safran, "Diasporas in Modern Societies" and "The Jewish Diaspora."

4. Clifford, "Diasporas," 302–38.

5. Safran, "Diasporas in Modern Societies," 83–99.

6. Cohen, *Global Diasporas*, 26.

7. Hall, "Cultural Identity and Diaspora."

8. Gilroy, *Black Atlantic*, 6.

9. Tölölyan, "Rethinking Diaspora(s)."

10. Thailand did not grant citizenship to children born to refugee parents. Refugee status is one of statelessness.

11. Vertovec, "Three Meanings of 'Diaspora,'" 149–80.

12. Some would argue that the Hmong dispersal began with their migration from southern China to Southeast Asia in the nineteenth century. Although I agree in terms of Hmong migration history, there is an important distinction between the two. In the former, little documentation exists to sustain a "collective memory," and due to time, ties to family and kin have been cut off. In the latter, documentation in many forms, both written and visual, exists, and many who experienced the dispersal are still living to tell their stories.

13. Vertovec, "Migrant Transnationalism and Modes of Transformation," 149.

14. Schein, "Hmong/Miao Transnationality," 273–74.

15. Dufoix, *Diasporas*, 62–69.

16. B. Anderson, *Imagined Communities*, 5–7.

17. Basch, Schiller, and Blanc, *Unbound Nations*, 7.

18. Ong, *Flexible Citizenship*, 110.

19. Today, *Miao* is a term used by the People's Republic of China for its fifth-largest minority group. This umbrella term for tribal minorities includes Hmong. Hmong is one of the four ethnic minority groups that fall under the Miao nationality in China. Hmong who lived in Vietnam, Laos, and Thailand were referred to as Méo. Writings before the mid-1970s used Miao or Méo. Since the mid-1970s, the term *Hmong* has been what people of Hmong origin have preferred to be called and is what people of Hmong ethnicity call themselves in their own language. Although those who are of Hmong ethnicity who currently live in China do not resent being called Miao, Hmong in the diaspora have argued that such terms as Miao/Méo have historical negative connotations. Not all Miao are Hmong.

20. Schein, "Hmong/Miao Transnationality," 276.

21. The extent to which this is occurring has not been documented. There are opportunities for research in this area. A number of Hmong Americans with financial resources have built hotels and other attractions in collaboration with family members in Laos. A few travel back and forth between Laos and the United States. One family in Minnesota has a home in this state, a home in Vientiane, Laos, and sends their children to attend school in Thailand.

22. Anderson and Lee, "Asian American Displacements," 15.

23. Long, *Ban Vinai*, 29.

24. Harrell-Bond and Voutira, "Anthropology and the Study of Refugees," 6–10.

25. Harrell-Bond, "The Experience of Refugees," 136.

26. Nyers, *Rethinking Refugees*, xv.

27. Interviewees for this book shared these various ways in which they and/or other people they knew were led to refugee camps by Hmong guides.

28. In some of the narratives, interviewees gave conflicting accounts of their understanding of why Americans were in Laos. Some talked about how they did not know anything about American anticommunist policies at the time, while others regurgitated the popular narratives that had been outlined in journalists' writings of how the Central Intelligence Agency (CIA) came to negotiate with Vang Pao.

29. Haines, *Refugees as Immigrants*, 8.

30. Kim, "Personal, Social, and Economic Adaptation," 103.

31. Portes and Zhou, "New Second Generation," 74–96.

32. Waters, Ueda, and Marrow, *New Americans*, 11.

33. Castles, "Factors That Make and Unmake Migration Policies," 29–61.

34. Menjívar, *Fragmented Ties,* 34–35.

35. DeWind and Kasinitz, "Everything Old Is New Again?" 1096–97.

36. Mahler, *American Dreaming,* 227.

37. Hein, *From Vietnam, Laos, and Cambodia,* 25.

38. Jacobson, *Special Sorrows,* 15–22.

39. As a member of the community being studied, I have participated in annual celebrations since the early 1980s.

40. Appadurai, *Modernity at Large,* 63–64.

Chapter 1: Hmong History and Migration Prior to America

1. Tapp, "State of Hmong Studies," 3–8.

2. Ibid., 61–96.

3. Michaud, "From Southwest China into Upper Indochina," 122.

4. Jenks, *Insurgency and Social Disorder in Guizhou,* 3.

5. See Culas and Michaud, "Contribution to the Study of Hmong (Miao) Migrations and History," 63–65; Tapp, *Hmong of China;* Schein, *Minority Rules,* 3–4.

6. Michaud, "From Southwest China into Upper Indochina," 123.

7. The first usage of the term *Hmong* by Westerners appears in Garrett, "Hmong of Laos."

8. Culas and Michaud, "Contribution to the Study of Hmong (Miao) Migrations and History," 66–68.

9. Saykao, "Root and the Fruit," 3–37.

10. D. Yang, *Hmong at the Turning Point,* 22–25.

11. Although Hmong women did not change their surnames when they married (and some still do not), many young women in America have opted to take their husband's last name upon marriage. Some elders fear that such practice may eventually lead to men and women of the same clan marrying one another, which is considered taboo and shameful.

12. G. Y. Lee, "Religious Presentation of Social Relationships."

13. I have chosen to include both Green and White Hmong spellings throughout the book if they are spelled differently. Although Green Hmong activists and scholars argue both *Mong* and *Hmong* should be used in written materials, I have elected to use only *Hmong.* As an individual of Green Hmong background, I understand the argument about inclusiveness; however, I also think that since *Hmong* has been used to refer to this ethnic group since the 1970s, it is best to continue to use this term for consistency.

14. Since migrating to the United States, some Hmong families have created new last names for their specific family. Frequently, they attach the clan name to a father's or grandfather's first name to ensure that others can still identify their clan affiliation. For example, one family in the Midwest takes the last name of Mouanoutoua. Here, "noutoua" is the ancestor's first name, and "Moua" designates the clan affiliation. Another family from the Thao clan completely removed the clan affiliation by taking only the ancestor's name "Saykao." Unless one knows the background of the family, it is impossible for anyone to know to which clan this family belongs. The Saykao family lives not only in the United States but also in Australia.

15. Michaud, "From Southwest China into Upper Indochina," 125–26.

16. The five entities made up the French Union. However, Cambodia and Laos were protectorates.

17. Evans, *Short History of Laos*, 39; Stuart-Fox, *History of Laos*, 42–46.

18. G. Y. Lee, "Refugees from Laos."

19. See Quincy, *Harvesting Pa Chay's Wheat*; Dommen, *Indochinese Experience of the French and the Americans*.

20. There is a discrepancy in the year Blia Yao Lor died. Historian Alfred McCoy writes that Lor died in 1933; ethnic-studies scholar Kou Yang suggests the year to be 1935.

21. Quincy, *Harvesting Pa Chay's Wheat*, 46.

22. Evans, *Short History of Laos*, 137.

23. Chan, *Hmong Means Free*, 19–20.

24. Quincy, *Harvesting Pa Chay's Wheat*, 84.

25. Chan, *Hmong Means Free*, 20–21; Stuart-Fox, *History of Laos*, 70–74.

26. Lair, interview.

27. See Quincy, *Harvesting Pa Chay's Wheat*; Warner, *Shooting at the Moon*; Conboy and Morrison, *Shadow War*; Castle, *At War in the Shadow of Vietnam*; Hamilton-Merritt, *Tragic Mountains*.

28. Hamilton-Merritt, *Tragic Mountains*, 88; Quincy, *Harvesting Pa Chay's Wheat*, 176.

29. Quincy, *Harvesting Pa Chay's Wheat*, 135–58.

30. Lair, interview.

31. Landry Papers.

32. Leary Papers, "Interview with James W. (Bill) Lair and Lloyd (Pat) Landry."

33. For a detailed history of Raven forward air-control operations, see Robbins, *Ravens*.

34. Lair, interview.

35. U.S. Congress, Senate, *United States Security Agreements and Commitments Abroad*.

36. Evans, *Short History of Laos*, 147. Also see Warner, *Shooting at the Moon*.

37. Manivanh, "Day We Lost Lee Lue." Kham Phiou Manivanh was another T-28 pilot. He witnessed Lee Lue's plane being shot down by enemies on the ground.

38. Leary Papers, "Interview with James W. (Bill) Lair and Lloyd (Pat) Landry," 1.

39. "Laos: Deeper into the Other War."

40. Branfman, *Voices from the Plain of Jars*.

41. Ronk, "Legend of Long Cheng."

42. Ranard, *Hmong*, 6.

43. Duffy, "Literacy and L'Armée Clandestine," 3.

44. Choua Thao, interview with author, Minneapolis, Minn., August 10, 2005. Thao, who was the Hmong nurse working directly with USAID staff to recruit and train the nurses, provided this estimate.

45. Hamilton-Merritt, *Tragic Mountains*, 334. These estimates do not take into account the thousands who died while trying to escape from Laos since 1975.

46. Mai Yer Her, interview with author, St. Paul, Minn., January 2, 2006.

47. Xang Vang, interview with author, St. Paul, Minn., October 11, 2005.

48. Mao Vang Lee, interview with author, St. Paul, Minn., August 8, 2005.

49. Yia Lee, interview with author, St. Paul, Minn., August 8, 2005.

50. May A Yang, interview with author, St. Paul, Minn., June 24, 2006.

51. May Ia Lee, interview with author, Brooklyn Park, Minn., October 24, 2005.

52. Mao Heu Thao, interview with author, St. Paul, Minn., October 7, 2005.

53. Sai Lee, interview with author, St. Paul, Minn., January 2, 2006.

54. Mai Yer Her, interview with author, St. Paul, Minn., January 2, 2006.

55. Sai Lee, interview with author, St. Paul, Minn., January 2, 2006.

56. Peteet, "Refugees, Resistance, and Identity."

57. Dang Her, interview with author, Maple Grove, Minn., October 25, 2005.

58. Hendricks, Downing, and Deinard, *Hmong in Transition*, 26.

59. M. Lee, "Mai Lee."

60. Mao Heu Thao, interview with author, St. Paul, Minn., October 7, 2005.

61. Yia Lee, interview with author, St. Paul, Minn., August 8, 2005.

62. May Ia Lee, interview with author, Brooklyn Park, Minn., October 24, 2005.

63. Very little is known about them. The only information is anecdotes from relatives residing in the United States. Some who resettled in China had moved back to Laos where they were able to inform their relatives in the United States of their whereabouts.

64. Hassoun, *Hmong du Laos en France*, 23.

65. T. T. Yang, "Hmong of Germany."

Chapter 2: A New Home in America

1. Nemes, "Welcome Refugees."

2. Daniels, *Coming to America*, 368–70.

3. Downing and Olney, *Hmong in Transitions*, 182–83.

4. Ibid., 18.

5. U.S. Department of Health and Human Services, Office of Refugee Resettlement, *Annual Report to Congress—2005*.

6. Downing and Olney, *Hmong in Transitions*, 185.

7. Ibid.

8. Proposals to solve secondary migration and dependency problems are outlined in a document by Derek M. Schoen, director, region 5, Chicago, U.S. Department of Health and Human Services. The document titled "Lessening Hmong Refugee Dependency: A Proposed Federal/State/Private Sector Strategy" outlines the issues and argues for building leadership as a way to eliminate major barriers to self-sufficiency. Other documents also show the involvement of Hmong community leaders in promoting work as outlined in a Lao Family Community of Minnesota board resolution calling for all Laotian refugees to "actively seek and accept employment now in order to achieve economic self-support at the earliest time possible." Box 2, vol. 3, Public Welfare Department Refugee Program Office, Minnesota Archives.

9. A sponsor to a refugee family, box 22, General/Multiethnic Collection. This letter was found in the refugee family's case file. It appears that the family did not know how to read it, and thus it is possible that the letter was brought to a bilin-

gual caseworker at the International Institute to read. Given that no other letters were found in this particular file, perhaps communication did not continue.

10. "Statement of Understanding," General/Multiethnic Collection. A copy of this signed statement is in almost all of the case files. The statement is also available in Hmong.

11. Sherman, "Hmong's Blue Ridge Refuge."

12. Ly Vang, interview with author, Minneapolis, Minn., August 18, 2005.

13. Shong Yang, interview with author, St. Paul, Minn., May 4, 2006.

14. Mai Yer Her, interview with author, St. Paul, Minn., January 2, 2006.

15. Xang Vang, interview with author, St. Paul, Minn., October 11, 2005.

16. Beck, "Ordeal of Immigration in Wausau," 88.

17. Jane Kretzman, interview with author, St. Paul, Minn., May 12, 2005.

18. Xang Vang, interview.

19. Chai Lue Kue, interview with author, Mohnton, Penn., March 29, 2008.

20. Pfeifer, "Hmong Alone Population Estimates."

21. Pipher, *Middle of Everywhere*, 284.

22. Pfeifer and Lee, "Hmong Population," 3–11.

23. Surprisingly, estimates from the American Community Survey in 2007 list Hmong populations only in twenty-seven states. Pfeifer, "Hmong Alone Population Estimates."

24. Pfeifer and Lee, "Hmong Population," 3–11. The states include California (65,095), Minn. (41,800), Wisconsin (33,791), North Carolina (7,093), Michigan (5,383), Colorado (3,000), Oregon (2,101), Georgia (1,468), Washington (1,294), Massachusetts (1,127), Kansas (1,004), and Rhode Island (1,001).

25. The Twin Cities of St. Paul and Minneapolis are contiguous, separated only by the Mississippi River. Thus, researchers tend to consolidate their populations when examining concentration.

26. States with more than 100 percent change were North Carolina (1,204 percent), Massachusetts (741 percent), Georgia (280 percent), Oregon (253 percent), Colorado (149 percent), Minnesota (135 percent) and Michigan (134 percent). Pfeifer and Lee, "Hmong Population," 5.

27. Ibid., 3–11.

28. Pfeifer, "Hmong Alone Population Estimates."

29. Tsong, "Volunteer Helps Anchorage's Growing Hmong Population Integrate."

30. Haines, *Case Studies in Diversity*, 1.

31. Roberts and Starr, "Differential Reference Group Assimilation among Vietnamese Refugees," 42–43.

32. Zhou, *Chinatown*, 14–15.

33. Lin, *Reconstructing Chinatown*, 6.

34. For a comprehensive history of refugee resettlement in Minnesota, see C. Y. Vang, *Hmong in Minnesota*.

35. Dang Her, interview with author, Maple Grove, Minn., October 29, 2005; Shoua Moua, interview with author, Maple Grove, Minn., October 29, 2005; and May Ia Lee, interview with author, Brooklyn Park, Minn., October 24, 2005.

36. Again, these data are only for those who received services from the International Institute of Minnesota. Other refugees did live in St. Paul and elsewhere.

37. Hein, *Ethnic Origins*, 101.

38. Case records, Boxes 21–27, General/Multiethnic Collection. Data for Hmong resettled cases were analyzed by this author. Residential patterns discussed here are the findings from analyzing all of the case records available in this collection.

39. Downing and Olney, *Hmong in Transitions*, 185.

40. "History of Hmong International New Year."

41. Crocker Stephenson, "Hmong Change Land That's Changing Them," *Milwaukee (Wisconsin) Journal Sentinel*, August 22, 1999, http://www.jsonline.com (accessed January 3, 2008).

42. "New Roots in Wausau—the Hmong," *Daily Herald (Wausau-Merrill, Wis.)*, August 29, 1984.

43. The celebration "Twenty Years from Home" was held in May 1995 as part of Wausau 2000—a COMMUNITY UNITED, an effort established in 1992 to identify concerns and challenges of assimilating minority populations in Wausau, Wisconsin. Event programs and newspaper article are available at Marathon County Historical Society located in Wausau.

44. Koltyk, *New Pioneers in the Heartland*, 4.

45. "Finding a Job Here Is Hard Work: Lack of Skills and Economy Are to Blame," *Daily Herald (Wausau-Merrill, Wis.)*, August 29, 1985, 5.

46. "Ginseng Fields Best Chance to Find Work," *Daily Herald (Wausau-Merrill, Wis.)*, August 29, 1984.

47. Tim Pirkl, "Hmong Launch Business: Shoemaking Firm Locates in Wausau," *Daily Herald (Wausau-Merrill, Wis.)*, June 13, 1989.

48. The Web site for the Wausau (Wisconsin) Area Hmong Mutual Association was http://www.wausauhmong.org.

49. United Hmong Association of North Carolina, *Needs Assessment Report*, 4.

50. North Carolina Department of Health and Human Services, "500 Hmong refugees to come to North Carolina."

51. United Hmong Association of North Carolina, *Needs Assessment Report*, 4.

52. Pfeifer and Lee, "Hmong Population," 9.

53. Kathleen Parrish, "A Common Thread Starts to Fray in Quilt Country," *Morning Call (Allentown, Pennsylvania)*, repr. Seattle Times, May 11, 2006, http://community.seattletimes.nwsource.com/archive (accessed June 12, 2007).

54. Desan, "Change of Faith for Hmong Refugees."

55. Shong Chai Hang, interview with author, Pottsdam, Penn., March 30, 2008.

56. Chai Lue Kue and May Houa Vang, interview with author, Mohnton, Penn., March 29, 2008.

57. Kao Nhia Kue, interview with author and observation, Mohnton, Penn., March 29, 2008; May Houa Vang, interview with author and observation, Mohnton, Penn., March 29, 2008.

58. May Houa Vang, interview with author, Mohnton, Penn., March 29, 2008.

59. Advertisement, Jack Elder, Tall Star Realty, Gentry, Arkansas, *Hmong Today*, http://www.hmongtoday.comfs (accessed November 12, 2007).

60. Hmong National Development, "Capacity Building." HND implemented a program for economic enhancement opportunities for small and disadvantaged poultry farmers program to assist Hmong poultry farmers about the risks of poultry production.

61. Mee Thao [pseud.] and Pao Thao [pseud.], interview with author, Danville, Arkansas, June 27, 2006. According to Mee and Pao, they have lost their farm due to flipping by the realtor, who collaborated with the banker to sell them the farm through a U.S. Department of Agriculture–backed loan. The realtor and the banker overpriced the farm, and once the new owners took ownership, the business did not generate enough income to sustain itself. The couple requested that their identities not be revealed, so pseudonyms are used.

62. Jeanette Jones [pseud.], interview with author, June 24, 2006. Jones, a realtor, indicated that her business had skyrocketed due to the Hmong. Her schedule was booked for the next three weeks to show farms to Hmong from Sheboygan, Wisconsin; Sacramento, California; Lincoln, Nebraska; and St. Paul, Minnesota. Jones requested that her real name not be given, so a pseudonym is used.

Chapter 3: Re-creation of Social Structures

1. Soyer, *Jewish Immigrant Associations and American Identity in New York, 1880–1939*; Olney, *We Must Be Organized.*

2. Basch, "Vincentians and Grenadians," 162–63.

3. Ueda, "Immigration in Global Historical Perspective," 14.

4. Niedzwiecki, Pich, Yang, Tran, and King, *Directory of Southeast Asian American Community-Based Organizations 2004*, i. Although those MAAs established to provide social services to refugees continue to use this term, the many organizations that emerged in the 1990s frequently refer to themselves as community-based organizations because many are engaged in broader issues than refugee basic-needs support. Thus, this author uses the terms interchangeably.

5. Ranard, "Mutual Assistance Associations," 1–2.

6. Abhay, "Leadership and Management," 9.

7. U.S. Department of Health and Human Services, *Annual ORR Report to Congress—2005*. A brief history of the Office of Refugee Resettlement is available on the department's Web site.

8. Dunnigan, Olney, McNall, and Spring, "Hmong," 161.

9. Xang Vang, interview with author, St. Paul, Minn., October 11, 2005.

10. Tong Vang, interview with author, St. Paul, Minn., August 8, 2005.

11. Tou Fu Vang and Leng Vang to the Commissioner of the Minnesota Department of Human Rights, August 2, 1977, vol. 2, Refugee Program Office Records. This letter from Hmong community leaders highlights the need for the organization and outlines the various struggles refugees were facing.

12. Ibid.

13. Dang Her, interview with author, Maple Grove, Minn., October 29, 2005.

14. Tou Fu Vang and Leng Vang to the Commissioner of the Minnesota Department of Human Rights, August 2, 1977, vol. 2, Refugee Program Office Records; Dang Her, Tong Vang, and Xang Vang, interviews with author, Maple Grove, St. Paul, and St. Paul, Minn., October 29, 2005, August 8, 2005, and October 11, 2005, respectively. Dang Her and Tong Vang are cofounders of the Hmong Association, and Xang Vang was its executive director when the organization became Lao Family Community of Minnesota.

15. Xang Vang, interview with author, St. Paul, Minn., October 11, 2005.

16. Four Lao Family organizations currently exist in the state of California in

the cities of Fresno, Merced, Sacramento, and Stockton. Milwaukee has the only LF organization in Wisconsin.

17. Her Dang, interview with author, Maple Grove, Minn., October 29, 2005.

18. In terms of community politics, board members are elected by LF members, thus limiting participation of others who may not perceive General Vang Pao's influence positively.

19. The chair of the Lao Family board of directors has included members from several clans. The only two executive directors from 1981 to 2008 were from the Vang clan. Lao Family's intimate ties to General Vang Pao has resulted in a resentment from some members of the Hmong population that the organization is biased toward other clan members for leadership positions. Retirement of Ying Vang has resulted in the hiring of Long X. Yang, which has been praised by some community leaders as a strategic direction for the organization as it is the oldest organization in the state.

20. Ly Vang, interview with author, Minneapolis, Minn., August 18, 2005. In 2005, AAHWM moved its offices to St. Paul and has continued to provide basic-needs support to Hmong families.

21. May Ia Lee, interview with author, Brooklyn Park, Minn., October 24, 2005.

22. Gaoly Yang, interview with author, St. Paul, Minn., September 14, 2005.

23. Ly Vang, interview with author, Minneapolis, Minn., August 18, 2005.

24. See Dunnigan, "Segmentary Kinship in an Urban Society"; Olney, *We Must Be Organized.*

25. P. Thao, "Mong Resettlement in the Chicago Area," 28.

26. The Hmong Youth Association of Minnesota was founded in the early 1990s but folded by the mid-1990s due to lack of funding and other leadership challenges.

27. For more organization information, see Hmong American Partnership's Web site, http://hmong.org.

28. Sao Sue Jurewitsch, "Hmong American Partnership Crisis Deepens: HAP Board and Yang Supporters' Feud Threatens Hmong Non-Profit's Future," *Hmong Times,* April 16, 2007.

29. Sao Sue Jurewitsch, "Hmong Times Interview: New HAP Executive Director Bao Ka Vang," *Hmong Times,* August 16, 2007.

30. For additional information, see Hmong Cultural Center's Web site, http://www.hmongcc.org.

31. For more information, see Center for Hmong Studies, Concordia University–St. Paul, http://www.csp.edu/hmongcenter.

32. "Hmong Arts Connection."

33. IRAC eventually changed its name to Southeast Asia Resource Action Center (SEARAC). It continues to operate out of Washington, D.C.

34. For more information, see Hmong National Development's Web site, http://www.hndinc.org.

35. For more information, see Wisconsin United Coalition of Mutual Assistance Associations, http://www.wucmaa.org.

36. See T. T. Vang, "Coming a Full Circle"; Kue, *Hmong Church History.*

37. *Lao* in this context refers to all people who live within the country of Laos and not just the ethnic Lao group.

38. T. T. Vang, "Coming a Full Circle," ix.

39. Ibid., 60.

40. Capecchi, "Hmong Combine Old Heritage with New Faith as Numbers Grow."

41. In addition to Kue, *Hmong Church History*, and T. T. Vang, "Coming a Full Circle," see Andrianoff and Andrianoff, *Chosen by the God of Grace.*

42. T. T. Vang, "Coming a Full Circle," ix.

43. Chou Vang, interview with author, Inver Grove Heights, Minn., May 13, 2006.

44. T. T. Vang, "Coming a Full Circle," 126–27.

45. Her, interview with Peter Chou Vang.

46. Ibid.

47. Green/Blue Hmong and White Hmong are the same ethnic group. The primary difference between the two is dialect and costumes.

48. Bertrais, "Txiv Plig Nyiaj Pov hais lus [Father Yves Bertrais 2002 Radio]." Transcription and translation by author.

49. Tapp, *Sovereignty and Rebellion*, 91.

50. T. T. Vang, "Coming a Full Circle," 166.

51. Sai Lee, interview with author, St. Paul, Minn., January 2, 2006.

52. Detzner, *Elder Voices*, 6.

53. Mai Yer Her, interview with author, St. Paul, Minn., January 2, 2006.

54. Nawyn, "Faith, Ethnicity, and Culture in Refugee Resettlement."

55. Her, interview with P. C. Vang.

56. Xao Vue, interview with author, Minneapolis, Minn., March 13, 2006.

57. Shoua Vue, interview with author, Minneapolis, Minn., May 3, 2006.

58. Chen, *Getting Saved in America*, 38.

59. Ranard, *Hmong*, 9.

60. The only formally trained Hmong American woman pastor, Bee Vue-Benson, does not serve a Hmong congregation.

61. Desan, "Change of Faith for Hmong Refugees," 47.

62. Ibid.

63. Nha Long Yang, interview with author, Maplewood, Minn., August 10, 2006. Dr. Yang is the senior pastor of St. Paul Hmong Alliance Church.

64. Ibid.

65. Kue, *Hmong Church History*, 111.

66. "Churches by Language and Ethnic Group." The information is through 2008.

67. "Churches."

68. "HBNA Member Churches."

69. Benhabib, *Claims of Culture*, 1.

70. Xang Vang, interview with author, St. Paul, Minn. October 11, 2005.

71. Shoua Vang, interview with author, Hugo, Minn., October 3, 2005.

72. Chou Vang, interview with author, Inver Grove Heights, Minn., May 13, 2006.

73. Miranda Joseph, *Against the Romance of Community*, 86–87.

74. Detzner, *Elder Voices*, 14.

75. Karner, *Ethnicity and Everyday Life*, 6.

76. Xao Vue, interview with author, Minneapolis, Minn., March 13, 2006.

77. Xiong and Xiong, "Critique of Timothy Vang's Hmong Religious Conversion and Resistance Study," 2–3.

78. Mao Heu Thao, interview with author, St. Paul, Minn., October 7, 2005.

79. Dang Her, interview with author, Maple Grove, Minn., October 29, 2005.

80. Ebaugh and Chafetz, *Religion and the New Immigrants*, 450.

81. Ong, *Flexible Citizenship*, 110.

82. Maile Vue, interview with author, Minneapolis, Minn., May 15, 2006.

83. Ebaugh and Chafetz, *Religion and the New Immigrants*, 431.

84. Nha Long Yang, interview with author, Maplewood, Minn., August 10, 2006.

Chapter 4: Continuity and Reinvention of Traditions

1. D. Yang, "Keeb Kwm Tsiab Peb Caug Hmoob [Hmong New Year Rituals]," *Haiv Hmoob* (St. Paul, Minnesota), November 1985, 38–42. In this community-newsletter article, Yang describes in Hmong language the importance of the New Year in Hmong society and takes the reader through the New Year process: "Nyob ntawm lub zos loj zos me, cim Tsiab Peb Caug Hmoob rub ntev plaub tsib hnub mus rau kaum tawm hnub. Sawv daws tau los noj sib cuag nyob sib fim, koom siab kom ntsws sib pab ua neej nyob kom vam meej nto moo lug mus yav tom ntej. Tej no tau ua rau peb haiv Hmoob nco ntsoov txog peb poj koob yam txiv tej kev cai dab qhuas. Txawm peb Hmoob yuav mus poob rau thaj av twg, lub teb chaws twg los lub nroog twg, sawv daws thiaj tseem pheej fwm lub tsiab peb caug Hmoob cia. . . . Vim qhov hais tias ib lub tsev npaj ib tug npua tsiab, ib lub zos Hmoob thiaj noj tsiab tsis tu ncua txog 4–5 hnub. Tus mab tus qhua tuaj txog Hmoob vaj Hmoob tsev los puav leej tau raug caw mus nrog Hmoog noj Hmoob haus tib si." (The English translation is the extract in the main text.)

2. When words are written in Hmong language in this book, I include both dialects unless such words are written in the same way in both Green and White Hmong. I provide the Green Hmong version followed by the White Hmong word. If I refer to the same word again in other sections of the book, I list only the Green Hmong version.

3. K. Yang, "Assessment of the Hmong American New Year and Its Implications for Hmong-American Culture," 5–6.

4. Lynch, "Hmong-American New Year Dress."

5. Shoua Vang, interview with author, Hugo, Minn., October 3, 2005.

6. K. Yang, "Assessment of the Hmong American New Year and Its Implications for Hmong-American Culture," 6.

7. Although married women do not engage in ball tossing, married men often do so with unmarried women.

8. Bourdieu, *Distinction*, 101.

9. Dang Her, interview with author, Maple Grove, Minn., October 29, 2005.

10. Buff, *Immigration and the Political Economy of Home*, 34.

11. Shoua Vang, interview with author, Hugo, Minn., October 3, 2005.

12. Tong Vang, interview with author, St. Paul, Minn., August 8, 2005.

13. Ly Vang, interview with author, Minneapolis, Minn., August 18, 2005.

14. Association of Hmong in Minnesota, "Happy New Year," 3.

15. Ibid.

16. Village leaders played important roles in the village context, and others such as Vang Pao were prominent during the Vietnam War era. However, the recognition and speeches that are delivered in diasporic New Year celebrations serve different purposes.

17. Ly Vang, interview with author, Minneapolis, Minn., August 18, 2005.

18. Yia Lee, interview with author, St. Paul, Minn., September 2, 2005.

19. Shong Yang, interview with author, St. Paul, Minn., May 4, 2006.

20. P. Levine, "Americanization and Globalization," 15.

21. Ly Vang, interview with author, Minneapolis, Minn., August 18, 2005.

22. Shong Yang, interview with author, St. Paul, Minn., May 4, 2006.

23. Chou Vang, interview with author, Inver Grove Heights, Minn., May 13, 2006.

24. Daobay Ly, interview with author, Minneapolis, Minn., October 25, 2005.

25. Benhabib, *Claims of Culture*, 184.

26. Ly Vang, interview with author, Minneapolis, Minn., August 18, 2005.

27. The controversy was due to the fact that the individual who sponsored the dance instructor was married to a Hmong American woman.

28. Toua Thao, interview with author, St. Paul, Minn., October 22, 2005.

29. Gaoly Yang interview with author, St. Paul, Minn., September 14, 2005.

30. Hmong New Year celebration video, 2002, private collection. The translation from Hmong to English is the author's.

31. Ly Vang, interview with author, Minneapolis, Minn., August 18, 2005.

32. Shong Yang, interview with author, St. Paul, Minn., May 4, 2006.

33. Al-Ali and Koser, *New Approaches to Migration?* 5.

34. Xang Vang, interview with author, St. Paul, Minn., October 11, 2005.

35. Ly Vang, interview with author, Minneapolis, Minn., August 18, 2005.

36. Mao Heu Thao, interview with author, St. Paul, Minn., October 7, 2005.

37. Neng Va Lo, interview with author, Woodbury, Minn., March 12, 2005.

38. Txong Pao Lee, interview with author, in St. Paul, Minn., May 8, 2006.

39. Shoua Moua, interview with author, Maple Grove, Minn., October 29, 2005.

40. Bauz L. Nengchu, interview with author, St. Paul, Minn., May 10, 2006.

41. Chao Lee, "Hmong New Year Eroding Its Tradition," *Hmong Tribune*, December 1998, 11.

42. Koua Yang, "A Forever and a Day Dream," *Hmong Tribune*, December, 11.

43. Daobay Ly, interview with author, Minneapolis, Minn., October 25, 2005.

44. Detzner, *Elder Voices*, 14.

45. Bauz L. Nengchu, interview with author, St. Paul, Minn., May 10, 2006. Bauz Nengchu's father had studied in France in the late 1950s and was living and working there in the early 1970s. Prior to the communist takeover of Laos, her father advised her to go to France in 1974, where she lived until 1979.

46. Chou Vang, interview with author, Inver Grove Heights, Minn., May 13, 2006.

47. Random interviews, Hmong New Year celebration videos, 2000–4. Private collection.

48. These titles are from the various pageants this author observed as well as an Internet search under "Hmong New Year beauty pageant."

Chapter 5: Political Activism

1. Even though Hmong may have status other than refugee, they use the description of perpetual refugee as a way to obtain resources for those in need.

2. See Lowe, *Immigrant Acts*, 5; Tuan, *Forever Foreigners or Honorary Whites*, 37; Wu, *Yellow*, 79–129.

3. Kasinitz, *Caribbean New York*, 7.

4. Ibid., 160–61.

5. Choua Thao, interview with author, Minneapolis, Minn., August 10, 2005.

6. Xang Vang, interview with author, St. Paul, Minn., October 11, 2005.

7. When Jesse Ventura was running for office, he visited with Hmong Americans in the Twin Cities, many of whom campaigned on his behalf.

8. This author was a lobbyist for a research and advocacy organization in St. Paul during this period and worked with community organizations on many hunger- and poverty-related issues.

9. During the 1995 veterans' recognition ceremony, a large sign with "America's most loyal allies" hung in the back of the stage.

10. See Hamilton-Merritt, *Tragic Mountains*; Warner, *Back Fire*; Conboy and Morrison, *Shadow War*.

11. Hamilton-Merritt, *Tragic Mountains*, 130.

12. Khaab, "Washington, DC Commencement, May 14–15, 1997."

13. Lao Veterans of America, "Hall of Fame." The word "Yov" on the plague is misspelled, thus the phrase as it is has no meaning. The spelling should be "Yuav." The sentence is in Lao and Hmong languages.

14. Lao-Hmong American Coalition.

15. Steve Thao, *Hmong Tribune*, August 4, 1998.

16. Vento was a twelve-term, Democrat congressman for the Fourth District in Minnesota, which includes the East Side of St. Paul, where many Hmong live.

17. "President Signs H.R. 371/P.L. 106-207 the 'Hmong Veterans' Naturalization Act of 2000.'"

18. Clinton, "Statement on Signing the Hmong Veterans Naturalization Act of 2000."

19. U.S. Department of State, "Excerpt House Passes Resolution on Lao-Hmong Recognition Day."

20. Emmett Timmons, "Minnesota Honors Lao War Veterans," *Asian American Press*, July 22, 2006.

21. Ibid. Chris Coleman and Norman Coleman are not related.

22. Schofield, *Brief History of the Hmong and the Secret War in Laos*; Eric Litke, "Brothers in Arms: U.S. Medic Pushed for Memorial," *Sheboygan (Wisconsin) Press*, http://www.sheboyganpress.com/article/99999999/SHE0101/101110007/1973 (accessed March 31, 2010). Schofield was in the Special Forces in Vietnam and Laos during the 1960s.

23. "Brothers in Arms: The Dedication of the Lao, Hmong and American Veterans Memorial," special commemorative program, *Sheboygan (Wisconsin) Press*, July 15, 2006, 5.

24. May Joseph, *Nomadic Identities*, 11.

25. Ibid.

26. Paul Demko, "A Face-Lift for the St. Paul City Council: Primaries Could

Mean a Stronger, Tougher Lineup," *City Pages,* September 3, 2003, www.citypages. com (accessed August 23, 2006).

27. Demko, "Party of Nine."

28. Ibid.

29. Xa Moua, "Christopher Moua (Rep) Runs for St. Paul City Council," *Hmong Times,* June 16, 2003.

30. "Hmong Candidates Seek Two of Four St. Paul School Board Positions: Kazoua Kong-Thao and Michael Yang," *Hmong Times,* April 1, 2003.

31. Kong-Thao, "Running for School Board."

32. At the celebration, this author conversed with Mee Moua about her campaign.

33. The telephone strategy has also been used by other larger-community candidates. Providing transportation and interpreting have been viewed by some opponents as unfair because voters who are assisted by volunteers supporting a particular candidate will likely vote for such candidate.

34. Wameng Moua, "Victorious Pakou Hang Prepares for Long Road Ahead," *Hmong Today,* June 1, 2007.

35. "About Us."

36. B. Anderson, *Imagined Communities,* 6.

37. B. Anderson, *Spectre of Comparisons,* 58–74.

38. Dufoix, *Diasporas,* 95.

39. P. Vang, "Against All Odds."

40. Ibid.

41. Ruth Hammond, "Rumors of War," *Twin Cities (Minnesota) Reader,* October 25–31, 1989, 8.

42. Ibid., 10.

43. Ibid., 10.

44. Ruth Hammond, "The Great Refugee Shakedown: The Hmong Are Paying to Free Laos—But What's Happening to the Money," *Washington Post,* April 16, 1989.

45. Tony Kennedy and Paul McEnroe, "Reality Gets in the Way of Loyalty to General," *(Minneapolis) Star Tribune,* July 4, 2005, http://www.startribune.com/local/11581761.html?elr=KArksUUUoDEy3LGDiO7aiU.

46. Gregg Aamot, "Old Tension Sparks Violence in Minnesota Area," *(Minneapolis) Star Tribune,* May 13, 2004.

47. Jo Napolitano, "Police See Arson in Destruction of Hmong Leader's Home," *New York Times,* April 29, 2004.

48. United Lao Council for Peace, Freedom, and Reconstruction, "Lao Conflict," 10.

49. Ruhi Hamid, "One Day of War."

50. United Lao Council for Peace, Freedom, and Reconstruction, "Lao Conflict," 10, 10, 11, 20–22.

51. Joshua Kurlantzick, "Guerrillas in Our Midst," *Boston Globe,* June 10, 2007.

52. T. Xiong, "Bush Signs Law Excluding Hmong From Patriot Act."

53. Scott, "Indictment Handed Down in Plot to Overthrow the Government of Laos." Scott was a United States Attorney, Eastern District of California.

54. *United States of America v. Harrison Ulrich Jack,* 4–5.

55. Weiner, *Legacy of Ashes*, 235.

56. Denny Walsh, "Hmong Make Their Case: General's Release Demanded by Crowd, Denied by Judge," *Sacramento (California) Bee*, June 12, 2007, http://www.sacbee.com.

57. Txiabneeb Vang, "All Shook Up!" June 6, 2007. This initial message from a Hmong American community member in Minnesota listed more than a hundred e-mail addresses, including this author, who received copies of the e-mail messages exchanged among Hmong Americans in the Midwest from June 6 through June 13, 2007.

58. Curt Brown, "Many Hmong Don't Back the General: 'This is our home now,'" *(Minneapolis) Star Tribune*, June 6, 2007, http://www.startribune.com.

59. This author observed the July 12, 2007, demonstration in Madison, Wisconsin, one of several held there.

60. Denny Walsh and Todd Milbourn, "Vang Pao Gains Bail," *Sacramento (California) Bee*, July 13, 2007, http://www.sacbee.com (accessed January 30, 2009).

61. Denny Walsh, "Feds Dropped Charges against Hmong Leader Vang Pao," *Sacramento (California) Bee*, September 18, 2009, http://www.sacbee.com/2009/09/18/2192606/feds-drop-charges-against-hmong.html (accessed March 31, 2010). Other sample headlines include: Eric Bailey and My-Thuan Tran, "Federal Charges Dropped against Hmong Leader Vang Pao," *Los Angeles Times*, September 19, 2009, http://articles.latimes.com/2009/sep/19/local/me-vang-pao19 (accessed March 31, 2010); Paul McEnroe and Richard Meryhew, "Overthrow Charges against Vang Are Dropped," *(Minneapolis) Star Tribune*, September 19, 2009, http://www.startribune.com/local/stpaul/59802237.html (accessed March 31, 2010); McClatchy News Service, "Hmong Leader Dropped from Charges," *Milwaukee (Wisconsin) Journal Sentinel*, September 18, 2009, http://www.jsonline.com/news/usandworld/59805812.html (accessed March 31, 2010); and Jesse McKinley, "U.S. Drops Case against Exiled Hmong Leader," *New York Times*, September 18, 2009. http://www.nytimes.com/2009/09/19/us/19general.html (accessed March 31, 2010).

62. "Hmong Grave Desecration Timeline."

63. Randolph, "Hmong Protest Grave Desecration."

64. "Resolution City of Saint Paul, Minnesota," *Hmong Times*, May 1, 2007.

65. Myron P. Medcalf, "Hmong Group Vandalized Grave Sites Not a Political Issue," *Minneapolis (Minnesota) Star Tribune*, October 26, 2007.

66. Hume, "St. Paul Mayor to Send Mission about Hmong Graves"; Cheryl Sherry, "Hmong Fight over Exhumed Bodies a 'Human Thing'" *Post-Crescent (Appleton, Wisconsin)*, October 28, 2007.

67. Kathy Mouacheupao, "St. Paul Delegation Reports on Hmong Graves in Wat Tham Krabok," *Twin Cities (Minnesota) Daily Planet*, October 15, 2007, http://www.tcdailyplanet.net/article/2007/10/13/st-paul-delegation-reports-hmong-graves-wat-tham-krabok.html.

68. Sao Sue Jurewitsch, "Two Minnesota Delegations Visit Thailand over Hmong Grave Desecration," *Hmong Times*, September 27, 2007, http//www.hmongtimes.com.

69. Frommer, "Senators Call on U.S. to Thailand on Hmong Refugees."

70. Chang, introduction, 3.

71. Nakanishi, "Beyond Electoral Politics," 112–13.

72. Zia, *Asian American Dreams*, 258–59.

73. Steve Thao, "Hit the Road Racism! KQRS Warned by Community," *Hmong Tribune*, August 24, 1998, 1, 3.

74. See *State of Wisconsin v. Chai Soua Vang.*

75. Curt Brown, "Hmong Leaders Say Suspect Doesn't Represent Community," *Star Tribune (Minneapolis–St. Paul)*, Wednesday, November 24, 2004, http://www.startribune.com (accessed December 3, 2006).

76. "National Southeast Asian American Groups Call for Healing and Unity after Shootings in Wisconsin."

77. Sample articles of this nature are Dirk Johnson, "Slaughter in the Woods," *Newsweek*, December 6, 2004, 28, and "In Rampage, Hunters Became the Hunted," Associated Press, *St. Petersburg (Florida) Times*, November 23, 20, 4, 1A.

78. Badillo, "Save a Hunter, Shoot a Hmong."

79. Wameng Moua, "Coalition Observations: Trial Was Biased," *Hmong Today*, November 3, 2005.

80. An example of article of this nature is Grinberg, "Trial Opens for Hmong Refugee Who Killed Six Deer Hunters."

81. Gramling, "Racial Justice Rally at Wis. Capitol."

Conclusion

1. G. Y. Lee, "Ethnic Minorities and Nation Building in Laos."

2. Patricia Leigh Brown, "A Doctor for Disease, a Shaman for the Soul," *New York Times*, September 19, 2009, http://www.nytimes.com/2009/09/20/us/20shaman.html (accessed March 31, 2010).

3. Elizabeth Thao, "First Nationally Recognized Hmong New Year Celebration in Laos Held on November 27, 2008," *Hmong Times*, January 28, 2009.

4. "Hmong Doctorates," Christian Hmong Fellowship. This is not a complete list. On its Web site, Christian Hmong Fellowship, dedicated to empowering young Hmong Americans, states that this data collection is meant to inspire young people to pursue higher education. The percentages are calculated by this author. Although the list contains many names with degrees, detailed information is available only for slightly more than 10 percent. For example, types of degrees obtained are identified, but where individuals received their degrees and their current practice/profession are not available. Of the 113 PhDs listed, information about degree, institution, and place of employment is available for only 25 individuals. The estimate of female PhDs is based on a count of women's names on the list so the estimate may actually be slightly higher since all gender-neutral names were assumed to be male.

5. K. Yang, "Hmong in America," 171.

6. Long Cheng, also spelled Long Tieng, was the so-called CIA secret base from which Vang Pao and American military advisers operated.

7. Sam Thong, the humanitarian headquarters where the hospital and schools were built, served as the showcase for visiting American dignitaries.

8. Chou Vang, interview with author, Inver Grove Heights, Minn., May 13, 2006.

9. Toua Thao, interview with author, St. Paul, Minn., October 22, 2005.

10. Gaoly Yang, interview with author, St. Paul, Minn., September 14, 2005.

11. Clint Eastwood, *Gran Torino.*

12. In the 1983 film from New Day Films *Becoming American: The Odyssey of a Refugee Family,* directors Ken Levine and Ivory Waterworth Levine capture the journey of a young Hmong family from a Thai refugee camp to Seattle, Washington. The film predicted that the young children of the refugees will unlikely ever see the homeland of their parents.

BIBLIOGRAPHY

Abhay, Krisna. "Leadership and Management: A Comparative Study of MAAs." *Refugee Participation Network.* Oxford: Refugee Studies Programme, University of Oxford, 1992, 9–12.

"About Lao Family Community of Minnesota Inc." *Lao Family Community of Minnesota Inc.* http://www.laofamily.org/about-lao-family.htm (accessed March 31, 2010).

"About Us." *St. Paul Public Schools.* http://www.spps.org/AboutUs.html (accessed March 31, 2010).

Affigne, Tony, and Pei-te Lien. "Peoples of Asian Descent in the Americas: Theoretical Implications of Race and Politics." *Amerasia Journal* 28, no. 2 (2002): 1–26.

Al-Ali, Nadje, and Khalid Koser, eds. *New Approaches to Migration? Transnational Communities and the Transformation of Home.* New York: Routledge, 2002.

Anderson, Benedict. *Imagined Communities: Reflections on the Origin and Spread of Nationalism.* Rev. ed. New York: Verso, 1991.

———. *The Spectre of Comparisons: Nationalism, Southeast Asia, and the World.* New York: Verso, 1998.

Anderson, Wanni W., and Robert G. Lee. "Asian American Displacements." In *Displacements and Diasporas: Asians in the Americas,* edited by Anderson and Lee, 3–22. New Brunswick: Rutgers University Press, 2005.

Andrianoff, Jean, and Andrianoff, Ruth. *Chosen by the God of Grace: The Story of the Birth of the Hmong Church through the Eyes of Ted and Ruth Andrianoff.* Camp Hill, Penn.: Christian, 2000.

Appadurai, Arjun. *Modernity at Large: Cultural Dimensions of Globalization.* Minneapolis: University of Minnesota Press, 1996.

Association of Hmong in Minnesota. "Happy New Year." *Hmong Newsletter* 1, no. 7 (1981): 3.

Badillo, Aimee J. "Save a Hunter, Shoot a Hmong: A Community Held Responsible—The Assignment of Blame by the Media." *Modern American* 1, no. 1, April 2005. *Vlex,* 2010. http://vlex.com/vid/hunter-shoot-hmong-assignment-blame-343429 (accessed March 12, 2010).

Baizerman, Michael, and Glen Hendricks. *A Study of Southeast Asian Refugee Youth in the Twin Cities of Minneapolis and St. Paul, Minnesota. Final Report.* Minneapolis: Southeast Asian Refugee Studies, University of Minnesota, 1986.

Basch, Linda. "The Vincentians and Grenadians: The Role of Voluntary Associations in Immigrant Adaptation to New York City." In *New Immigrants in*

New York, edited by Nancy Foner, 159–94. New York: Columbia University Press, 1987.

Basch, Linda G., Nina Glick Schiller, and Cristina Blanc. *Unbound Nations: Transnational Projects, Postcolonial Predicaments, and Deterritorialized Nation-States*. Langhorne, Penn.: Gordon and Breach, 1994.

Beck, Roy. "The Ordeal of Immigration in Wausau." *Atlantic Monthly*, April 1994, 84–97.

Benhabib, Seyla. *The Claims of Culture: Equality and Diversity in the Global Era*. Princeton: Princeton University Press, 2002.

Bertrais, Yves. "Txiv Plig Nyiaj Pov hais lus [Father Yves Bertrais 2002 Radio]." By Xia Vue Yang. *Hmong RPA (Sheboygan, Wisconsin)*, August 1, 2002. http://www.hmongrpa.org/hmongrpa1.mp3 (accessed March 31, 2010).

Bourdieu, Pierre. *Distinction: A Social Critique of the Judgment of Taste*. Translated by Richard Nice. Cambridge, Mass.: Harvard University Press, 1984.

Branfman, Fred. *Voices from the Plain of Jars: Life under an Air War*. New York: Harper & Row, 1972.

Brothers in Arms. Sheboygan: Sheboygan (Wisconsin) Press, 2006.

Buff, Rachel. *Immigration and the Political Economy of Home: West Indian Brooklyn and American Indian Minneapolis, 1945–1992*. Berkeley: University of California Press, 2001.

Capecchi, Christina. "Hmong Combine Old Heritage with New Faith as Numbers Grow." *Catholic Spirit, Heritage: Roots & Traditions, Cultures & Customs of Catholic Minnesota*. http://extra.thecatholicspirit.com/heritage/hmong-combine-old-heritage.html (accessed March 31, 2010).

Castle, Timothy N. *At War in the Shadow of Vietnam: U.S. Military Aid to the Royal Lao Government, 1955–1975*. New York: Columbia University Press, 1993.

Castles, Stephen. "The Factors That Make and Unmake Migration Policies." In *Rethinking Migration: New Theoretical and Empirical Perspectives*, edited by Alejandro Portes and Josh DeWind, 29–61. New York: Berghahn Books, 2007.

Center for Hmong Studies. Concordia University–St. Paul, Minn. http://www.csp.edu/hmongcenter (accessed July 2006).

Chan, Sucheng. *Hmong Means Free: Life in Laos and in the United States*. Philadelphia, Penn.: Temple University Press, 1994.

Chang, Gordon. "Asian Americans and Politics." In Chang, *Asian Americans and Politics*, 13–38.

———, ed. *Asian Americans and Politics: Perspectives, Experiences, Prospects*. Stanford, Calif.: Stanford University Press, 2001.

———. Introduction. In Chang, *Asian Americans and Politics*, 1–12.

Chen, Carolyn. *Getting Saved in America: Taiwanese Immigration and Religious Experience*. Princeton: Princeton University Press, 2008.

"Churches." *Hmong District of the Christian and Missionary Alliance*. http://www.hmongdistrict.org (accessed April 12, 2008).

"Churches by Language and Ethnic Group." *Ethnic Christian Church Directory*. http://www.ethnicchurch.com/Language.aspx (accessed March 31, 2010).

Clifford, James. "Diasporas." *Cultural Anthropology* 9, no. 3 (1994): 302–38.

Clinton, William J. "Statement on Signing the Hmong Veterans Naturalization Act of 2000." May 26, 2000. *The American Presidency Project*. Edited by John

Woolley and Gerhard Peters. University of California, Santa Barbara. http://
www.presidency.ucsb.edu/ws/index.php?pid=58559&st=&st1= (accessed March
31, 2010).

Cohen, Robin. *Global Diasporas: An Introduction.* Seattle: Washington University Press, 1997.

Conboy, Kenneth, and James Morrison. *Shadow War: The CIA's Secret War in
Laos.* Boulder, Colo.: Paladin Press, 1995.

Cooper, Robert. "The Hmong of Laos: Economic Factors in Refugee Exodus and
Return." In Downing and Olney, *Hmong in Transitions,* 23–40.

Culas, Christian, and Jean Michaud. "A Contribution to the Study of Hmong
(Miao) Migrations and History." In Tapp, Michaud, Culas, and Lee, *Hmong/
Miao in Asia,* 61–96.

Daniels, Roger. *Coming to America: A History of Immigration and Ethnicity in
American Life.* 2nd ed. New York: HarpersCollins, 2002.

del Rosario, Carina A., ed. *A Different Battle: Stories of Asian Pacific American
Veterans.* Seattle: University of Washington Press, 1999.

Demko, Paul. "Party of Nine: The Ward One Race in St. Paul Promises to Be One
Nasty Scrum." *City Pages,* April 9, 2003. http://www.citypages.com/2003–
04–09/news/party-of-nine (accessed March 31, 2010).

Desan, Christine. "A Change of Faith for Hmong Refugees." *Cultural Survival Quarterly* 7, no. 3 (Fall, 1983): 45–48. http://www.culturalsurvival.org/
ourpublications/csq/article/a-change-faith-hmong-refugees (accessed March
31, 2010).

Detzner, Daniel F. *Elder Voices: Southeast Asian Families in the United States.*
Walnut Creek, Calif.: AltaMira Press, 2004.

DeWind, Josh, and Philip Kasinitz. "Everything Old Is New Again? Processes
and Theories of Immigrant Incorporation." *International Migration Review*
31, no. 4 (1997): 1096–111.

Dommen, Arthur J. *The Indochinese Experience of the French and the Americans:
Nationalism and Communism in Cambodia, Laos, and Vietnam.* Bloomington:
Indiana University Press, 2001.

Donnelly, Nancy. *Changing Lives of Hmong Women.* Seattle: University of Washington Press, 1997.

Downing, Bruce T., and Douglas Olney, eds. *The Hmong in Transitions.* Minneapolis: Center for Urban and Regional Affairs / University of Minnesota, 1982.

Duffy, John. "Literacy and L'Armée Clandestine: The Writings of Hmong Military
Scribes." *Hmong Studies Journal* 3 (2000): 1–32.

———. *Writing from These Roots: Literacy in a Hmong-American Community.*
Honolulu: University of Hawaii Press, 2007.

Dufoix, Stéphane. *Diasporas.* Berkeley: University of California, 2008.

Dunnigan, Timothy. "Segmentary Kinship in an Urban Society: The Hmong of
St. Paul–Minneapolis," *Anthropological Quarterly* 55, no. 3 (1982): 126–36.

Dunnigan, Timothy, Douglas P. Olney, Miles A. McNall, and Marline Spring.
"Hmong." In Haines, *Case Studies in Diversity,* 145–66.

Eastwood, Clint, dir. *Gran Torino.* Burbank, Calif.: Warner Brothers, 2008.

Ebaugh, Helen Rose, and Janet Saltzman Chafetz, eds. *Religion and the New Immigrants: Continuities and Adaptations in Immigrant Congregations.* Walnut
Creek, Calif.: Altamira Press, 2000.

Evans, Grant. *A Short History of Laos: The Land In Between.* New South Wales, Australia: Allen and Unwin, 2002.

Faderman, Lillian. *I Begin My Life All Over: The Hmong and the American Immigrant Experience.* Boston: Beacon Press, 1999.

Fadiman, Anne. *The Spirit Catches You and You Fall Down: A Hmong Child, Her American Doctors, and the Collision of Two Cultures.* New York: Farrar, Straus, and Giroux, 1997.

Faruque, Cathleen Jo. *Migration of Hmong to the Midwestern States.* Lanham, Md.: University Press of America, 2002.

Frommer, Fred. "Senators Call on U.S. to Press Thailand on Hmong Refugees." *Minnesota Public Radio,* June 26, 2008. http://minnesota.publicradio.org/display/web/2008/06/26/senatorshmong/?refid=0.

Garrett, Wilbur E. "The Hmong of Laos—No Place to Run." *National Geographic,* January 1974, 78–111.

Geddes, William. *Migrants of the Mountain: The Cultural Ecology of the Blue Miao (Hmong Njua) of Thailand.* Oxford: Clarendon Press, 1976.

General/Multiethnic Collection. Boxes 21–27, Case Records, Immigration History Research Center, International Institute of Minnesota, University of Minnesota.

Gilroy, Paul. *The Black Atlantic: Modernity and Double Consciousness.* Cambridge, Mass.: Harvard University Press, 1993.

Goldfarb, Mace. *Fighters, Refugees, Immigrants: A Story of the Hmong.* Minneapolis, Minn.: Carolrhoda Books, 1982.

Gramling, Jonathan. "Racial Justice Rally at Wis. Capitol: Is Justice Being Served?" *Asian Wisconzine* 4, no. 1(January 2008). http://www.asianwisconzine.com/0108RacialJusticeRally.html (accessed April 12, 2010).

Grinberg, Emanuella. "Trial Opens for Hmong Refugee Who Killed Six Deer Hunters." *CourtTV News,* October 3, 2005, http://news.findlaw.com/court_tv/s/20050909/09sep2005160714.html (accessed March 31, 2010).

Haines, David, ed. *Case Studies in Diversity: Refugees in America in the 1990s.* Westport, Conn.: Greenwood Press, 1997.

———, ed. *Refugees as Immigrants: Cambodians, Laotians, and Vietnamese in America.* Totowa, N.J.: Rowman and Littlefield, 1989.

Hall, Stuart. "Cultural Identity and Diaspora." In *Identity: Community, Culture, Difference,* edited by Jonathan Rutherford, 222–37. London: Lawrence and Wishart, 1990).

Hamid, Ruhi. "One Day of War." *British Broadcasting Corporation (BBC)/Frontlines: Part One,* May 27, 2004.

Hamilton-Merritt, Jane. *Dr. Jane Hamilton-Merritt.* http://www.tragicmountains.org (accessed April 20, 2008).

———. *Tragic Mountains: The Hmong, the Americans and the Secret War for Laos, 1942–1992.* Bloomington: Indiana University Press, 1999.

Harrell-Bond, B. "The Experience of Refugees as Recipients of Aid." In *Refugees: Perspectives on the Experience of Forced Migration,* edited by Alastair Ager, 136–68. London: Pinter, 1999.

Harrell-Bond, B. E., and E. Voutira. "Anthropology and the Study of Refugees." *Anthropology Today* 8, no. 4 (1992): 6–10.

Hassoun, Jean-Pierre. *Hmong du Laos en France: Changement Social, Initiatives et Adaptations [Hmong from Laos in France: Social Change, Initiatives and Adaptations]*. Paris: Presses Universitaires de France, 1997.

"HBNA Member Churches." *Hmong Baptist National Association*, 2010. http://www.hbna.org/directory (accessed March 30, 2010).

Hein, Jeremy. *Ethnic Origins: The Adaptation of Cambodian and Hmong Refugees in Four American Cities*. New York: Russell Sage Foundation, 2006.

———. *From Vietnam, Laos, and Cambodia*. New York: Twayne, 1995.

Hendricks, Glen L., Bruce T. Downing, and Amos S. Deinard, eds. *The Hmong in Transition*. Staten Island, N.Y.: Center for Migration Studies, 1986.

Her, PaMang. "PaMang Her." Interview with Peter Chou Vang. Transcribed and translated by Leona Lor. Edited by Paul Hillmer. Hmong Oral History Project, Concordia University, St. Paul, Minn., 2005.

"History of Hmong International New Year." *Hmong International New Year*, 1998–2010. http://www.hmongnewyear.us/index.htm (accessed March 28, 2010).

Hmong American Partnership. http://www.hmong.org/ (accessed June 2006).

"Hmong Arts Connection: Our Mission." *Hmong American Institute for Learning*, August 18, 2009. http://www.hmonghail.org (accessed March 31, 2010).

Hmong Cultural Center. http://www.hmongcc.org (accessed March 31, 2010).

"Hmong Doctorates." *Christian Hmong Fellowship*. http://www.christianhmong fellowship.org/doctors.html (accessed March 31, 2010).

"Hmong Grave Desecration Timeline." Human Rights Program. *University of Minnesota*. http://hrp.cla.umn.edu/projresearch/gd/timeline.html (accessed March 31, 2010).

Hmong National Development. "Capacity Building." *Hmong National Development Inc*. http://hndinc.org/content/view/24/41/ (accessed March 31, 2010).

Hume, Bob. "St. Paul Mayor to Send Mission about Hmong Graves." Office of the Mayor of Saint Paul, Minnesota. *Presszoom.com*. http://presszoom.com/story_141151.html (accessed March 31, 2010).

Jacobson, Matthew Frye. *Special Sorrows: The Diasporic Imagination of Irish, Polish, and Jewish Immigrants in the United States*. Cambridge, Mass.: Harvard University Press, 1995.

Jenks, Robert D. *Insurgency and Social Disorder in Guizhou: The "Miao" Rebellion, 1854–1873*. Honolulu: University of Hawaii Press, 1994.

Johnson, Dirk. "Slaughter in the Woods." *Newsweek*, December 6, 2004, 28.

Joseph, May. *Nomadic Identities: The Performance of Citizenship*. Minneapolis: University of Minnesota Press, 1999.

Joseph, Miranda. *Against the Romance of Community*. Minneapolis: University of Minnesota Press, 2002.

Karner, Christian. *Ethnicity and Everyday Life*. London: Routledge, 2007.

Kasinitz, Philip. *Caribbean New York: Black Immigrants and the Politics of Race*. Ithaca: Cornell University Press, 1992.

Khaab, Ntxawg. *The Washington, DC, Commencement, May 14–15, 1997*. Milwaukee, Wis.: Ntxawg Video, 1997.

Kim, Young Yun. "Personal, Social, and Economic Adaptation: 1975–1979 Arrivals in Illinois." In Haines, *Refugees as Immigrants*, 86–104.

Koltyk, Jo Ann. *New Pioneers in the Heartland*. Needham Heights, Mass.: Allyn and Bacon, 1998.

Kong-Thao, Kazoua. "Running for School Board." Speech presented at the National Conference on Hmong Women. University of Minnesota, Minneapolis, September 2005.

Kue, Naolue Taylor. *A Hmong Church History.* Thornton, Colo.: Hmong C&MA District, 2000.

Ladson-Billings, Gloria. "Racialized Discourses and Ethnic Epistemologies." In *The Landscape of Qualitative Research: Theories and Issues,* edited by Norman K. Denzin and Yvonna S. Lincoln, 398–432. Thousand Oaks, Calif.: Sage, 2003.

Lair, Bill. Interview by Steve Maxner. December 11, 2001. Transcribed by Tammi Mikel Lyon. Bill Lair Collection, the Vietnam Archive Oral History Project. Vietnam Center and Archive, Office of International Affairs, Texas Tech University. http://www.virtual.vietnam.ttu.edu/star/images/oh/OH0200-part1.pdf (accessed October 17, 2008).

Landry, Lloyd (Pat). Papers. The CAT, Air America Archive, The History of Aviation Collection, McDermott Library, University of Texas at Dallas.

Lao-Hmong American Coalition. Home page. http://www.laohmong.org (accessed January 18, 2008).

"Laos: Deeper into the Other War." *Time,* March 9, 1970, http://www.time.com/time/magazine/article/0,9171,878776,00.html (accessed March 31, 2010).

Lao Veterans of America. "Hall of Fame." http://www.laoveterans.com/photo.html (accessed March 31, 2010).

Leary, William M. Papers. "Interview with James W. (Bill) Lair and Lloyd (Pat) Landry, Bangkok, Thailand, July 3, 1933 [sic]." U.S. Special Operations in Laos: 1955–1965, CAT, Air America Archive, History of Aviation Collection, McDermott Library, University of Texas at Dallas. http://www.utdallas.edu/library/uniquecoll/speccoll/aamnote/sepcop65.pdf (accessed March 2, 2010).

Lee, Gary Yia. "Diaspora and the Predicament of Origins: Interrogating Hmong Postcolonial History and Identity." *Hmong Studies Journal* 8 (2007): 1–25.

———. "Ethnic Minorities and Nation Building in Laos: The Hmong in the Lao State." *Gary Yia Lee,* 1995. http://www.hmongnet.org/hmong-au/hmonglao.htm (accessed June 12, 2006).

———. "Refugees from Laos: Historical Background and Causes." *Gary Y. Lee,* 1990. http://hmongnet.org/hmong-au/refugee.htm (accessed March 3, 2008).

———. "The Religious Presentation of Social Relationships: Hmong World View and Social Structure." *Lao Studies Review* 2 (1994–95): 44–60. http://www.global.lao.net/laostudy/hmrelate.htm.

Lee, Mai. "Mai Lee." Interviewed, translated, and transcribed by Mai Neng Vang (granddaughter). Edited by Paul Hillmer. Hmong Oral History Project, Concordia University, St. Paul, Minnesota, 2005. http://homepages.csp.edu/hillmer/Interviews/Mai_Lee.html (accessed June 28, 2008).

Levine, Ken, and Ivory Waterworth Levine, dirs. *Becoming American: The Odyssey of a Refugee Family,* Harriman, N.Y.: New Day Films, 1983.

Levine, Paul. "Americanization and Globalization." In *Transnational America: Contours of Modern US Culture,* edited by Russell Duncan and Clara Juncker, 13–26. Copenhagen: Museum Tusculanum Press, 2004.

Lin, Jan. *Reconstructing Chinatown: Ethnic Enclave, Global Change.* Minneapolis: University of Minnesota Press, 1998.

Lo, Fungchatou. *The Promised Land: The Socioeconomic Reality of the Hmong People in Urban America, 1976–2000.* Bristol, Ind.: Wyndham Hall Press, 2000.

Long, Lynellen. *Ban Vinai: The Refugee Camp.* New York: Columbia University Press, 1993.

Lowe, Lisa. *Immigrant Acts: On Asian American Cultural Politics.* Durham, N.C.: Duke University Press, 1996.

"LVA Hall of Fame." *Lao Veterans of America Inc.* http://www.laoveterans.com/photo.html (accessed March 31, 2010).

Lynch, Annette F. "Hmong-American New Year Dress: A Material Culture Approach." PhD diss., University of Minnesota, 1992.

Mahler, Sarah J. *American Dreaming: Immigrant Life on the Margins.* Princeton: Princeton University Press, 1995.

Manivanh, Kham Phiou. "The Day We Lost Lee Lue: Hmong Ace Pilot Serving in the Secret War." http://us.geocities.com/koratmahknut/warinlaos/hmonglao/theday.htm (accessed October 9, 2009).

Marlowe, Thom. "The Hidden War in Laos." *Asia Magazine,* September 19, 1971, 40–45.

McCormack, Dennis X. http://www.usenet.com/newsgroups/soc.culture.hmong/msg02337.html (accessed January 18, 2008).

McCoy, Alfred W. *The Politics of Heroin: CIA Complicity in the Global Drug Trade.* Rev. ed. Chicago: Lawrence Hill, 2003.

Menjívar, Cecilia. *Fragmented Ties: Salvadoran Immigrant Networks in America.* Berkeley: University of California Press, 2000.

Michaud, Jean. "From Southwest China into Upper Indochina: An Overview of Hmong (Miao) Migrations." *Asia Pacific Viewpoint* 38, no. 2 (August 1997): 119–30.

Morrison, Gayle L. *Sky Is Flying: An Oral History of the CIA's Evacuation of the Hmong from Laos.* Jefferson, N.C.: McFarland, 1999.

Moua, Mai Neng, ed. *Bamboo among the Oaks.* St. Paul: Minnesota Historical Society Press, 2002.

Nakanishi, Don T. "Beyond Electoral Politics: Renewing a Search for a Paradigm of Asian American Politics." In Chang, *Asian Americans and Politics,* 102–29.

"National Southeast Asian American Groups Call for Healing and Unity after Shootings in Wisconsin." *Southeast Asia Resource and Action Center,* December 15, 2004. http://www.searac.org/pr-3ohndsearac-12-15-04.pdf (accessed March 31, 2010).

Nawyn, Stephanie J. "Faith, Ethnicity, and Culture in Refugee Resettlement." *American Behavioral Scientist* 49, no. 11 (2006): 1509–27.

Nemes, Paul. "The Welcome Refugees: Why the West Opened Its Arms to Fleeing Hungarians in 1956." *Central Europe Review* 1, no. 19 (November 1, 1999). http://www.ce-review.org/99/19/nemes19.html.

Niedzwiecki, Max, Sophy Pich, KaYing Yang, Thanh Tran, and Barry King. *Directory of Southeast Asian American Community-Based Organizations 2004: Mutual Assistance Associations (MAAs) and Religious Organizations Providing Social Services.* Washington, D.C.: Southeast Asia Resource Action Center, 2004.

North Carolina Department of Health and Human Services. "500 Hmong refugees to come to North Carolina: Donations and assistance needed." News release. http://www.dhhs.state.nc.us/pressrel/7–2–04a.htm (accessed February 14, 2008).

Nyers, Peter. *Rethinking Refugees: Beyond States of Emergency.* New York: Routledge, 2006.

Olney, Douglas Philip. "We Must Be Organized: Dual Organizations in an American Hmong Community." PhD diss., University of Minnesota, 1993.

Ong, Aihwa. *Flexible Citizenship: The Cultural Logics of Transnationality.* Durham, N.C.: Duke University Press, 1999.

Pentagon Papers: The Defense Department History of Decisionmaking on Vietnam. Senator Gravel ed. 5 vols. Boston: Beacon Press, 1971.

Peteet, Julie. "Refugees, Resistance, and Identity." In *Globalizations and Social Movements: Culture, Power, and the Transnational Public Sphere,* edited by John A. Guidry, Michael D. Kenny, and Mayer N. Zald, 183–209. Ann Arbor: University of Michigan Press, 2000.

Pfeifer, Mark. "'Hmong Alone Population' Estimates: 2007 American Community Survey." *Hmong Studies Journal,* Fall 2008. http://www.hmongstudies.org/2007SEAAmericanCommunitySurvey.html (accessed March 31, 2010).

Pfeifer, Mark E., and Serge Lee. "Hmong Population, Demographic, Socioeconomic, and Educational Trends in the 2000 Census." In Thao, Schein, and Niedzweicki, *Hmong 2000 Census Publication,* 3–11.

Pipher, Mary. *The Middle of Everywhere: Helping Refugees Enter the American Community.* Orlando, Fla.: Harcourt, 2002.

Portes, Alejandro, and Josh DeWind, eds. *Rethinking Migration: New Theoretical and Empirical Perspectives.* New York: Berghahn Books, 2007.

Portes, Alejandro, and Min Zhou. "The New Second Generation: Segmented Assimilation and Its Variants." *Annals of the American Academy of Political and Social Science* 530 (November 1993): 74–96.

"President Signs H.R. 371/P.L. 106-207 'Hmong Veterans' Naturalization Act of 2000,' The." Social Security Legislative Bulletin. Legislative Archive of the 106th Congress. *Social Security Administration,* June 24, 3000. http://www.ssa.gov/legislation/legis_bulletin_061300.html (accessed March 31, 2010).

Quincy, Keith. *Harvesting Pa Chay's Wheat: The Hmong and America's Secret War in Laos.* Spokane: Eastern Washington University Press, 2000.

———. *The Hmong: History of a People.* Cheney: East Washington University Press, 1988.

Ranard, Donald A., ed. *The Hmong: An Introduction to Their History and Culture.* Washington, D.C.: Center for Applied Linguistics, 2004. http://www.cal.org/co/hmong/hmong_fin.pdf.

———. "Mutual Assistance Associations: Refugee Self-Help Groups Play Key Role." *America: Perspectives on Refugee Resettlement* 8 (May 1990): 1–4.

Randolph, Toni. "Hmong Protest Grave Desecration." *Minnesota Public Radio,* March 3, 2006. http://minnesota.publicradio.org/display/web/2006/03/03/hmong_graves_meeting/(accessed March 31, 2010).

Ratliff, Martha. "Vocabulary of Environment and Subsistence in the Hmong-Mien Proto-Language." In Tapp, Michaud, Culas, and Lee, *Hmong/Miao in Asia,* 147–66.

Refugee Program Office Records. Minnesota Historical Society. Minnesota History Center, Minnesota Department of Public Welfare, Minnesota State Archives, St. Paul.

Robbins, Christopher. *Ravens: The Men Who Flew in America's Secret War in Laos.* New York: Crown, 1987.

Roberts, Alden E., and Paul D. Starr. "Differential Reference Group Assimilation among Vietnamese Refugees." In Haines, *Refugees as Immigrants*, 40–85.

Ronk, Don. "The Legend of Long Cheng: War's End Unveils a Forbidden Valley." *Asia Magazine*, April 21, 1974, 16–20.

Rosaldo, Renato. *Culture and Truth: The Remaking of Social Analysis.* Boston: Beacon, 1989.

Safran, William. "Diasporas in Modern Societies: Myths of Homeland and Return." *Diaspora* 1, no. 1 (1991): 83–99.

———. "The Jewish Diaspora in a Comparative and Theoretical Perspective." *Israel Studies* 10, no. 1 (Spring 2005): 36–60.

Savina, François Marie. *Histoire des Miao.* Hong Kong: Impr. de la Société des Missions étrangères de Paris, 1924.

Saykao, Pao. "The Root and the Fruit: Hmong Identity." Keynote address, Hmong National Development (HND) annual conference. Milwaukee, Wis., April 2002.

Schein, Louisa. "Hmong/Miao Transnationality: Identity beyond Culture." In Tapp, Michaud, Culas, and Lee, *Hmong/Miao in Asia*, 273–90.

———. *Minority Rules: The Miao and the Feminine in China's Cultural Politics.* Durham, N.C.: Duke University Press, 2000.

Schofield, Steve R., prod. *A Brief History of the Hmong and the Secret War in Laos.* Newton, Wis., 2004.

Scott, McGregor W. "Indictment Handed Down in Plot to Overthrow the Government of Laos." News release. *U.S. Attorney's Office, Eastern District of California*, June 14, 2007. http://www.usdoj.gov/usao/cae.

Sherman, Spencer. "The Hmong's Blue Ridge Refuge." *APF Reporter* 9, no. 1 (1986). http://www.aliciapatterson.org/APF0901/Sherman/Sherman.html (accessed March 31, 2010).

Southeast Asian Task Force. "Home Away from Home." St. Paul, Minn.: Ramsey County Community Human Services, 1993.

Soyer, Daniel. *Jewish Immigrant Associations and American Identity in New York, 1880–1939.* Cambridge, Mass.: Harvard University Press, 1997.

State of Wisconsin v. Chai Soua Vang. Criminal complaint by Gary Gillis, Sawyer County Sheriff's Department, November 2004. http://images.ibsys .com/2004/1129/3955960.pdf (accessed March 31, 2010).

Stuart-Fox, Martin. *A History of Laos.* Cambridge: Cambridge University Press, 1997.

Tapp, Nicholas. *The Hmong of China: Context, Agency, and the Imaginary.* Boston: Brill Academic, 2003.

———. *Sovereignty and Rebellion: The White Hmong of Northern Thailand.* Oxford: Oxford University Press, 1989.

———. "The State of Hmong Studies." In Tapp, Michaud, Culas, and Lee, *Hmong/Miao in Asia*, 3–38.

Tapp, Nicholas, Jean Michaud, Christian Culas, and Gary Yia Lee, eds. *Hmong/Miao in Asia.* Chiang Mai, Thailand: Silkworm Books, 2004.

Thao, Bo, Louisa Schein, and Max Niedzweicki, eds. *Hmong 2000 Census Publi-*

cation: Data and Analysis. Washington, D.C.: Hmong National Development and Hmong Cultural and Resource Center, 2004.

Thao, Paoze. "Mong Resettlement in the Chicago Area, 1978–1978: Educational Implications." PhD diss., Loyola University, 1994.

Tölölyan, Khachig. "Rethinking Diaspora(s): Stateless Power in the Transnational Moment." *Diaspora* 5, no. 1 (1996): 3–36.

Tsong, Nicole. "Volunteer Helps Anchorage's Growing Hmong Population Integrate." *Alaska History and Cultural Studies.* http://www.akhistorycourse.org/articles/article.php?artID=298 (accessed March 31, 2010).

Tuan, Mia. *Forever Foreigners or Honorary Whites: The Asian American Experience Today.* New Brunswick: Rutgers University Press, 1998.

Ueda, Reed. "Immigration in Global Historical Perspective." In Waters, Ueda, and Marrow, *New Americans,* 14–28.

United Hmong Association of North Carolina. *Needs Assessment Report,* 2005. http://www.uhanc.org (accessed March 16, 2008).

United Lao Council for Peace, Freedom, and Reconstruction. "The Lao Conflict: Background, Basic Strategies & Intelligence." February 15, 2007. http://www.justice.gov/usao/cae/press_releases/docs/2007/06–14–07jackexhibit2.pdf.

United States of America v. Harrison Ulrich Jack, General Vang Pao, Lo Cha Thao, Lo Thao, Youa True Vang, Hue Vang, Chong Yang Thao, Seng Vue, Chue Lo, and Nhia Kao Vang. California Criminal Complaint, U.S. District Court Eastern District of Sacramento, California, June 4, 2007. Case Number 207MJ0178. http://www.thedailypage.com/media/2007/06/05/06–04–07JackComplaint.pdf (accessed March 31, 2010).

U.S. Congress. Senate. Committee on the Judiciary. *Refugee Problems in South Vietnam and Laos.* Hearings before the Subcommittee to Investigate Problems Connected with Refugees and Escapees. 89th Congress, 1st sess., July and September 1965.

U.S. Congress. Senate. Committee on Foreign Relations. *Contribution to the Expenses of the International Commission for Supervision and Control of Laos, Report No. 357.* 88th Congress, 1st sess., July 15, 1963.

U.S. Congress. Senate. Committe on Foreign Relations. *United States Security Agreements and Commitments Abroad, Part 2, Kingdom of Laos, Ninety-first Congress, First and Second Sessions.* Hearings of October 20–22, 28, 1969, before the Subcommittee on U.S. Security Agreements and Commitments Abroad.

U.S. Department of Health and Human Services. Administration for Children and Families, Office of Refugee Resettlement. *Annual ORR Report to Congress—2005.* http://www.acf.hhs.gov/programs/orr/data/05arc7.htm (accessed January 3, 2008).

U.S. Department of Health and Human Services. Office of Refugee Resettlement. *Hmong Resettlement Study.* Washington, D.C.: N.p., 1985.

U.S. Department of State. Office of International Information Programs. "Excerpt House Passes Resolution on Lao-Hmong Recognition Day." *Washington File, U.S. Department of State,* November 14, 2001. http://usinfo.org/wf-archive/2001/011114/epf314.htm (accessed March 31, 2010).

University of Wisconsin Extension and Applied Population Laboratory. *Wisconsin's Hmong Population, Census 2000 Population and Other Demographic Trends.* Madison: 2003.

Vang, Chia Youyee. *Hmong in Minnesota.* St. Paul: Minnesota Historical Society Press, 2008.

Vang, Pao. "Against All Odds: The Laotian Freedom Fighters." *Heritage Foundation*, March 19, 1987. http://www.heritage.org/Research/AsiaandthePacific/HL96.cfm.

Vang, Timothy T. "Coming a Full Circle: Historical Analysis of the Hmong Church Growth—1950–1998." PhD diss., Fuller Theological Seminary, Pasadena, Calif., September 23, 1998.

Vertovec, Steven. "Migrant Transnationalism and Modes of Transformation." In Portes and DeWind, *Rethinking Migration,* 149–80.

———. "Three Meanings of 'Diaspora,' Exemplified among South Asian Religions." *Diaspora* 6, no. 3 (1997): 277–99.

Warner, Roger. *Back Fire: The CIA's Secret War in Laos and Its Link to the War in Vietnam.* New York: Simon and Schuster, 1995.

———. *Shooting at the Moon: The Story of America's Clandestine War in Laos.* South Royalton, Vt.: Steerforth Press, 1998.

Waters, Mary C., Reed Ueda, and Helen B. Marrow, eds. *The New Americans: A Guide to Immigration since 1965.* Cambridge, Mass.: Harvard University Press, 2007.

Wausau (Wisconsin) Area Hmong Mutual Association. http://www.wausauhmong.org (accessed January 3, 2008).

Weiner, Tim. *Legacy of Ashes: The History of the CIA.* New York: Anchor Books, 2008.

Wisconsin United Coalition of Mutual Assistance Associations. http://www.wucmaa.org (accessed May 12, 2008).

Wu, Frank H. *Yellow: Race in America beyond Black and White.* Cambridge, Mass.: Basic Books, 2003.

Xiong, Nao, and Yang Sao Xiong. "A Critique of Timothy Vang's Hmong Religious Conversion and Resistance Study." *Hmong Studies Journal* 9 (2008): 1–22.

Xiong, Tsia. "Bush Signs Law Excluding Hmong from Patriot Act." *AsianWeek*, January 9, 2008. http://www.asianweek.com/2008/01/09/bush-signs-law-excluding-hmong-from-patriot-act/ (accessed April 13, 2010).

Yang, Dao. *Hmong at the Turning Point.* Minneapolis: World Bridge, 1993.

———. "Keeb Kwm Tsiab Peb Caug Hmoob ["Hmong New Year Rituals]." *Haiv Hmoob (St. Paul, Minnesota)* 1, no. 2, November 1985, 38–43.

Yang, Kou. "An Assessment of the Hmong American New Year and Its Implications for Hmong-American Culture." *Hmong Studies Journal* 8 (2007): 1–32.

———. "The Hmong in America: Twenty-five Years after the Secret War in Laos." *Journal of Asian American Studies* 4, no. 2 (2001): 165–74.

———. "The Passing of a Hmong Pioneer: Nhiavu Lobliayao (Nyiaj Vws Lauj Npliaj Yob), 1915–1999." *Hmong Studies Journal* 3 (2000): 1.

Yang, Tou T. "Hmong of Germany: Preliminary Report on the Resettlement of Lao Hmong Refugees in Germany." *Hmong Studies Journal* 4 (2003): 1–14.

Yau, Jennifer. "The Foreign-Born Hmong in the United States." *Migration Policy Institute,* 2005. http://www.migrationinformation.org/USFocus/display.cfm?ID=281fs (accessed March 31, 2010).

Zhou, Min. *Chinatown: The Socioeconomic Potential of an Urban Enclave.* Philadelphia, Penn.: Temple University Press, 1995.

Zia, Helen. *Asian American Dreams: The Emergence of an American People.* New York: Farrar, Straus and Giroux, 2000.

INDEX

Abhay, Khamphay, 139
acculturation, 94
activism, political, 123, 131
Aderholt, Harry "Heinie," 128
advisers, 27
Affigne, Tony, 122
agency, 15, 47, 50, 54
agrarian lifestyle, 34, 44, 54
Air America, 28
Alaska, 55–56, 63, 120
Allman, Timothy, 30
American Community Survey (ACS),
  54
American exceptionalism, 90
Americanization process, 85, 105, 117
ancestral worship, 18, 92, 141
ancestry, 5–8
anchor families, 63
Anderson, Benedict, 8, 136
Andrianoff, Ted and Ruth, 80
animist traditions, 79, 85, 92–93, 95
Annam, 20
anticolonial movements, 22
anticommunism, 11, 24, 138, 139,
  156
Appadurai, Arjun, 16
Argentina, 42
Arkansas, 15, 54, 65–67, 120
army, clandestine, 27–28, 32, 37,
  40–41, 52, 99
Asian Americans, 123, 126, 135, 159
assimilation, downward, 12
Association for the Advancement
  of Hmong Women in Minnesota
  (AAHWM), 73, 75, 89
Association of Hmong Community
  United Methodist Church, 87

Association of Hmong in Illinois
  (AHI), 75
Association of Hmong in Minnesota,
  71
asylum, 10–11
Australia, 42, 120, 138–39
authenticity, 97–98, 101, 109

Badillo, Aimee J., 147
ball tossing, 100, 105, 108
Ban 52 (Lak Ha Sip Song), 155
Ban Namphong, xx, 38, 39, 40, 41, 83
Ban Nam Yao, 43
Ban Vinai, xxi, 39, 40
Barnard, Tom, 145
Barney, G. Linwood, 82
Basch, Linda G., 8
beauty pageants, 102, 104–5, 111,
  116–17, 119, 120–21
Beck, Roy, 52
Benhabib, Seyla, 89
Bertrais, Yves, 82
Bhabha, Homi K., 97, 150
births, 93
Blanc, Cristina, 8
Bollywood, 107–8
Bostrom, Dan, 134
Bourdieu, Pierre, 101
Brennan, Edmund, 140
British Broadcasting Corporation
  (BBC), 138
Burma (Myanmar), 18
Bush, George W., 129, 139

California, 13, 55, 56, 60, 63, 75, 78,
  87, 120
Cambodia, 20, 21

CHIA YOUYEE VANG is an assistant professor of history at the University of Wisconsin–Milwaukee and the author of *Hmong in Minnesota*.

*The University of Illinois Press
is a founding member of the
Association of American University Presses.*

---

*University of Illinois Press
1325 South Oak Street
Champaign, IL 61820-6903
www.press.uillinois.edu*